S0-BOG-408

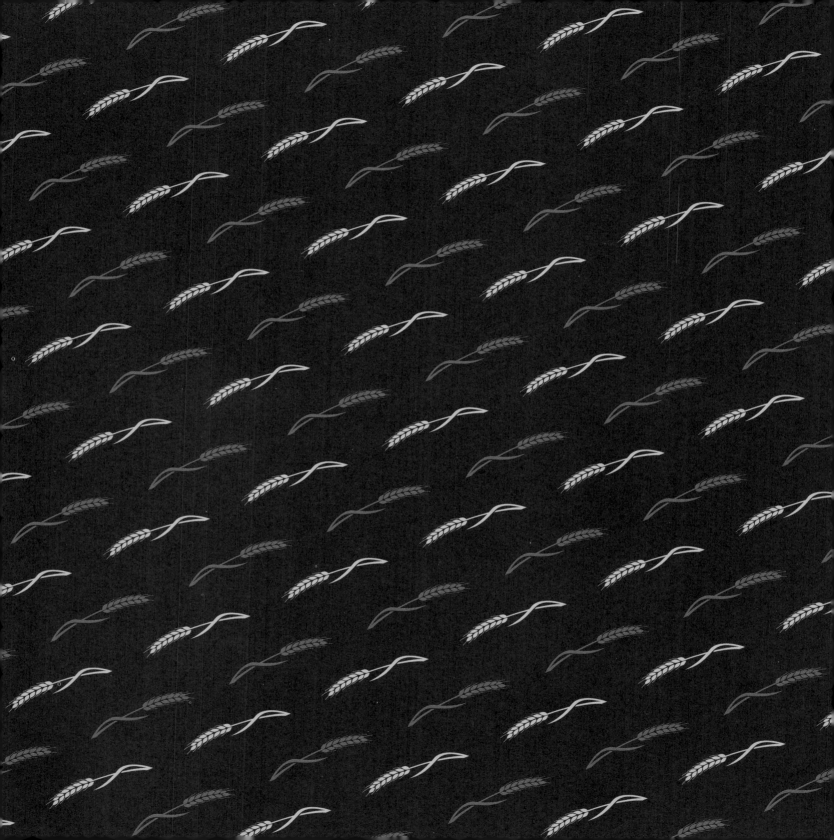

KNEADERS

BAKERY 25 YEARS & CAFE

A CELEBRATION *of* OUR RECIPES *and* MEMORIES

Colleen Worthington

SHADOW
MOUNTAIN
PUBLISHING

To our guests
with gratitude and love

Photos on pages vi, 1, 2, 3, 46, 47, 75, 100, 111, 142, 216, 217, 262, provided by the author; photo of Ally Condie on page 345 by Erin Summerill.

All other photos: Nick Bayless Photography
Food Styling: Erin Bayless

Any trademarks, service marks, product names, or named features are the property of their respective owners, and they are used herein for reference and comparison purposes only. This book was not prepared, approved, licensed, or endorsed by any of the owners of the trademarks or brand names referred to in this book. There is no express or implied endorsement for any products or services mentioned in this publication.

© 2023 KNDRS, LLC

All rights reserved. No part of this book may be reproduced in any form or by any means without permission in writing from the publisher, Shadow Mountain Publishing®, at permissions@shadowmountain.com or PO Box 30178, Salt Lake City, Utah 84130. The views expressed herein are the responsibility of the author and do not necessarily represent the position of Shadow Mountain Publishing.

Visit us at ShadowMountain.com

Library of Congress Cataloging-in-Publication Data
Names: Worthington, Colleen, 1947– author. | Kneaders Bakery & Cafe.
Title: Kneaders Bakery & Cafe: a celebration of our recipes and memories / Colleen Worthington.
Description: Salt Lake City, Utah: Shadow Mountain, [2023] | "25 years." | Summary: "The owner of the popular southwestern United States restaurant chain Kneaders shares favorite recipes and memories from family and friends"—Provided by publisher.
Identifiers: LCCN 2023009703 | ISBN 9781639931514 (hardback)
Subjects: LCSH: Kneaders Bakery & Cafe. | Cooking, American. | Baked products. | BISAC: COOKING / Courses & Dishes / Bread | COOKING / Courses & Dishes / General | LCGFT: Cookbooks.
Classification: LCC TX715. W93038 2023 | DDC 641.5973—dc23/eng/202303154
LC record available at https: //lccn.loc.gov/2023009703

Printed in China
RR Donnelley, Dongguan, China

10 9 8 7 6 5 4 3 2 1

CONTENTS

A PLACE
at the
TABLE

Colleen and Gary Worthington

"Morning, Sunshine." Those were the first words Gary ever said to me. It was a gorgeous June day at Brigham Young University in Provo, Utah. I was working at my campus job in catering and Gary was picking up some of the orders. When he came through the door, tall, suntanned, and smiling, and said those words to me, I have to admit I melted. Right away, we both knew something was happening. It was as if we had agreed on that greeting in some other time and place so that we would recognize each other.

And we did.

It would be easy to say that was the beginning, and in many ways it was. The beginning also goes back before us, to our parents and grandparents.

One of my favorite memories as a child was sitting on the kitchen counter while my mother made what she called "Grandma's Cookies." (You can find the recipe on page 258.) It took about two hours and many steps to make these cookies, but I loved being there for every moment of it. I loved watching my mother and spending time with her.

Being the youngest of the family was such a blessing to me because I was able to have many special one-on-one times with my parents. I was born when my mother, Althea Ashby Kimball, was forty-two years old. By the time I was eighteen, she was sixty years old and had begun the battle with cancer that eventually took her life. She was a schoolteacher, and she taught children with reading struggles in the morning and differently abled children in the afternoon. She had so much patience and love for people who weren't always accepted by others. My mother taught me that taking care of other people is the most important work anyone can do, and that helping someone who is struggling is meaningful for both people.

My father, Eddie Kimball, put himself through college by working at the National Guard armory mucking out the horse stalls. Growing up on a farm taught him valuable skills. He often told us, "You will always have a job if you can do something with your hands and something with your head." Skills like sewing, cooking, and cleaning were as valuable as math and English to him. My dad taught me that anything is possible if you are willing to work hard and long enough. I've tried to put these lessons from both of my parents into practice as we've built Kneaders over the past twenty-five years.

My parents loved Gary right from the start, and I think part of that was because they recognized that he came from a family that believed these things, too. Gary's father, Jethro Worthington, was a fireman and a farmer in Grantsville, Utah, where Gary grew up. Although there was not much money, there was love from many generations and having family all around (a much greater blessing than money). Gary's sister, Peggy, had special needs and required extra attention. Since Gary was the oldest in the family, he often helped with Peggy or helped his mother with family chores so she could tend to her. I'm sure that is part of what has made Gary such a gentle soul and also such a great leader.

The first time I met Gary's mother, Mary, she took me to her pantry and showed me her beautiful bottles of Lemon Elberta peaches and Bartlett pears. Making jam was also her specialty—apricot pineapple, strawberry peach, and raspberry. She took great pride in her pantry. Every bottle was a work of art. Mary was also a wonderful bread baker. Twice a week, the delicious aroma of fresh-baked bread filled the house. She baked beautiful white loaves to make sandwiches for lunch and for late-night snacks of bread and milk (served with salt and pepper).

Our wedding day.

For Mary, food was not only good for the body, it was also good for the soul. It brought comfort to everyone she met. You could never visit the Worthington home without her fixing a meal for you, and your hands were always loaded with food when you left. This was such a blessing to Gary and me when we were poor college students! We often made the two-hour drive from our home in Provo to Grantsville, near Salt Lake City, on Sundays. (Gas was only .25 a gallon then, if you can believe it.) We'd eat her big Sunday dinners and then, before we headed back to our house, she'd pack a sack for us with leftovers, bread, jam, and bottled fruit.

Gary also dearly loved his Nana and her pumpkin pie. He was privileged to live next door to her while he was growing up. It was Nana's custom to bake pies and leave them on her windowsill to cool. When Nana made pumpkin pie, she always made two large pies and a small one. Gary would find a reason to visit Nana and sneak that little pie for himself. Being a grandma myself, I'm pretty sure that Nana knew exactly what she was doing. Years later, my daughter Amy asked Gary's mother, Mary, to teach her how to make Nana's Pumpkin Pie. It had become quite a ritual for Mary and was a legend in our family. To our surprise, Amy learned a lot that had never been written down in the recipe. So when you get to that special recipe on page 297, we're happy to tell you that we've included all of those tips. You're part of the family now.

Gary and I both grew up knowing that we are loved by our Heavenly Father and our family. Those two beacons would become our guiding lights.

Education was also very important to our families. My mother's family had ten children. All ten of them graduated from college, including the six daughters. My mother was born in 1905 and my father in 1903. It was not common in those days to attend college. But every sacrifice was made so that they could.

Gary was the first of his family to go on a mission for our church and to go to college and graduate. He earned all of his own money to pay for his mission and college by himself.

We both feel and know that sacrifices make us stronger. Everything we have we owe to our Heavenly Father. We are not self-made but a product of His love and of the sacrifice of His Son.

Once Gary and I began dating, things moved quickly. After that first June meeting, we were married on November 16, 1966. We both graduated from Brigham Young University. Gary majored in business management with minors in economics, accounting, and statistics. I graduated with a degree in family relations and human development, with minors in clothing and textiles, food

and nutrition, and physical education. We loved learning as many things as we could and tried to take full advantage of our time in school. Gary went on to do graduate work toward a master's degree in public administration and started a construction business. I became a mother, which had always been my dream. We had six amazing children—Laura, Angie, Christy, Tami, James, and Amy. Every one of them is loved and treasured so much (and you will hear more about them throughout this cookbook—they've each played such a part in the Kneaders story). We also have twenty-two grandchildren and seven great-grandchildren, with two more on the way.

When Gary left the construction business, we opened nine Subway sandwich stores and ran them for years. Eventually, Subway asked us to be open on Sundays, which was against our belief system. We decided it was time to retire, and we sold our stores.

But retirement was boring. We loved people too much and we loved serving them. So after eight years,

Family photo from 1996, one year before opening Kneaders.
From left to right: Amy, Christy, Laura, Gary, Colleen, James,
Angie, and Tami.

we retired from retirement. Our children say they were not surprised. They knew we couldn't sit still for long.

Because of our upbringings, we knew that we wanted to instill the values of hard work and helping others in our own children. We also knew how fun it can be working as a team and with our family. We know that the hardest and best times of your life often happen side-by-side and hand-in-hand.

Gary and I began learning everything we could about baking artisan bread. We read, went to school, studied, and practiced. In our attempts to make the perfect bread, we ruined our home oven by squirting water on the coils to make the steam needed for a good crust and an attractive color. So Gary bought a small steam-injected oven and put it in our garage, where we practiced baking ciabatta bread. Eventually, we produced our first successful loaf.

At first, Kneaders was just one building in North Orem, Utah, off of State Street. Gary oversaw the construction of the store. We were open from 7:00 a.m. to 7:00 p.m, so the only time we could bake was at night. Gary came in right after we closed at 7:00 p.m. to do all the baking. Our son James, who was in high school at the time, came in and helped. Gary took some of the bread to our neighbors to try it out, so when Kneaders opened, they were all primed.

Gary made up many of our recipes, including our Hazelnut 12-Grain Hearth Bread and our Paesano Bread. You can always tell when Gary bakes. It's truly special.

Throughout everything we've done—raising children, serving in our church, work—Gary and I have been partners. We've always found ways to help each other. A family business is hard, but you can do it, and it's so rewarding.

Our granddaugher Emily Bishop's rendition of our first Kneaders location.

This is what it is to build something. It is laughing when a little one gets flour everywhere and taking a moment in the "snow." It is dancing in St. Marco's Square for our twenty-fifth wedding anniversary. It is honoring your values and teaching them to your children while you are working side-by-side. It is falling in bed side-by-side exhausted, too tired to talk. It is finding moments for conversations in a myriad of moments throughout shared days and endeavors. It is making something special for a loved one, with love.

We know you are building families and lives, too. You always have a place at our table. And it is an honor to share these recipes in the hopes that we might have a place in gathering your loved ones with you around yours.

See NANA'S PUMPKIN PIE heritage recipe on page 297.

A PLACE AT THE TABLE

BREAKFAST

Blueberry Lemon Muffin Tops

Makes 12 muffin tops • Prep Time: 35 minutes • Total Time: 55 minutes

After opening the bakery in 1997, I spent some time in Maryland with my daughter Angie, whose husband, Scott, was attending medical school. Their oldest daughter, Erika, was about three years old. I love books and Erika loves books. When I visited, I brought her the book *If You Give a Moose a Muffin*, by Laura Joffe Numeroff. To make it even more fun, I brought along the ingredients for blueberry muffins, which we made together. We shared those treats with eager family members—such a sweet memory for all of us. When I returned home, we began making our first muffins at the bakery. The guests loved them just as much as that little family in Maryland.

2¾ cups all-purpose flour, divided

1 cup sugar, divided

2 tablespoons butter, room temperature

Zest of 2 lemons, divided

2 teaspoons baking powder

½ teaspoon baking soda

¼ teaspoon salt

1 egg

1 cup buttermilk

½ cup oil

1 teaspoon vanilla

1½ cups frozen blueberries

Nonstick baking spray

GLAZE

1½ cup powdered sugar

¼ cup lemon juice

¼ teaspoon vanilla

1. Make the crumble topping by mixing ¼ cup flour, ¼ cup sugar, the butter, and ½ teaspoon lemon zest (reserving the rest for the muffins) with a fork until crumbly. Spread out on a baking sheet to dry.

2. Preheat the oven to 400 degrees F.

3. In a mixing bowl, whisk together remaining flour and sugar, baking powder, baking soda, salt, and remaining lemon zest.

4. In another bowl, mix together the egg, buttermilk, oil, and vanilla until well combined.

5. Mix the dry and wet mixtures together and fold in blueberries.

6. Place paper baking cups in a standard muffin pan and coat baking cups and the top of the muffin pan with nonstick baking spray.

7. Fill each cup just to the rim.

8. Sprinkle the crumble mix on each muffin. More is better. The pieces will expand as they rise.

9. Bake 5 minutes, then turn the oven down to 375 degrees F. and bake for 15 minutes more, or until golden brown. Cool.

11. For the glaze, whisk together powdered sugar, lemon juice, and vanilla until well combined. Glaze muffins when they have cooled.

Granddaughter Erika Bishop and grandma Colleen reminiscing.

Raspberry Almond Muffin Tops

Makes 12 muffin tops • Prep Time: 30 minutes • Total Time: 50 minutes

Muffins are an easy place for a beginning baker to start. It's as easy as 1, 2, 3. First, combine all of the dry ingredients together in a bowl. Second, combine all of the wet ingredients in another bowl. Third, pour the wet ingredients in with the dry ingredients. Remember not to overmix—you do want some lumps in the batter. Once you've poured the batter into the tins, all that's left to do is to bake and enjoy.

---

1 (2.25-ounce) package slivered almonds

3½ cups all-purpose flour, divided

1 cup + 2 tablespoons granulated sugar, divided

4 tablespoons (½ stick) salted butter, cold

1 teaspoon almond extract

2 teaspoons baking powder

½ teaspoon salt

2 large eggs

1 cup buttermilk

¾ cup (1½ sticks) unsalted butter, melted

½ teaspoon vanilla

¼ teaspoon lemon zest

1½ cups fresh raspberries, frozen for 30 minutes

Nonstick baking spray

1. Preheat oven to 325 degrees F. Spread slivered almonds on a half-sheet baking pan and toast for 15 minutes, stirring once or twice to avoid burning. Remove from oven and allow to cool. Turn oven up to 425 degrees F.

2. In a medium bowl, blend together with a pastry cutter or a fork 1½ cups flour, ¼ cup + 2 tablespoons sugar, salted butter, and almond extract. Set crumble mixture aside.

3. In a large bowl, whisk 2 cups flour, ¾ cup sugar, baking powder, and salt together.

4. In a medium bowl, mix eggs, buttermilk, unsalted butter, vanilla, and lemon zest together until incorporated.

5. Pour the wet ingredients into the dry ingredients and gently stir with a spatula to combine.

6. Add raspberries and gently fold into the batter.

7. Place paper baking cups in a standard muffin pan and coat baking cups and the top of the muffin pan with nonstick baking spray.

8. Fill each cup just to the rim.

9. Sprinkle the crumble mix on each muffin. More is better. The pieces will expand as they rise.

10. Bake 5 minutes, then turn the oven down to 375 degrees F. and bake for 15 minutes more, or until golden brown. Allow to cool, then glaze with Raspberry Glaze and top with toasted almonds.

RASPBERRY GLAZE

½ cup heavy cream

Juice from 3–4 macerated raspberries

¼ cup powdered sugar

1. Mix heavy cream, raspberry juice, and powdered sugar until well combined.

2. Drizzle on cooled Raspberry Almond Muffin Tops and sprinkle immediately with toasted almonds.

Tasty Tips

- You can make your own buttermilk by mixing 1 cup whole milk with 2 tablespoons lemon juice. Let it stand for 5 minutes or until the milk curdles, and use in any recipe calling for buttermilk.
- Freezing the fresh raspberries for 30 minutes before adding to the mixture will keep them from bleeding juice into the muffin batter.

Chocolate Zucchini Muffin Tops

Makes 24 muffin tops • Prep Time: 15 minutes • Total Time: 35 minutes

When I was a little girl, my mom fixed zucchini squash a hundred different ways. I loved it, and her creativity always impressed me. The best was when she fixed it like whipped potatoes with lots of cheese, cream, and butter. Zucchini adds a lot of moisture to baked goods, just like applesauce, without adding any unwanted flavor. Enjoy these flavorful chocolate muffin tops with zucchini, and be sure to pay attention to the tip at the end.

---

4 cups flour, divided

1¼ cups brown sugar, divided

2 tablespoons (¼ stick) butter, room temperature

1 cup granulated sugar

3 eggs

1 cup vegetable oil

2 cups zucchini, grated and peeled

3 tablespoons vanilla

½ cup Dutch cocoa powder

1 tablespoon baking soda

1 tablespoon baking powder

1 teaspoon salt

3 tablespoons cinnamon

1 tablespoon nutmeg

1 cup semi-sweet or dark chocolate chips, as desired

Nonstick baking spray

1. Preheat the oven to 375 degrees F. In a small mixing bowl, mix together ¼ cup flour, ¼ cup brown sugar, and butter with a fork. Set crumble mixture aside.

2. In a large mixing bowl, combine granulated sugar, 1 cup brown sugar, eggs, oil, zucchini, and vanilla.

3. In a medium mixing bowl, whisk together 3¾ cups flour, baking soda, baking powder, salt, cinnamon, and nutmeg.

4. Pour the dry ingredients into the wet ingredients and gently stir with a spatula to combine.

5. Place paper baking cups in a standard muffin pan and coat baking cups and the top of the muffin pan with nonstick baking spray.

6. Fill each cup just to the rim.

7. Sprinkle the crumble mix on each muffin. More is better. The pieces will expand as they rise. Bake for 17–20 minutes or until a toothpick inserted in the center comes out clean.

Tasty Tips

- This recipe also works well without the cocoa powder and chocolate chips.

Refrigerator Bran Muffin Tops

Makes 48 muffin tops • Prep Time: 10 minutes • Total Time: 30 minutes

Good news: you can keep this muffin batter in the refrigerator for up to 28 days. Even more good news: I think the batter gets better as it ages. When our children were little, we made giant batches in the winter and cooked them up a dozen at a time for breakfast. They made the house smell so good and comforted the soul.

We made them at Kneaders during the recession of 2007–2009. It was a time when a lot of our guests needed something to warm their spirits. Having this cozy breakfast on offer was something I felt I should do—as if they were my family members, and I was sending them out into the world with something warm and good.

---

2 cups boiling water

2 cups dates, chopped

5 teaspoons baking soda

1 cup shortening

2 cups granulated sugar

4 eggs

4 cups bran buds

2 cups bran flakes

1 teaspoon salt

5 cups flour

1 quart buttermilk

1 cup nuts

Nonstick baking spray

1. Preheat oven to 375 degrees F.

2. In a medium bowl, pour boiling water over dates and let cool. Add baking soda.

3. In a large mixing bowl, cream together shortening, sugar, and eggs.

4. Add bran buds, bran flakes, and salt. Mix until incorporated.

5. Alternate adding flour and buttermilk in 1-cup increments.

6. Stir in cooled date mixture and nuts.

7. Place paper baking cups in a standard muffin pan and coat baking cups and the top of the muffin pan with nonstick baking spray.

8. Fill each cup just to the rim.

9. Bake muffin tops for 20 minutes.

Tasty Tips

- In just 30 minutes you can have a batch of muffins ready to take to a neighbor who needs your attention.

Gary's Family Scones with Pie Filling

Makes 40 scones • Prep time: 15 minutes • Total time: 5 hours

We used to have a giant Christmas tree in our backyard, and just after Thanksgiving on the first Monday in December, Gary would make a huge batch of scones and invite the neighbors over. We would sing Christmas carols, light the tree, and eat the scones with pie filling and whipped cream. Gary's parents picked out that tree when he was ten, and he and the tree were the same size. We moved that Christmas tree to our home from Gary's parents' house in Grantsville, Utah, about fifty years ago. This event was one of our touchstone traditions as our children were growing up, and I can still smell the pine and hear my neighbors singing when I eat these scones.

---

4 tablespoons dry yeast

¼ cup warm water (90–100 degrees F.)

1 quart hot water

⅔ cup sugar

2 tablespoons salt

7–8 cups flour

8 cups shortening

1 (21-ounce) can cherry pie filling

1 (21-ounce) can blueberry pie filling

1 (21-ounce) can raspberry pie filling

Whipped Cream Topping (see recipe on page 227)

1. In a medium bowl, dissolve the yeast in ¼ cup warm water. Set aside to proof.

2. Using a stand mixer with dough hook attachment, combine water, sugar, salt, and 4 cups of flour. Mix for 3 minutes. Add yeast and enough flour to make a soft dough, about 4 more cups.

3. Add dough to a lightly oiled bowl, cover, and let rise until doubled. Punch down. Repeat once more.

4. Pinch off a 2-inch ball of dough. Flatten until it is the thickness of a dime (sometimes we use a rolling pin). Repeat until all dough is used.

5. In a large skillet or electric frying pan, heat Crisco until it is 350–360 degrees F. Carefully put scones in the oil in small batches. Cook until golden brown, then immediately remove from the pan and drain on a paper towel–lined plate.

6. Allow to cool and fill with cooled cherry, blueberry, or raspberry pie filling and add a dollop of Whipped Cream Topping to each scone.

Tasty Tips
- Treasure family traditions. They are the strings that hold families together.

Baked Breakfast Scones

Makes 8 scones • Prep Time: 20 minutes • Total Time: 35–40 minutes

Scones sound fancy, but don't let them intimidate you. They really are so simple to make. Try your hand at our easy version of this tasty breakfast pastry, and serve it up to your family with butter and homemade—or Kneaders— jam. A special thanks to Monica Kate, one of our executive pastry chefs, who developed this scone base recipe and the variations.

---

1 (2.25-ounce) package
  slivered almonds

½ cup powdered sugar

½ teaspoon vanilla

1 tablespoon water

2 cups flour

3 tablespoons sugar

1 teaspoon baking powder

½ teaspoon baking soda

½ teaspoon salt

6 tablespoons butter, frozen

½ cup dried currants

2 ounces cream cheese,
  room temperature

½ cup buttermilk

1 egg

2 tablespoons heavy cream

1. Preheat oven to 325 degrees F. Spread slivered almonds on a half-sheet baking pan and toast for 15 minutes, stirring once or twice to avoid burning. Remove from oven and allow to cool. Set aside.

2. Turn oven up to 400 degrees F.

3. In a small bowl, mix together powdered sugar, vanilla, and water. Set glaze aside.

4. Whisk together flour, sugar, baking powder, baking soda, and salt in a medium mixing bowl.

5. Using the large holes on a box grater, grate the frozen butter into the dry ingredients.

6. Use your fingers to gently mix the butter in. Fold in currants.

7. In a blender, combine cream cheese, buttermilk, egg, and heavy cream. Blend until smooth.

8. Pour the liquid ingredients into the dry ingredients. Stir with a fork until the dough just comes together.

9. Turn out dough onto a lightly floured surface. Knead a few times to work in any remaining dry ingredients. The less you handle the dough, the more tender your scones will be.

10. Pat the dough into an 8-inch circle. Using a large chef knife, cut circle into 6–8 wedges, depending on the size you want.

11. Place the wedges 1 inch apart on a parchment-lined half-sheet baking pan. Bake for 15–17 minutes, or until golden brown. While scones are still slightly warm, drizzle generously with glaze. Immediately add toasted almonds.

Cranberry Orange White Chocolate Scones

- Substitute dried cranberries for currants.
- Add ½ cup white chocolate chips.
- Decrease buttermilk to ⅓ cup. Add the zest and flesh of ¼ orange to the wet ingredients in the blender.
- Use orange juice in place of water in glaze.

Dark Chocolate Cherry Almond Scones

- Substitute dried cherries for currants.
- Add ½ cup dark chocolate chips.
- Add ¼ teaspoon almond extract to the wet ingredients in the blender.
- Use almond extract in place of vanilla in glaze.

Apricot Hazelnut Vanilla Bean Scones

- Substitute chopped dried apricots for currants.
- Add ½ cup chopped and roasted hazelnuts and ½ cup white chocolate chips.
- Add ½ teaspoon vanilla extract to the wet ingredients in the blender.
- Add a generous pinch of powdered vanilla bean to the glaze.

Cranberry Orange White Chocolate Scones

Dark Chocolate Cherry Almond Scones

Avocado Toast for Two

Serves 2 • Prep Time: 10 minutes • Total Time: 20 minutes

This recipe is our research and development chef Ryker Brown's version of Kneaders-style avocado toast. This was first published in our monthly newsletter. Avocados have a buttery consistency with a rich nutty flavor, so they make a perfect companion for our Hazelnut 12-Grain Hearth Bread. This combination of nuts, grains, and healthy fats makes for a delicious and satisfying breakfast—or lunch or dinner, if you feel so inclined!

---

1 loaf Kneaders Hazelnut 12-Grain Hearth Bread, sliced

1 tablespoon butter

1 avocado

1 lime

1 pinch ground black pepper

1 teaspoon kosher salt

1 Fresno chili pepper or jalapeño pepper, thinly sliced

2 scallions, thinly sliced

2 eggs

1 tablespoon white wine vinegar

1. In a medium sauté pan, melt butter and add two slices of Kneaders Hazelnut 12-Grain Hearth Bread. Toast until golden brown and remove from heat. Place toast on serving plates.

2. In a small mixing bowl, mix avocado, lime juice, salt, and pepper. Gently smash with a fork until all ingredients are incorporated.

3. Place avocado on toast and garnish with peppers and scallions.

4. In a small saucepan over high heat, bring 4 cups of water to boil. Reduce heat to a simmer and add vinegar. Gently swirl the water, then immediately drop in two cracked eggs. Poach for 2–3 minutes or until desired doneness.

5. Using a slotted spoon, place one egg on top of each slice of avocado toast.

Tasty Tips

- Looking for a sweet flavor? Add a thin spread of Kneaders Apricot Jam before adding the avocado. Delicious!

Rosemary Potato Bread Easter Strata

Serves 12 • Prep Time: 10 minutes • Total Time: 2 hours + 8 hours chill time

A strata is an egg casserole with lots of bread—a savory bread pudding. It gets even better if you make it the day before and let it sit overnight so that the flavor soaks in. That makes this dish especially wonderful for the holidays—it gets you out of the kitchen and having fun with your family. This yummy strata is one we like to serve on Easter mornings, but any morning will do.

---

1 pound Italian sausage

1 loaf Kneaders Rosemary Potato Bread, cut into 1-inch cubes

4 ounces sliced mushrooms

3 ounces fresh spinach leaves

2 cups grated Colby jack cheese

8 eggs

3 cups half-and-half

1 teaspoon salt

1 teaspoon ground mustard

1. Cook sausage over medium-high heat until evenly browned. Drain and set aside. Sauté mushrooms until softened, about 7 minutes.

2. Layer bread cubes, sausage, mushrooms, spinach, and cheese in a 9x13 baking dish.

3. In a large mixing bowl, beat together eggs, half-and-half, salt, and mustard.

4. Pour egg mixture over layered ingredients in the baking dish.

5. Cover and refrigerate 8 hours or overnight.

6. Remove from the refrigerator 30 minutes before cooking and preheat oven to 350 degrees F.

7. Bake for 50–60 minutes or until a knife inserted in the center comes out clean.

Tasty Tips

• Substitute 1 cup asparagus for the mushrooms.
• Substitute 3 cups skim milk for the half-and-half.

Cinnamon Rolls

Makes 12 rolls • Prep Time: 25 minutes • Total Time: 3 hours

As a family, we practiced making cinnamon rolls for weeks prior to opening Kneaders. We experimented over and over again, trying to get them consistent. The first morning we opened, our cinnamon rolls came out of the oven at 6:45. By 7:00 we had quickly frosted them and put them in the display case. By 11:00 they were all gone—they were the first product we sold out of that day. Twenty-five years later, our cinnamon rolls still remain in the top three pastries we sell chainwide. Here's our basic cinnamon roll recipe, plus a few variations that you may want to try.

CREAM CHEESE ICING

8 ounces cream cheese,
    room temperature

¼ cup butter, room temperature

¼ cup granulated sugar

1 teaspoon vanilla

BASIC CINNAMON ROLL DOUGH

2¼ teaspoons active dry yeast

1 cup warm water

¾ cup + 1 teaspoon granulated
    sugar, divided

1 egg, slightly beaten

½ cup milk, scalded then
    cooled to warm

¼ cup canola oil

1½ teaspoons salt

4½ cups all-purpose flour, divided

Nonstick baking spray

1 teaspoon ground cinnamon

¼ cup butter, melted

1. For the icing, cream together cream cheese, butter, and sugar until smooth. Stir in vanilla. Set aside.

2. Preheat the oven to 350 degrees F.

3. In a small bowl, dissolve yeast in water with 1 teaspoon of sugar. Let sit for about 10 minutes until it begins to bubble and grow.

4. In a large mixing bowl, combine egg, milk, oil, ½ cup sugar, salt, yeast mixture, and 1½ cups of the flour. Mix well. Cover and allow to rest about 20 minutes or until bubbly and double in volume.

5. Slowly work in remaining 3 cups of flour. Mix until well incorporated. Turn dough onto a lightly floured surface and knead until smooth and elastic.

6. Place dough in a lightly oiled bowl. Turn once to coat. Cover and let rise until doubled. Spray a 9x13 baking dish with nonstick baking spray.

7. Roll dough into a 12x18-inch rectangle. Brush with melted butter.

8. In a small bowl, mix remaining ¼ cup sugar and cinnamon. Sprinkle dough with cinnamon and sugar. Roll dough into a cylinder starting on the long side of the rectangle. Cut into 1-inch-thick slices. Place cinnamon rolls in the prepared baking dish about an inch apart. Allow to rise until double in size.

9. Bake for 30 to 35 minutes, or until golden brown. Allow to cool 10 minutes, then frost with Cream Cheese Icing.

See CARAMEL PECAN and RASPBERRY CREAM CHEESE CINNAMON ROLLS varations of this recipe on page 22.

BREAKFAST

21

Caramel Pecan Cinnamon Rolls

½ cup butter, melted

¾ cup light brown sugar

½ cup pecans, chopped

1. Make the basic cinnamon roll recipe (page 21) through step 5.

2. In a small bowl, mix melted butter and brown sugar. Pour into the prepared baking dish. Sprinkle pecans evenly over brown sugar mixture. Place cinnamon rolls on top of the mixture about an inch apart.

3. Bake according to basic instructions.

4. Remove from the oven. Immediately turn the pan upside down onto a parchment-lined half-sheet baking pan. The caramel pecan mixture will run over the cinnamon rolls.

5. Let cool for 15 minutes, then serve.

Raspberry Cream Cheese Cinnamon Rolls

GLAZE

1½ cups confectioners' sugar

1 teaspoon vanilla

⅓ –½ cup milk

CREAM CHEESE FILLING

½ cup butter, room temperature

2 ounces cream cheese,
   room temperature

RASPBERRY FILLING

1 (12-ounce) package frozen raspberries

¼ cup granulated sugar

1 tablespoon cornstarch

1. For the glaze, mix all ingredients together until smooth and at a desired consistency. Set glaze aside.

2. Make the basic cinnamon roll recipe (page 21) through step 4.

3. While the dough is rising, prepare cream cheese filling.

4. When the dough is ready to roll out, prepare the raspberry filling.

5. For the cream cheese filling, mix together butter and cream cheese until incorporated. Set aside.

6. For the raspberry filling, toss the frozen raspberries, sugar, and cornstarch together until berries are evenly coated.

7. Roll dough into a 12x18 rectangle. Spread the cream cheese mixture evenly over the dough. Sprinkle raspberry mixture evenly over cream cheese filling. Roll and cut according to instructions in basic recipe. Place in prepared baking pan. Bake according to basic instructions.

8. Allow to cool for 10 minutes, then drizzle glaze over cinnamon rolls.

Buttermilk Caramel Syrup

Makes 3 cups • Prep Time: 10 minutes • Total Time: 10 minutes

We are so excited to share with you this recipe from the Vincent family. This is certainly not our Kneaders Famous Caramel Syrup, but it was the beginning of it. This recipe is our go-to when we are fixing French toast for a crowd. It is so delicious.

---

1 cup buttermilk

1 cup butter

1 teaspoon baking soda

2 cups granulated sugar

2 tablespoons corn syrup

2 teaspoons vanilla

1. In a large saucepan over medium-high heat, combine buttermilk, butter, baking soda, sugar, and corn syrup.

2. Stirring continually, bring to a boil for 5 minutes.

3. Remove from heat and add vanilla. It will foam up, but continue to stir until vanilla is incorporated.

Tasty Tips

- Substitute 1 cup brown sugar for granulated sugar to kick up the caramel flavor.

The
ANCHORS

James and Amy's family, clockwise from bottom left:
Jarett, Amy, Jackson, James, Jordan, Jace, Jett.

James and Amy Worthington

Our son James was a teenager when we started Kneaders. He was there when we had tubs of flour in the kitchen, an oven in the garage, and no idea how to bake bread. He worked graveyard shifts with Gary baking bread during his senior year of high school because we couldn't find anyone to cover those shifts. When I asked James recently about his memories of the beginning of Kneaders, he told me that he remembers me saying, "When we own a business, more opportunities to help people present themselves."

James and his wife, Amy, have loved helping people since our early days as a company. They've done everything from scrub floors and prep food in the back to design our gift baskets and develop new recipes. Now, James is the CEO and Amy continues to work in research and development. Their five boys (Jackson, Jordan, Jace, Jett, and Jarett) have done everything from cleaning the stores late at night to appearing in our ads. It has been a true family endeavor on their part.

If you've been to Kneaders, it's likely that you've had our famous Chunky Cinnamon French Toast. James is the one who came up with that recipe. He was attending Brigham Young University and his dorm didn't have a kitchen. So, James and his roommates started going over to the girls' dorm (where they *did* have kitchens) and making them French toast. We introduced our version of his French toast recipe in our stores in 2004.

Gary first met Amy at Kneaders. James and Amy had just started dating, and she was visiting James at the store. She was sitting on one of the dough benches and Gary opened the door just as James was leaning in to kiss Amy. She turned bright red—it was not how she'd imagined being introduced to James's family!

Amy liked coming into the bakery. Her parents, Danny and Carol Hansen, valued hard work in their home. When she met us, Amy thought, *Here's another family that works like mine.* I think we recognized that in her as well. From day one, Amy and James have always worked well together. They roll up their sleeves and jump right in.

Amy began working in the store in 2002, the summer before she and James got married. She started off as the prep person for the salads and made dressings by hand. She also did research and development on some of the menu items, like Artichoke Portobello Soup, Three-Cheese Cauliflower Soup, and Barbecue Chicken Salad. She has a wonderful creative touch and has often helped with the gift baskets and with buying retail to sell in our stores.

Before James and Amy had even graduated from Brigham Young University, they opened the Fort Union store. They ran the Fort Union Kneaders from 2003–2008. During that time, James completed his MBA at the University of Utah—and they had twins! In fact, James started his MBA program the day the twins were born. They were eight weeks early. Because they were so tiny, they had to remain in the NICU for six weeks. James would go up and help Amy feed the twins at the hospital before going to work at the Fort Union store, stop by again to feed them on his way to the University of Utah for school, and then again on his way back. Amy went back and forth between the hospital, home, and the store as well. We posted pictures in their store announcing the birth of the twins, and their patrons were so excited and often asked how the babies were doing. One patron even made them blankets. Their first outing, once they were healthy enough to leave the hospital, was to attend our Kneaders Halloween party, dressed as two tiny pumpkins.

Those twin boys, Jackson and Jordan, are now adults and have worked at the bakery for several years. They've learned that when a job isn't done well or a guest isn't happy, you work hard to make it right.

During the pandemic, the twins became friends with a ninety-year-old gentleman named Bert who came in for French toast every day at 10:58 a.m. When he didn't come in for a few days, Jordan worried about him. Later, they found out from a relative that Bert had passed away. Because they'd brought him food for a month and a half, this was hard for the boys. They'd come to love Bert and looked forward to seeing him. Later, Bert's family came in and celebrated his birthday in his honor at Kneaders. That was a tender moment for their family and for ours. Amy and James loved that the boys were able to see how we bring smiles to our customers and how they also bring those smiles to us. The same recipe that their dad invented as a college student was one they were able to share with Bert when they were teenagers themselves.

One of Amy and James's other five boys, Jace, recently texted Amy for a school assignment and asked her what made their family unique. When Amy asked him what *he* thought, he said, "We help people." It was an unconscious echo of what I had said to James years ago. When we are able to fund scholarships, raise money for worthy medical causes, help people find holiday work, or hand out loaves of bread at a shelter—it means the world. And it happens because of our customers, who come in time and time again and share their lives with us.

For James and Amy, and for all of us, the theme of Kneaders is *people.* Customers, employees, and family. All of the people we have served and worked with over the years have had huge impacts on where we are as a business and who we are as individuals. When we have the chance to see our family—children and grandchildren especially—experience that same connection and growth, it brings us true joy.

See JAMES'S CHUNKY CINNAMON FRENCH TOAST on page 26.

25

James's Chunky Cinnamon French Toast

Makes 8 slices • Prep Time: 5 minutes • Total Time: 10 minutes

Read James and Amy's story on pages 24–25.

2 large eggs, beaten

1 cup heavy cream

2 teaspoons vanilla extract

1 loaf Kneaders Chunky
Cinnamon Bread

1 (12-ounce) bottle Kneaders Famous
Caramel Syrup (or see recipe for
Buttermilk Caramel Syrup on page 23)

1. Slice Kneaders Chunky Cinnamon Bread into 8 thick slices, setting aside bread ends.

2. In a pie pan, shallow bowl, or 8x8 baking pan, whisk the eggs, heavy cream, vanilla extract, and cinnamon until fully combined.

3. Heat a large skillet or griddle over medium heat (350 degrees F.).

4. Dip the bread into the egg mixture, flipping over so both sides of the bread are soaked.

5. Add the bread to the skillet or griddle, being careful not to tear the slices. Cook until the French toast is golden brown on both sides.

6. Repeat with remaining slices of bread.

7. Serve the French toast hot with Kneaders Famous Caramel Syrup.

Tasty Tips

• Serve with fresh fruit and Whipped Cream Topping (see recipe on page 227).

French Toast Soufflé

Serves 12 • Prep Time: 20 minutes • Total Time: 1 hour 20 minutes

Having overnight guests? Need a quick breakfast? This can be prepared the night before. Pop it in the oven an hour before breakfast and let it cook while you're getting ready for the day. The aroma will fill your house and your guests will be charmed. Top with fresh fruit and serve with maple syrup.

---

1 (8-ounce) package cream cheese, softened

½ cup butter

1 cup maple syrup

1 loaf Kneaders Chunky Cinnamon Bread

12 eggs

2 cups half-and-half

1 teaspoon vanilla

Fresh fruit for topping

1. Preheat the oven to 350 degrees F.

2. Put the cream cheese, butter, and maple syrup in a microwave-safe bowl. Microwave for 30 seconds and beat until smooth.

3. Break Chunky Cinnamon Bread into 1½-inch pieces. Put them in a 9x13 baking dish.

4. Pour the cream cheese mixture over the top of the bread.

5. In a medium bowl, beat the eggs, half-and-half, and vanilla until frothy. Pour egg mixture over the bread in the pan.

6. Bake for 60 minutes.

7. Top with fresh blueberries or strawberries, powdered sugar, and syrup. Serve hot.

Mother's Day Overnight Peach Cobbler French Toast

Serves 6 • Prep Time: 30 minutes • Total Time: 1 hour + 8 hours chill time

Mothers are special to us at Kneaders. On Mother's Day, you can count on me crying. I'm still not quite sure why. Maybe it's just become a tradition. Every year at Kneaders we serve Chunky Cinnamon French Toast the day before Mother's Day to moms for free. It's my favorite day to work; there are so many happy people. I see lots of past employees with their cute kids as well as former neighbors with their daughters who are now mothers. Life goes on. We love being part of that at Kneaders.

In this recipe you will really enjoy the brown sugar and peach topping. It tastes like a peach cobbler that my grandma used to make.

---

1 cup brown sugar

½ cup butter

2 tablespoons water

1 (29-ounce) can sliced peaches, drained

12 (¾-inch thick) slices of Kneaders French Country Sourdough Bread

5 eggs

¾ cup heavy cream

1 tablespoon vanilla

Pinch of cinnamon

1. In a saucepan over medium-high heat, stir together brown sugar, butter, and water. Bring to a boil.

2. Reduce heat to low and simmer for 10 minutes, stirring frequently.

3. Pour brown sugar mixture into a 9x13 baking dish, covering the bottom evenly.

4. Layer the peaches over the brown sugar mixture.

5. Layer slices of bread over peaches.

6. In a separate bowl, whisk together eggs, heavy cream, and vanilla.

7. Slowly pour egg mixture over the bread slices to coat evenly.

8. Dust top with cinnamon.

9. Cover with foil and refrigerate for 8 hours or overnight.

10. Preheat the oven to 350 degrees F. Remove the dish from the refrigerator about 30 minutes before baking.

11. Bake covered for 20 minutes, then remove foil and bake for 25–30 minutes or until bread is golden brown.

Tasty Tips
- You can substitute any canned fruit for the sliced peaches. Apples or pears are good choices.

Overnight Chunky Cinnamon French Toast

Serves 6–8 • Prep Time: 20 minutes • Total Time: 1 hour 10 minutes + 8 hours chill time

Our most popular breakfast by far at Kneaders is our Chunky Cinnamon French Toast.

As much as we wish you could, we you can't spend every morning at Kneaders. But we're happy to share the next best thing—waking up to the rich aroma of baked French toast inside the comfort of your own home! You can create our bestselling breakfast by using thick slices of our famous Chunky Cinnamon Bread and baking them until the bread's cinnamon swirl and frosting are irresistibly caramelized. And the flavor doesn't stop there! We suggest topping it off with freshly sliced strawberries, whipped cream, and our famous caramel syrup to complete this scrumptious breakfast.

---

1 loaf day-old Kneaders
  Chunky Cinnamon Bread

7 eggs

1 tablespoon brown sugar

1 tablespoon vanilla

3 cups milk

¾ teaspoon salt

2 tablespoons butter

1 (12-ounce) bottle Kneaders Famous
  Caramel Syrup (or see recipe for
  Buttermilk Caramel Syrup on page 23)

1. Slice the Chunky Cinnamon bread into 8 pieces.

2. Generously butter a 9x13 glass baking dish.

3. Place 6 bread slices in the baking dish. Cut the remaining 2 slices into smaller pieces to fill in any spaces in the pan.

4. Mix eggs, brown sugar, vanilla, milk, and salt together. Pour the mixture over the bread slices.

5. Cut the butter into small pieces and dot evenly over the top of the bread slices.

6. Cover the baking dish and refrigerate overnight or at least 4 hours.

7. Preheat the oven to 350 degrees F. Uncover and bake for 40–50 minutes.

8. Serve hot with Kneaders Famous Caramel Syrup.

Tasty Tips
• Be sure to cut the slices thick when you are working with our Chunky Cinnamon Bread.

Stuffed French Toast

Serves 6 • Prep Time: 25 minutes • Total Time: 45 minutes

When I was little, my sister Linda and I would make my Mom breakfast in bed for Mother's Day. Usually it was undercooked French toast with syrup and fresh orange rings with a glass of milk. Trying to make it extra special, we would add a vase of flowers—the last of the lilacs mixed with dandelions. She loved it.

This is Chef Ryker's recipe for Mother's Day happiness. What a special treat!

---

1 (2.25-ounce) package slivered almonds

3 cups fresh strawberries, quartered

2 cups fresh raspberries

1 cup fresh blueberries

2 tablespoons granulated sugar

1 teaspoon lemon zest

4 eggs, beaten

1 teaspoon vanilla extract

2 cups heavy cream

1 loaf Kneaders Chunky Cinnamon Bread, sliced into 12 pieces

6 tablespoons (⅜ cup) mascarpone cheese

6 tablespoons (⅜ cup) Kneaders Pleasant Grove Strawberry Jam

1 tablespoon unsalted butter

Powdered sugar, to garnish

Maple syrup

1. Preheat oven to 325 degrees F. Spread slivered almonds on a half-sheet baking pan and toast for 15 minutes, stirring once or twice to avoid burning. Remove from oven and allow to cool. Set aside.

2. In a large mixing bowl, toss strawberries, raspberries, and blueberries with sugar and lemon zest. Set aside.

3. In a large mixing bowl, whisk together eggs, vanilla, and heavy cream.

4. Spread mascarpone cheese on 6 bread slices. Spread jam on remaining 6 slices and sandwich together with mascarpone bread slices.

5. Melt butter in a large nonstick skillet over medium heat. Dip each sandwich in the heavy cream mixture on both sides and place in the heated skillet. Cook on each side for about 3 minutes or until dark golden brown.

6. Cut each sandwich in half and garnish with almonds, berries, and powdered sugar. Serve warm with maple syrup.

Lemon Ricotta "Soufflé" Pancakes

Makes 6–8 pancakes, depending on size • Prep Time: 10 minutes • Total Time: 30 minutes

If you're in need of a breakfast that cooks up quickly but still feels special, this recipe fits the bill. You will love the brightness that the lemon zest gives these creamy ricotta pancakes, taking them to the next level. They are light, fluffy, fast—and sure to impress.

2½ cups Kneaders Homestyle Buttermilk Pancake Mix

1½ cup water

Zest of 1 lemon

½ cup ricotta cheese

½ cup egg whites (4 eggs), whipped

1 cup fresh blueberries

1 (12-ounce) bottle Kneaders Famous Caramel Syrup (or see recipe for Buttermilk Caramel Syrup on page 23)

1. Heat a large nonstick skillet to medium heat.

2. Whip egg whites to stiff peaks and set aside.

3. In a mixing bowl, whisk together the pancake mix and water. Add the lemon zest and ricotta cheese and whisk thoroughly. Gently fold in the whipped egg whites until well combined.

4. Spoon ¼–½ cup of batter onto the preheated skillet and cook for 1–2 minutes or until golden brown.

5. Turn the pancake over and cook for another minute or until cooked through. Repeat with remaining batter.

6. Serve pancakes warm with fresh blueberries and Kneaders Famous Caramel Syrup.

Tasty Tips

- You can use other fresh fruit—raspberries, blackberries, or fresh peach slices would also work well.

Pecan Pancakes

Makes 8–16 pancakes, depending on size • Prep Time: 15 minutes • Total Time: 20–25 minutes

When our daughters Christy and Amy lived in Texas, we became obsessed with pecans and started adding them to everything. This recipe for pecan pancakes was our favorite. We hope y'all enjoy this little bit of Texas.

2 eggs

1¾ cups buttermilk

½ cup butter, melted then cooled to room temperature

2 teaspoons vanilla

1¾ cups flour

2 tablespoons sugar

1 teaspoon baking soda

1 teaspoon salt

½ cup chopped pecans

1 (12-ounce) bottle Kneaders Famous Caramel Syrup (or see recipe for Buttermilk Caramel Syrup on page 23)

1. In a medium bowl, beat the egg, buttermilk, butter, and vanilla together until well blended.

2. In a separate bowl, whisk the flour, sugar, baking soda, and salt together.

3. Fold the wet ingredients into the dry ingredients until they are incorporated.

4. Scoop batter in ¼-cup or ½-cup increments onto a hot oiled skillet.

5. Sprinkle pecans on the batter side of each pancake.

6. Flip each pancake when bubbles stay open or it's golden brown.

7. Serve with butter and Kneaders Famous Caramel Syrup.

SALADS

Aloha Summer Pasta Salad

Serves 8–12 • Prep Time: 15 minutes • Total Time: 25 minutes + 30 minutes chill time

For all of you who have been asking, here is this flavorful Hawaiian pasta recipe. In 2015 we started our limited-time summer offers by making food from different regions of the world. Who doesn't love the islands? This was such a fun time for us at Kneaders. For this first promotion, all the stores had a decorating contest. I remember that Cilla and Ben Toa at our Baseline Gilbert store in Arizona won that contest, hands down. All our stores presented paper leis to our customers as they entered during the promotion, and many stores had talent come to entertain guests on Friday and Saturday nights. My favorite song of that summer was "Somewhere Over the Rainbow," ukulele-style.

1 (27-ounce) package colored
   twist pasta

¾ cup Poppy Seed Dressing
   (see recipe on page 57)

2 avocados, chopped in ½-inch pieces

2 cups fresh pineapple tidbits,
   chopped in ½-inch pieces

½ cup red onion, chopped
   in ¼-inch squares

1. Cook pasta according to instructions for al dente, about 10 minutes.

2. While pasta is boiling, pour the dressing into a separate bowl and add the avocado, pineapple, and onion. Let soak until the pasta is finished cooking. (This will help bring more flavor to the ingredients and keep the avocado from turning brown.)

3. Drain pasta and toss with poppy seed mixture.

4. Refrigerate for 30 minutes or more before serving.

Tasty Tips

- Try substituting mangoes or other tropical fruits for the pineapple.
- To help the pasta cool quickly, drain it and rinse it with cold water. Be sure to let it dry before adding the dressing.

Berry Delight Salad

Serves 6 • Prep Time: 5 minutes • Total Time: 10 minutes

As I was growing up, having salad for dinner meant iceberg lettuce, tomatoes, onions, cucumbers—and maybe some grated cheese. Fruit salads were made with fruit cocktail and Jell-O. It wasn't until I was a freshman in college that I tasted my first fresh fruit salad with greens. I became obsessed immediately! I love fresh fruit, especially fresh berries. I'm sure this love comes from the time spent at my grandpa Ashby Fox's farm in Highland, Utah. He grew fresh fruits and vegetables for his family of ten children on several acres. My favorite memories revolved around picking strawberries, blueberries, and raspberries. To be perfectly truthful, most of the berries ended up in my mouth. They never would have made it into a salad. I was amazed that my grandpa always knew I'd been eating them. I guess the juice dripping from the corners of my mouth was the clue. I hope you enjoy these berries as much as I did at the Fox farm.

---

1 quart spinach, not packed

1 quart romaine lettuce, chopped in 1-inch squares

2 cups fresh strawberries, hulled and halved

1 cup fresh blueberries

1 cup fresh raspberries

1 cup fresh blackberries

½ cup chopped red onion

½ cup feta cheese

½ cup walnut halves

1 batch Blueberry Pomegranate Vinaigrette dressing

Fill a large serving bowl with the spinach and romaine lettuce, distributing them evenly. Add the fresh berries and the red onion and toss lightly. Sprinkle the salad with feta cheese and almonds. Serve with Blueberry Pomegranate Vinaigrette dressing (see recipe on page 56).

BLT Macaroni Salad

Serves 8–10 • Prep Time: 15 minutes • Total Time: 35 minutes + 2 hours chill time

When we first introduced our sandwiches twenty-three years ago, we also began making our deli salads. We wanted to have something to serve in the box lunches that we often cater for businesses or other groups. This recipe comes from one of Amy Peterson's sisters-in-law, Julie Riley. We added cheddar cheese for creaminess. This salad was a huge success in those lunches.

While taking pictures for this cookbook, I was bewildered to realize there is no *L* (lettuce) in this salad! I had never noticed that before, and no one has ever mentioned it to me. I guess it's just a BT salad, but I promise you will love the tangy dressing, sweet tomatoes, and salty bacon with every bite.

4–6 cups water

4 cups medium sized elbow macaroni

1¼ cups sour cream

2½ cups mayonnaise

2 tablespoons salt

1 tablespoon pepper

1 cup + 1 tablespoon white Italian vinegar

1 cup Parmesan cheese

½ cup chopped green onions

3 cups grape tomatoes, cut in half

1½ cups chopped celery

½ cup cheddar cheese, cut in small cubes

3 strips bacon, cooked and cut into ½-inch squares

1. In a large saucepan or Dutch oven over high heat, boil the water and add macaroni, following the instructions on the package for medium-done noodles.

2. While the noodles are boiling, whisk together the sour cream, mayonnaise, salt, pepper, white Italian vinegar, and Parmesan cheese in a medium bowl. Set aside.

3. Drain the noodles and rinse immediately with cold water. Let dry.

4. Mix the noodles with the sauce.

5. Add the green onions, tomato, and celery and mix. Add bacon and cheddar cubes and mix.

6. Chill for two hours.

Tasty Tips

• Serve on a bed of lettuce (to make it a true "BLT").

The WISHER

Gary, Jacob, and Colleen in the Kneaders kitchen.

Jacob Hutchings

"What are we baking today, Mom?" four-year-old Jacob would ask each morning. He loved the comfort, sweetness, and delicious aromas of home cooking. His mom knew that the stability of routine and the warmth of a home steeped in love would help her son through a period filled with pain, uncertainty, and confusion as Jacob struggled with an aggressive brain tumor.

He said, "I want to be a baker because I want to spank the dough." Make-A-Wish granted Jacob his wish. Part of that was time spent with us at Kneaders. He handed out free cookies and made a special loaf of bread that he shared with customers that day. We ended the day the best way we know how—with a big flour fight.

Jacob was four and a half when he came to visit us, and all he wanted was to "pat the dough." He had seen cartoon characters pat the dough, and he wanted to do that too. So Gary made this recipe especially for him—a "loaf" made of individual rolls for a maximum amount of patting and shaping for Jacob. Each roll had a different topping on it, and when Gary and Jacob put it in the oven, Gary told Jacob, "These are like all the friends surrounding you."

Jacob brought his friends and a cousin with him, and we put his name up on the marquee in front of the store. Our food supplier had a baker's hat and an apron made especially for Jacob. At that time, our daughter Amy was Miss Pleasant Grove. She dressed up with her crown and gifted him with baking supplies to take home. The employees decorated the store by filling it with balloons. It was one of the most special days we have had. Near the end of the visit, I carried Jacob through the bakery so he could choose baked goods to take with him. When we got to the cheesecakes, I asked him if he wanted a piece to take home. The entire time, Jacob had been so grateful and thankful for everything and everyone. So his answer surprised me a little—he asked if he could have a whole cheesecake. That was fine with me, but it seemed a bit out of character. Then he looked at me and said, "Can I take it to the hospital to give to all my nurses and to the doctors and workers?" In all of Jacob's struggles, his thoughts were to take care of those who took care of him.

On our twentieth anniversary, Justin and Jacob made Jacob's Loaf again, and it was later featured in the Make-A-Wish newsletter (which had also featured Jacob's story the first time he visited us). We sold Jacob's Loaf in Orem all through that anniversary year. In the time that has passed since his Make-A-Wish visit, Jacob has continued baking in his home with the commercial baking pans, whisks, and other equipment that we gave him.

See recipe for JACOB'S LOAF on page 156.

Gary, Jacob, and Jacob's dad loading the oven.

Gary and Jacob shaping the dough.

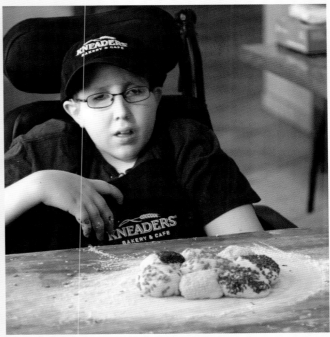

Jacob at the twentieth anniversary of Kneaders with a ready-for-the-oven Jacob's Loaf.

Broccoli Sunflower Salad

Serves 6–8 • Prep Time: 10 minutes • Total Time: 10 minutes

This recipe was the very first side salad that was served every day at Kneaders for 20 years. We have changed the dressing over the years; it's a little more tangy now, but everything else is the same. It's also delicious when made with half-cauliflower, half-broccoli. A fun addition to try is adding bacon pieces and substituting your favorite nuts for the sunflower seeds.

---

6 cups broccoli, cut into bite-size pieces

5⅓ cups spinach, loosely packed

1⅓ cups red grapes

⅓ cup raisins

⅓ cup sunflower seeds

1 batch Creamy Broccoli Salad Dressing

1. Put broccoli in a large mixing bowl.

2. Add the spinach, red grapes, raisins, and sunflower kernels and toss.

3. Mix Creamy Broccoli Salad Dressing (see recipe on page 55) into the salad until everything is well coated.

4. Store in the refrigerator.

Tasty Tips

• All the boys like it with added bacon bits.

Chicken Raspberry Pecan Salad

Serves 6 • Prep Time: 15 minutes • Total Time: 15 minutes

Pairing raspberries with feta cheese is a combination loved by our guests. Feta cheese is a Greek cheese made from a mixture of sheep and goat's milk and has a naturally salty taste. This makes a perfect companion to fresh raspberries. And of course, spinach is a superfood. No wonder Popeye ate so much of it! I'm not a big fan of canned spinach (I'll leave that for Popeye), but I love the underlying sweetness of fresh spinach, especially in a salad.

8 cups fresh baby spinach greens

3 precooked boneless skinless chicken breasts, cut in bite-size pieces

½ cup feta cheese

½ cup raspberries

¼ cup Cinnamon Sugar Pecans (see recipe below)

5 slices red onion to garnish

1 batch Poppy Seed Dressing

1. In a medium serving bowl, layer spinach.

2. Add chicken and gently toss by hand.

3. Top with feta cheese, raspberries, and Cinnamon Sugar Pecans.

4. Garnish with sliced red onions and serve with Poppy Seed Dressing (see recipe on page 57).

Cinnamon Sugar Pecans

Makes 3 cups • Prep Time: 5 minutes • Total Time: 35 minutes

¼ cup sugar

2¼ teaspoons ground cinnamon

¼ teaspoon salt

½ teaspoon allspice

1 egg white

3 cups pecans

1. Preheat the oven to 250 degrees F.

2. In a medium bowl, beat the egg white until foamy. Add the pecans. Toss until well coated.

3. Mix sugar, cinnamon, and salt in a small bowl.

4. Add spice mixture to the pecans and toss until coated evenly.

5. Spread pecans in a single layer on a parchment-lined baking sheet.

6. Bake for 30 minutes, stirring once. Let cool completely. Store in an airtight container for up to 2 weeks.

Citrus Salad

Serves 4 • Prep Time: 5 minutes • Total Time: 10 minutes

This well-loved salad was the favorite of almost all of our home office training crew when it was on the menu. When you are out on the road training for two weeks, you get really tired of hamburgers. It was always refreshing to go to one of our stores and have this healthy, crunchy, salty, and sweet citrus salad. I have a feeling this might become a fast favorite of yours, too.

---

2 quarts mixed greens

1 medium sweet orange, peeled and cut into rings, then quartered, or 1 (6-ounce) can mandarin oranges, drained

2 grilled chicken breasts, cut into strips

½ cup sunflower kernels

½ cup dried cranberries

½ cup shaved Parmesan cheese

1 batch Balsamic Vinaigrette Dressing

1. Fill a serving bowl with mixed greens.

2. Add the oranges, grilled chicken, sunflower kernels, and dried cranberries.

3. Hand toss until evenly distributed.

4. Top the salad with shaved Parmesan cheese.

5. Serve with Balsamic Vinaigrette Dressing (see recipe on page 55).

UTENSILES

Paris, France

1893

SALT

PEPPER

Dressings

Balsamic Vinaigrette Dressing

Makes 1 cup • Total Time: 5 minutes

Don't you just love balsamic vinegar dressing? I sure do. It's zesty and has an underlying sweetness. It's my go-to dressing with any salad we have at Kneaders. Turkey Bacon Avocado Salad—yes! Thai Salad—yes! Raspberry Nut Salad—yes! And if you can't get to Kneaders, you just need a cool summer evening, fresh vegetables and fruits from your garden, and this dressing. Life doesn't get any better. This version of the dressing was developed by Ryker Brown for Kneaders Bakery.

¼ cup balsamic vinegar

1½ teaspoons granulated garlic

½ teaspoon kosher salt

¾ teaspoon coarse black pepper

1 tablespoon brown sugar

½ cup + 1 teaspoon mild
   flavored olive oil

Add all ingredients into a blender and blend until incorporated. Store for up to 2 weeks in a covered jar in the refrigerator. Shake to reconstitute.

Creamy Broccoli Salad Dressing

Makes 1 cup • Prep Time: 5 minutes • Total Time: 10 minutes

Our Poppy Seed Dressing is such a versatile dressing. By adding sour cream and mayo to it, now you have a creamy dressing that's perfect for serving with raw vegetables.

1/3 cup Poppy Seed Dressing
   (see recipe on page 57)

1/3 cup sour cream

1/3 cup mayonnaise

1. Place poppy seed dressing and sour cream in a bowl and whisk until smooth.

2. Add mayonnaise to the dressing and mix until smooth. Store in the refrigerator.

Blueberry Pomegranate Vinaigrette Dressing

Makes 1½ cups • Prep Time: 15 minutes • Total Time: 20 minutes

You can't resist this combination of blueberries and pomegranate. It's a dressing that may surprise you.

Seeds of 1 small pomegranate

½ cup fresh blueberries

¼ cup extra virgin olive oil

2 teaspoons apple cider vinegar

2 teaspoons real maple syrup

Salt and pepper to taste

1 pint jar with lid

1. Add all ingredients to a blender. Blend until combined.

2. Place a fine mesh sieve over a bowl and pour the dressing into it. You can use the back of a spoon to press the liquid through the sieve. Discard any seed pulp.

3. Use immediately or refrigerate in a covered jar for up to 5 days.

Lemon Garlic Vinaigrette Dressing

Makes 1 cup • Prep Time: 10 minutes • Total Time: 15 minutes

You'll find a handful of recipes in this cookbook that were never served at the bakery—this is one of them. We really did try to make it work, but making fresh zest every day wasn't cost-effective. There is no substitute for fresh lemon juice and fresh lemon zest! That bright taste cannot be manufactured.

Juice of 2 lemons

Zest of 1 lemon

2 garlic cloves, finely grated

½ cup avocado oil

Salt to taste, starting with 1/8 teaspoon

Pepper to grind on top of dressed salad

Add all ingredients to a blender and blend until incorporated. Store for up to 2 weeks in a covered jar in the refrigerator. Shake to reconstitute.

Poppy Seed Dressing

Makes 2 cups • Total Time: 5 minutes

In the early 2000s, my oldest sister, Elaine, shared a tasty poppyseed dressing with us at the bakery. She also made a delicious chicken salad with almonds and mozzarella cheese. It was delightful. Elaine gave us permission to make it our very first salad and dressing at Kneaders. And it's a beautiful color. It tastes both refreshing and sweet, so add it to any salad to ramp up the flavor.

⅓ cup red wine vinegar

1 cup granulated sugar

1½ teaspoons poppy seeds

1 tablespoon ground mustard

1 cup canola oil

½ teaspoon salt

¼ teaspoon pepper

Add all ingredients to a blender and blend until incorporated. Store for up to 2 weeks in a covered jar in the refrigerator. Shake to reconstitute.

Maria's Caprese Salad

Serves 8 • Prep Time: 10 minutes • Total Time 20 minutes

When we were at a Dallas gift market, we asked Frank Duty, our Orem store operator and a longtime Texas resident, where to eat. He gave us the name of a great Texas steakhouse where they made a delicious caprese salad. They've since stopped making it, but it's still a family favorite. After a few revisions, it became part of our Italian Summer. I love the variety of flavors in this dish—the tang of the balsamic vinegar reduction, the creaminess of the fresh mozzarella, and the crispness of the bacon.

---

2 heads (16 leaves) romaine lettuce

4 roma tomatoes, sliced into 16 slices

8 slices fresh mozzarella, cut in half

16 basil leaves, chopped in half

Balsamic vinegar reduction, such as Roland Original Glaze

Ranch dressing

8 slices cooked bacon, chopped

1. Wash the lettuce and pat dry. Trim the bottom of the leaves so they are the length of the plates you want to use for your salads. Place 2 leaves of lettuce on a plate, with the edges toward the outside of the plate.

2. Alternating the tomato and mozzarella, place 2 tomato slices and 2 mozzarella slices on top of each lettuce bed.

3. Place 1 piece of basil on top of each tomato slice and mozzarella slice.

4. Drizzle with balsamic vinegar reduction and ranch dressing.

5. Sprinkle bacon over each salad.

Roasted Root Vegetable Salad

Serves 8 • Prep Time: 25 minutes • Total Time: 60 minutes

Don't you just love those one-pan dishes where everything bakes for 35 minutes at 400 degrees and then—like magic—dinner is done? Ryker Brown used that idea for this recipe for roasted vegetables, which can be a dinner in itself if you add salad greens and dressing. Something really good happens when you roast vegetables instead of boiling them.

During the COVID-19 quarantines, Gary and I had a lot of fun trying different combinations of roasted meats and veggies. It goes like this: Wash and slice any veggies that you have, such as onions, mushrooms, sweet potatoes, carrots, potatoes, squash, or zucchini. Drizzle olive oil on a sheet pan. Add vegetables and chicken tenders and turn over so that they are oiled on both sides, then sprinkle with salt and pepper. Place the pan in the oven. After 15 minutes, turn everything over and continue to roast for 15–20 more minutes until done. Take it out of the oven and dish it up all hot and juicy onto your festive ceramic plates. Gary and I recommend you eat slowly and binge your favorite show. COVID-19 did have some blessings: lots of time together and lots of one-pan cooking at home.

1½ cups parsnip, peeled
and diced large

1½ cups carrot, peeled and diced large

1 cup onion, peeled and diced large

2 cups butternut squash,
peeled and diced large

1½ cups turnip, peeled and diced large

2 cups rutabaga, peeled
and diced large

Salt and pepper to taste

¼ cup garlic, peeled and chopped

½ teaspoon fresh thyme, chopped

½ teaspoon fresh rosemary, chopped

2 tablespoons Italian parsley, chopped

3 tablespoons extra virgin olive oil

2 (5-ounce) bags spring mix

1 batch Balsamic Vinaigrette Dressing

1. Preheat oven to 400 degrees F.

2. In a large mixing bowl, toss all ingredients except the greens thoroughly, then spread out on a parchment-lined half-sheet pan and place in the oven.

3. Roast for 30–35 minutes, or until vegetables are soft and deep golden brown, turning them over once halfway through.

4. Remove from the oven and serve immediately on top of mixed greens.

5. Drizzle with Balsamic Vinaigrette Dressing (see recipe on page 55).

Tasty Tips

- You can substitute any vegetable in the recipe for an equal amount of any other vegetable, if desired.

Southwest Barbecue Chicken Salad

Serves 8 • Prep Time: 15 minutes • Total Time: 30 minutes

It's hard to say which part of this salad is the best. Is it the grilled chicken tossed in BBQ sauce, the crisp romaine, the fresh tortilla strips, or the cotija cheese? Or maybe it's the cilantro ranch dressing that ties it all together. There's enough protein in this delightful salad that you don't have to add anything else to make it a one-dish meal.

1 bunch cilantro, stems removed and chopped fine, divided

1 cup ranch dressing

2 heads romaine lettuce, washed and chopped

1 cup barbecue sauce, such as Sweet Baby Ray's, divided

4 grilled chicken breasts, cooked, sliced, and tossed in ½ cup barbecue sauce

1 (15-ounce) can black beans, rinsed and drained

1 (11-ounce) can shoepeg corn, rinsed and drained

1 cup cherry tomatoes, cut in half

2 avocados, diced

4 ounces cotija cheese or feta cheese, crumbled

1 (3.5-ounce) bag tortilla strips, such as Fresh Gourmet, Santa Fe Style

1. Blend together ¼ cup chopped cilantro with ranch dressing. Set aside.

2. In a large bowl, toss the romaine with the remaining cilantro.

3. Top the greens with chicken, black beans, corn, tomatoes, avocado, and cotija cheese.

4. Add the cilantro ranch dressing and toss until everything is well coated.

5. Drizzle the salad with remaining barbecue sauce. Top with the tortilla strips.

6. Serve immediately.

Southwest Quinoa Salad

Serves 10–12 • Prep Time: 15 minutes • Total Time: 25 minutes

One of my favorite research and development chefs, Justin Garner, developed this beautiful recipe for us. Take a look at all the protein in this vegetarian recipe! The quinoa adds a mild nutty flavor and a satisfying crunch. You'll also enjoy the fresh veggies and chopped lemony cilantro. This hard-to-resist salad is one you can make a batch of, divide into separate containers, refrigerate, and eat all week long.

---

3 cups dried quinoa (enough to make 6 cups cooked quinoa)

2 red peppers, ribs and seeds removed, diced

14 green onions, diced

1 cup loosely packed cilantro, chopped

1 (15-ounce) can sweet corn, drained

1 (15-ounce) can black beans, drained and rinsed

DRESSING

¼ cup olive oil

6 tablespoons fresh-squeezed lime juice

4 teaspoons minced garlic

2 teaspoons cumin

1 teaspoon oregano

2 teaspoons salt

½ teaspoon pepper

1. In a stockpot over high heat, bring 6 cups of water to a boil. Add 3 cups of uncooked quinoa and bring back to a rolling boil. Cover and boil for 5 minutes. As soon as the quinoa seeds start to open, take them off the heat. Quinoa will be firm and dry but not hard.

2. Place the red pepper, green onions, and cilantro in a large bowl, add the corn and black beans, and mix together.

3. In a small bowl, mix the olive oil, lime juice, garlic, and spices together until combined.

4. Add the quinoa and the olive oil mixture to the bell pepper mixture in the large bowl. Toss the ingredients until they are all incorporated.

5. Cool and serve.

Tasty Tips

- Serve in a Kneaders Sourdough Bread Bowl and top with a sunny-side up fried egg.

SANDWICHES

BBQ Pulled Pork Sandwiches

Makes 36 sandwiches • Prep Time: 15 minutes • Total Time: 7 hours

Slow cooked and delicious, these pulled pork sandwiches are easy to make for a crowd (and the crowd will be pleased!). With tender pork, light fluffy rolls, and a burst of flavors, everyone will be asking for more. It's easy to double or even triple the recipe. Let the slow cooker work its magic and Kneaders do the rolls, and it will be easy for you to sit back and enjoy the party!

A fun note: Tami shared this recipe on the local television show *Good Things Utah*. They'd asked us to share a tailgate recipe. Well, our favorite item for tailgating is anything served on our scrumptious soft rolls. In fact, we just love those rolls with a piece of provolone cheese, some ranch dressing, and any kind of meat. But that wasn't quite fancy enough for TV. This BBQ pulled pork recipe, however, is fit for a king. I like mine with an extra shot of barbecue sauce.

1½ tablespoons chili powder

¾ teaspoon salt

½ teaspoon freshly ground black pepper

1 (3.5-pound) pork shoulder roast

1 onion, roughly sliced

2 cloves garlic, minced

1½ cups barbecue sauce, divided (such as Sweet Baby Ray's)

4 cups water

3 dozen Kneaders Soft Rolls

Coleslaw, for garnish (optional)

Cilantro, for garnish (optional)

Red onion, for garnish (optional)

1. In a small bowl, combine the chili powder, salt, and pepper and rub the mixture on the pork roast until it is thoroughly coated.

2. Place the sliced onion and garlic in the bottom of a slow cooker. Then add the roast and ½ cup barbecue sauce. Pour the water over the roast. Cook the roast on high until it is very tender and the meat falls off the bone, about 6 hours.

3. Remove the pork from the slow cooker and place on a platter. Strain and discard the cooking liquid from the slow cooker, keeping the onion.

4. Return the pork and onion to the slow cooker. Shred the pork. Add remaining cup barbecue sauce. Cook on high until it's heated through, about 8 minutes.

5. To assemble the sandwiches, split each roll in half and place about 3 tablespoons pork inside. Garnish with coleslaw or cilantro and red onion if desired.

Tasty Tips

• Be sure to get a pork shoulder roast. With just the right amount of fat, it is both juicy and tender. Be careful not to overshred, and leave some larger chunks. If the shredded meat gets dry, just add more sauce.

Chicken Cilantro Sandwich

Serves 6 • Prep Time: 15 minutes • Total Time: 30 minutes

I know that some of you think that cilantro tastes like soap. I still love you, but you will want to move on to a different recipe. Now, if you're like me and you can't get enough cilantro, you've got to give this a try. Don't hesitate to use the sauce as a dip. To quote one of my friends: "It will change your life." Yum!

CILANTRO SAUCE

4 ounces cream cheese, softened

1½ teaspoons sour cream

3.5 ounces salsa verde

½ teaspoon black pepper

½ teaspoon celery salt

¼ teaspoon ground cumin

1 teaspoon garlic powder

¼ cup chopped fresh cilantro

1½ teaspoons lime juice

SANDWICH

2 loaves Kneaders Ciabatta Bread

6 chicken breasts

12 slices provolone cheese

1 head red leaf lettuce

3 tomatoes, sliced

1 red onion, sliced

1. Combine all cilantro sauce ingredients in a blender. Blend until smooth and creamy.

2. Cut off the ends of each loaf of ciabatta bread, then slice the bread into thirds. Cut open each third horizontally to make the top and bottom for each sandwich.

3. With a meat mallet, flatten chicken out to be ¼ inch thick. Grill or panfry each chicken breast until browned and cooked through.

4. Place each piece of ciabatta bread cut side down on a griddle. Grill until golden brown.

5. Spread cilantro sauce on bread. Stack with chicken, cheese, lettuce, tomato, and red onion.

Tasty Tips

• Fresh cilantro keepers are available online. They keep cilantro fresh for up to 3 weeks. Worth the money!

Ciabatta Muffuletta Sandwich

Olive Salad: Prep Time: 20 minutes • Chill Time: 24 hours / Sandwich: Prep Time: 10 minutes • Chill Time: 8 hours

We have a lot of customers who remember and love this sandwich. They keep asking for the recipe. Well, now it is yours, and we are so pleased to share it with you. You will enjoy these blended Mediterranean flavors—salty, sharp, and tangy. Our ciabatta bread is made for this sandwich. It can hold up well when piled high with ingredients. The olive salad takes a day to make, but it keeps for several days.

OLIVE SALAD

½ cup green queen stuffed olives, chopped

1 cup black olives, chopped

½ cup chopped red onion

½ cup celery, thinly sliced down the stalk, then chopped

½ teaspoon finely minced garlic

½ cup sweet roasted red peppers, drained and chopped

½ tablespoon Extra Virgin Olive Oil

½ tablespoon apple cider vinegar

Freshly ground sea salt

Freshly ground black pepper

SANDWICH

1 loaf Kneaders Ciabatta Bread

6 slices ham, thinly sliced

12 thin slices Genoa salami

8 artichoke hearts, drained and chopped

½ cup feta cheese

12 fresh basil leaves

Freshly ground sea salt

Freshly ground black pepper

1. For the salad, in a medium bowl, mix together olives, red onion, celery, garlic, and red peppers. In a small bowl, mix olive oil and vinegar. Pour over the salad. Salt and pepper to taste. Store covered in the refrigerator for 24 hours before using.

2. For the sandwich, cut off the ends of the ciabatta bread, then cut the bread in half horizontally. Layer with a generous amount of olive salad, ham, genoa salami, artichokes, feta, and basil. Salt and pepper to taste.

3. Wrap tightly in parchment paper and refrigerate for 8 hours with a 5-pound weight on top.

4. Once chilled, cut into 6 sandwiches. Grill on a panini press for 4 minutes on high heat. Serve warm.

Tasty Tips
- Use a gallon of milk as a weight.

The
ENGINEERS

Tami and David's family, left to right: Elle Vincent, Abbie Vincent Douglas, Seth Douglas, David Vincent, Tami Worthington Vincent.

Tami and David Vincent

Some of the great things about being part of a family—a work family, a family of friends, a family of people related to one another—are the traditions that are created together. Even if the traditions are born out of necessity! Our daughter Tami and her husband, David, who have worked with us since the very beginning, have noted that having all hands on deck during the holidays has become one of our family's traditions. We opened our first store in December 1997, and the holidays have been a fulfilling and busy time for us ever since.

David is now the Chief Financial Officer for Kneaders, and Tami started our Abbie & Ellie candy company. But, like many of our family members who have helped us get the business going, they have done just about every job imaginable.

Opening a brand-new business during the holidays was the beginning of our nonstop holiday seasons. David and Tami were there from the ground up. They were newlyweds, and they tried new recipes, worked behind the counter and at the register, and helped clean the building. David learned to bake from Gary and made many of our loaves of bread for the first few years.

After a couple of years of being married and going to school and working in Utah, Dave decided to transfer to the University of Michigan in Ann Arbor to finish his undergraduate degree in mechanical engineering. When it came time to graduate, Dave had several internship offers, including one with Ford Motors. But he felt like he wanted to work for Kneaders and he and Tami wanted to be closer to family, so they decided to come back to Utah. We were thrilled, because we really needed their help and expertise but hadn't wanted to pressure them.

Dave went right back to doing whatever was needed at the store. His engineering degree has come in handy as he's helped us figure out not only machinery, but also all the other moving parts of running a business. Dave learned how to bake, he managed a store, and he did the finances for the company. Dave still bakes at Thanksgiving and Christmas, and I feel like you can always tell the difference when Justin, Gary, and Dave are baking. The bread tastes extra special. We often met Dave and Tami at the Orem Kneaders on Sunday afternoons. Dave always made his own BLT sandwich. He'd ask us, "Do you want some?" We always answered "Yes!" without hesitation.

During Dave and Tami's time in Michigan, we had started making gift baskets to sell, and we had lost the supplier for our chocolate pretzel rods. So, of course, we decided just to make them ourselves, and we started our own candy company. We bought recipes from my nephew Greg and a steam kettle from eBay for 300 dollars. Tami became an engineer in her own right—she ran and managed the entire Abbie & Ellie candy company (which is named after Dave and Tami's two daughters). During the holidays, Tami got everyone she could to come help with the pretzel rods. For several years, Dave and James came in to work at Kneaders for their twelve hours, and then they would go home and switch with Tami and Amy, who would come in and work through the night while Dave and James cared for the kids. They did that for days until everything was ready.

One Thanksgiving was particularly memorable. We make so many pies and rolls for Thanksgiving that it is always a crazy time, with everyone working around the clock to get it all done. That year, we had done our prep work and had our soft rolls all prepped and ready to bake. When David and the others went to bake them off, we realized that four to five hundred dozen rolls had been made with expired yeast that our vendor had sent over without realizing. We looked at each other and realized this wouldn't work. We had to start all over, which meant that we were driving around delivering rolls to customers at 11:00 P.M. the night before Thanksgiving so

Abbie and Ellie.

that they'd have them in time for their Thanksgiving dinners. Because everything has a domino effect, it meant that we also got behind on our pie baking, so Dave and the others were delivering pumpkin pies at 11:00 P.M. as well. The customers were understanding when they saw how hard we were trying to make it right.

During the holidays, we work long hours at the store—even the grandchildren. There isn't a grandchild who hasn't worked at one of our stores or helped with the business at one time or another. Thanks to Dave and Tami and our other children, employees, and their families, one of our most treasured holiday traditions is being a part of our customers' lives at the most wonderful time of the year.

See recipes for DAVE'S BLT SANDWICH on page 76, and PEPPERMINT BARK on page 321.

Dave's BLT Sandwich

Makes 4 sandwiches • Prep Time: 5 minutes • Total Time: 15 minutes

What makes this BLT special? It's our wonderful Country White Bread that we make fresh every day. You can't beat fresh. And, of course, our Kneaders Sauce is another factor. When deciding the base dressing for our sandwiches, we took mayo and mustard and mixed them together in different ratios. It was good, but it lacked tang. When we added sour cream, the sauce was perfect! We probably tried about fifty combinations before we decided on the final recipe. Now that you know the ingredients, you can experiment and mix up your family's own favorite blend of Kneaders Sauce.

Read Tami and David Vincent's story on pages 74–75.

---

8 slices Kneaders White Country bread

½ cup Kneaders Sauce (see introduction to this recipe)

4 large leaves green leaf lettuce

16 large pieces bacon, cooked

2 tomatoes, sliced

4 slices provolone cheese

1. Using a spatula, spread Kneaders Sauce on one side of each slice of bread.

2. On one slice of bread, put a slice of provolone cheese, one leaf of lettuce, and 4 pieces of bacon. Top with 4 tomato slices and salt and pepper to taste. Top with another slice of bread. Repeat until you have 4 sandwiches.

Tasty Tips

• Candied bacon puts this sandwich over the top.

Hot Ham and Cheese Sandwich

Serves 6 • Prep Time: 10 minutes • Total Time: 25 minutes

Hot ham and cheese sliders are the perfect appetizer (try them on Kneaders Soft Rolls). But if you're looking for a main course entree try this recipe on Kneaders crusty, flavorful Ciabatta Bread.

2 loaves Kneaders Ciabatta Bread

12 slices Black Forest ham

12 slices Swiss cheese

8 tablespoons butter, softened

½ cup chopped sweet onion

1½ tablespoons Dijon mustard

1½ tablespoons poppy seeds

1. Preheat oven to 350 degrees F.

2. Cut the ends off the ciabatta bread, and slice the loaves into thirds. Cut open each slice horizontally to make the tops and bottoms of the sandwiches.

3. In a small bowl, combine butter, onion, mustard, and poppy seeds. Mix well.

4. Spread the butter mixture on both halves of the sliced bread.

5. Place two slices of ham and two slices of cheese on each bottom half. Put the top half on top of the cheese and ham. Wrap each sandwich in aluminum foil.

6. Place the wrapped sandwiches on a half-sheet baking pan and bake for 15 minutes.

Tasty Tips

- Buy Ciabatta Bread from Kneaders at 5 p.m. Nothing is as good as hot Ciabatta bread! Try substituting whole grain mustard for Dijon to give the sandwiches more texture.

Gourmet Picnic Sandwich

Makes 8 sandwiches • Prep Time: 15 minutes • Chill Time: 8 hours

Inspiration for this sandwich came from a trip to Verona, Italy. Just outside the Roman Colosseum, grand white tents with white lights had been set up for a bread, deli meat, and cheese fair. At one of the tents was a sandwich made on a large loaf of bread called miche, a French sourdough. A variety of cold cuts and cheeses stuffed the bread. The merchant sliced off wedges for us to enjoy. I know it's an interesting combination—French bread, Swiss cheese, and Italian cold cuts outside a Roman Colosseum. What made it even more magical was that Michael Bublé, a Canadian, was performing in the Colosseum. And the song he was singing? "It's a Beautiful Day."

I made my own recipe in a smaller version reminiscent of Italy and this magical experience. It's great for picnics and outings and for your own beautiful days.

---

1 loaf Kneaders Paesano Bread

2 tablespoons olive oil

½ pound Swiss cheese, sliced

½ pound provolone cheese, sliced

½ pound Muenster cheese, sliced

1 pound shaved Black Forest ham

1 pound shaved pastrami

1 pound shaved roast beef

½ cup fresh basil leaves

2 Roma tomatoes, sliced

½ red onion, sliced in rings

Freshly ground sea salt

Freshly ground black pepper

1 (9-ounce) bottle lemon garlic finishing sauce, such as Bittersweet Herb Farm (available online)

1. Cut a thin layer of bread off the top of the loaf. Remove the inside of the bread to make a bread bowl. Rub olive oil on the inside of the loaf.

2. Layer half of each of the cheeses (Swiss, provolone, Muenster) on the bottom of the loaf.

3. Layer half of each of the meats (ham, pastrami, roast beef).

4. Layer half of the basil leaves, tomato, and onion.

5. Season with salt and pepper.

6. Drizzle with lemon garlic finishing sauce, to taste.

7. Repeat all layers. Replace the top of the loaf.

8. Wrap the bread tightly with parchment paper. Place in the fridge for 8 hours with a 5-pound weight on top to mesh all the layers together.

9. When ready to serve, unwrap and cut into 8 wedges.

Tasty Tips

- Make the day before so the flavors can meld together. Use a gallon of milk as a weight.

Hawaiian Hammy Sammy

Serves 6 • Total Time: 20 minutes

This idea came from my favorite bakery in Ann Arbor, Michigan: Zingerman's Bakehouse. I attended two different trainings at Zingerman's, and they always fed my creativity and helped spark ideas of things we could do at Kneaders. One such idea—having limited-time offers around a culture's food—was born at one of those Zingerman's training sessions. It is something that has been delightful for our employees as well as our guests.

Many of the recipes included in this book are from our summer events: Italian Summer, Fiesta Summer, All-American Summer, and Aloha Summer. Everyone enjoys the food, and our guests ask for more.

2 loaves Kneaders Ciabatta Bread

¼ cup butter, melted

6 fresh pineapple rings, grilled

18 ounces Black Forest ham, thickly sliced

Salt and pepper

12 slices Muenster cheese

¾ cup chutney sauce, such as Stonewall Kitchen Major Grey's Mango Chutney (available online)

1. Cut the ends off each loaf of ciabatta bread, then slice each loaf into thirds. Cut open each slice horizontally to make a top and a bottom for each sandwich.

2. Lightly butter each slice of bread on the cut side and grill facedown until browned.

3. Grill pineapple rings just until grill marks appear.

4. Grill the ham in 3-ounce bunches for each sandwich. Allow it to warm and brown. Salt and pepper the ham, flip over, and place 2 slices Muenster cheese on top of the ham. Allow the cheese to melt.

5. Take the bottom slice of bread and place it on top of the Muenster cheese. Flip the ham, cheese, and bun combo over and place it on a plate. Layer with a grilled pineapple ring.

6. On each top slice of bread, spread 1–2 tablespoons chutney sauce. Place the tops on the sandwiches and enjoy.

Tasty Tips

- Fresh pineapple rings are a little more work but taste much better than canned rings.

Pot Roast French Dip Sandwich

Serves 8 • Prep Time: 20 minutes • Total Time: 9 hours

Necessity is often the mother of invention. This recipe came about for my granddaughter Katelyn's wedding reception.

Katelyn's favorite sandwich at Kneaders is the French dip. We wanted to make an extra-special version of it for her reception. We tested and tried different recipes, and this was the perfect one. We slow-cooked chuck roast beef overnight instead of using sliced deli beef.

I think it tastes like Sunday dinner—you know, the kind of meal that always brings you home. So many people liked it at the reception that we did a limited-time offer at Kneaders as well. Here's hoping we get to do that limited-time offer again.

---

4 tablespoons butter

2 ribs celery, thinly sliced

1 yellow onion, thinly sliced into rings

3 pounds chuck roast beef

1 cup water

2 (1.1-ounce) envelopes onion soup mix, such as Lipton Beefy Onion

AU JUS SAUCE

2 cups water

2 beef bouillon cubes

¼ cup balsamic reduction glaze, + more for drizzling

2 Kneaders Baguettes

12 slices Swiss cheese

1. In a skillet, melt butter. Sauté celery and onion. Add to the slow cooker.

2. Place the roast, water, and the soup mix in the slow cooker. Cover and cook on high for 6–8 hours, until the beef is tender.

3. Turn off the slow cooker and let rest for 20 minutes. Remove beef from pot. Cut beef into bite-size pieces.

4. For the au jus sauce, strain the beef drippings into a saucepan and skim off the fat. Add water and beef bouillon cubes. Mix and cook on medium heat until reduced. Add balsamic reduction glaze. Stir until incorporated.

5. Slice open baguettes and cut each into fourths. Stack pulled roast beef inside and top each sandwich with 2 slices Swiss cheese. Drizzle on balsamic reduction glaze. Serve each sandwich with a small cup of au jus.

Tasty Tips

• For a quick dip, use Johnny's French Dip Au Jus Concentrate Sauce (available online) for dipping your sandwiches.

Triple-Double Grilled Cheese Sandwich

Serves 5–10 • Prep Time: 15 minutes • Total Time: 25 minutes

This sandwich was part of a spring promotion that launched during March Madness. In basketball, a triple-double is a single-game performance by a player who accumulates a double-digit number in three of five categories: points, rebounds, assists, steals, or blocked shots.

At Kneaders, a Triple-Double has three pieces of French Country Sourdough Bread and two kinds of cheese, but what makes it a real winner is the amazing pesto butter on the outside of the bread that has been grilled to perfection. I'm sure by now you know I love our breads! The most amazing fact is that when breads are grilled, baked, toasted, or warmed in any way, they taste even better.

PESTO BUTTER

3 tablespoons fresh basil, finely minced

½ teaspoon minced garlic

1 cup butter, softened

¼ cup grated Parmesan cheese

SANDWICH

1 loaf Kneaders French Country
    Sourdough Bread

10 slices provolone cheese

10 slices Muenster cheese

1. For the pesto butter, blend fresh basil and garlic in a food processor. Transfer to a bowl and add butter and Parmesan cheese. Cover and refrigerate until needed.

2. For the sandwich, slice the bread into 15 slices. Each sandwich uses 3 slices of bread.

3. On the grill, toast 5 slices of bread on both sides. These will be the middle pieces of bread on the sandwiches.

4. Butter one side of each of the remaining bread slices with the pesto butter. Place them butter side down on the grill.

5. Place 2 slices provolone cheese each on 5 buttered bread slices. Place 2 slices Muenster cheese on remaining 5 buttered bread slices. Allow cheese to melt.

6. When the bread is toasted and the cheese is melted, build your sandwich. Start with one provolone slice, add one toasted slice, and finish with one Muenster slice. Grill for 2 more minutes on each side.

Tasty Tips

- This pesto butter is also good as a topping on baked salmon; add before baking.

Open-Faced Grilled Cheese Sandwich

Serves 2 • Prep Time: 2 minutes • Total Time: 5 minutes

When Gary and I met, it was truly love at first sight, but his love for me had nothing to do with my cooking skills. I had none. Gary and I spent a lot of time together that first summer. He would come to visit and pick a yellow rose from the fence by the student center to give to me. Since he brought the rose, I provided the meal: open-faced grilled cheese sandwiches. Fancy, right?

This recipe is reminiscent of those late nights. Little did I know then that someday we would make the world's best bread together. French Country Sourdough bread is always in season at Kneaders.

---

2 slices Kneaders French
    Country Sourdough Bread

2 teaspoons butter, softened

4 slices cheddar cheese

Dash of garlic salt

1. Preheat the oven to broil on high. Place a half-sheet baking pan on the middle shelf to warm while the oven heats up. When you are ready to prepare the sandwiches, pull the sheet from the oven.

2. Spread the softened butter on each slice of bread. Place the bread, butter side down, on the heated pan. Top each slice of bread with 2 slices of cheese and a dash of garlic salt.

3. Put the baking sheet on the top shelf and broil until the cheese is melted, bubbling, and golden around the edges.

4. Serve with a crisp salad—or just lots of kisses.

Tasty Tips

• Switch up your cheese and bread for variety.

Tailgate Hot Chicken Sandwich

Serves 6 • Prep Time: 15 minutes • Total Time: 35 minutes

I came from a family that was big into football. My dad (Edwin "Eddie" Kimball) was in athletics for a lifetime. He played college football, then coached, and worked as the athletic director at Brigham Young University. The first song I learned to sing was "Rise and Shout," the university fight song. My dad sang it to wake me up every morning.

Whether you are attending the big game or watching it on TV, you'll enjoy this easy, spicy gameday sandwich. Be sure to load up with plenty of guacamole and sour cream. Go Blue!

---

1 loaf Kneaders Ciabatta
   Bread, unsliced

2 cups shredded rotisserie chicken

2 cups grated pepper jack cheese

1 cup ranch dressing

½ cup fire roasted diced
   green chile peppers

Salt and pepper

Guacamole of choice, for serving

Sour cream, for serving

1. Preheat the oven to 350 degrees F. Line a half-sheet baking pan with aluminum foil.

2. Slice the ciabatta loaf in half horizontally. Place each half on the foil, cut side up.

3. In a medium bowl, combine shredded chicken, cheese, dressing, and green chiles. Add salt and pepper to taste.

4. Spread the mixture generously on the two halves of bread, making an open-faced sandwich. Loosely wrap each half in foil to keep in moisture. Be careful to keep the foil off the cheese mixture; make a tent with toothpicks, or spray the sandwich side of the foil with non-stick baking spray. Keep refrigerated until ready to bake.

5. Bake for 15 minutes or until the cheese is melted.

6. Slice each half into thirds. Serve with guacamole and sour cream.

Tuscan Bistro Sandwich

Serves 3–6 • Prep Time: 10 minutes • Total Time: 8 hours 10 minutes

The star of the Italian Summer promotion in 2015 was this Tuscan Bistro Sandwich. We loved serving gelato, caprese salad, and citrus cannoli, but the best part for me was sitting under the red umbrellas on the patio at Kneaders and eating this sandwich while songs like "Santa Lucia" and "'O Sole Mio" played over the speakers. If you try this sandwich with someone you love, it might be fun to end your date with "arrivederci."

---

1 loaf Kneaders Ciabatta Bread

Balsamic vinegar glaze, such as Roland's Balsamic Reduction, for drizzling

Extra-virgin olive oil, for drizzling

3 slices provolone cheese

8 slices Genoa salami

8 slices Milano salami

8 slices prosciutto

Freshly ground sea salt

Freshly ground black pepper

8 fresh basil leaves, cut into 1-inch pieces

½ red onion, thinly sliced

1. Slice the whole loaf of ciabatta horizontally.

2. Drizzle the balsamic vinegar glaze and olive oil over the cut sides of bread. Layer the bottom half of bread with cheese and meats. Lightly salt and pepper the sandwich. Spread fresh basil pieces evenly over the meats, then add onion rings. Replace the top half of bread.

3. Wrap the sandwich in plastic wrap and refrigerate for 8 hours.

4. When ready to eat, cut the sandwich into 3-inch strips and serve.

Tasty Tips

• Remove all casings from the meat.

SOUPS

Artichoke Portobello Soup

Serves 6–8 • Prep Time: 20 minutes • Total Time: 50 minutes

Known online as "Kneaders's Best Soup," this delicious dish is high in nutrition and low in calories. It was developed by my daughter-in-law Amy Hansen Worthington. Everything she makes is exceptional. While in college, Amy worked in research and development for us, and one of her first projects was this artichoke soup. As if the high-nutrition, low-calorie news weren't already good enough, this soup also freezes well. So make up a big batch and enjoy it later, too.

½ cup butter, divided

½ cup sliced green onion

2 carrots, peeled and sliced

2 ribs celery, sliced

2 portobello mushrooms, chopped

1 bay leaf

½ teaspoon thyme

½ teaspoon oregano

⅛ teaspoon cayenne pepper

4 cups chicken broth

14 ounces marinated artichoke
 hearts, drained and sliced

3 tablespoons all-purpose flour

1 cup heavy cream

Salt and freshly ground pepper to taste

1. In a large saucepan over medium heat, melt ¼ cup butter. Sauté the onion, carrot, and celery until they begin to caramelize, about 8 minutes. Add chopped mushrooms and sauté an additional 3–4 minutes.

2. Add the bay leaf, thyme, oregano, cayenne, broth, and artichokes. Simmer for 15–20 minutes.

3. In a separate pan, melt the remaining ¼ cup butter over low heat. Stir in the flour and cook, stirring constantly, until it is thickened. Stir the flour mixture into the soup.

4. Slowly add the heavy cream to the soup. Salt and pepper to taste. Cook until the broth has slightly thickened and is heated through. Remove the bay leaf before serving.

Tasty Tips

- Soup takes the bite out of a frosty night. Share with a friend.

Butternut Squash Bisque

Serves 6–8 • Prep Time: 20 minutes • Total Time: 1 hour

Recently I learned that butternut squash is a fruit, not a vegetable as one might think! (After all, the grocery stores keep it in the vegetable section.) No wonder we all like it so much. Eating a bowl of butternut squash soup is about as close to eating pumpkin pie as you can get without having to admit that you're actually eating dessert. The trick is to add enough warm spices to make it sweet without adding sugar.

This soup is a staple during the colder winter months because it's so creamy and warm. Using freshly ground nutmeg to finish this soup means you'll be met with *wows* from family and guests alike. In fact, I think I should make some right now.

SOUP

2 tablespoons butter

½ cup diced yellow onion

1 cup diced carrots

4 cups peeled and cubed butternut squash

3 cups vegetable or chicken stock

Salt and ground black pepper to taste

1 cup heavy cream

GARNISH

½ cup sour cream

2 tablespoons club soda or lemon-lime soda

Cinnamon, for sprinkling

Ground nutmeg, for sprinkling

1. In a large pot over medium heat, melt the butter. Add the onion and sauté for 8 minutes, until golden brown. Mix the carrots and squash into the pot. Pour in vegetable stock. Season with salt and pepper. Bring to a boil, then reduce heat and simmer until vegetables are tender, about 5–7 minutes.

2. Work in small batches here so you don't get burned. In a blender, puree the soup mixture until smooth.

3. Return the soup to the pot. Add the heavy cream. Heat through, but do not let the soup boil.

4. For the garnish, mix together the sour cream and soda. Use a spoon to drizzle a spiral (or any other shape) on top of each bowl of soup. Serve warm with a dash of nutmeg and cinnamon.

Tasty Tips

- Freshly ground nutmeg can make this soup extra flavorful. Whole nutmeg and grinders can be easily purchased online. The garnish puts this soup over the top. It's easy and worth the time.

Clam Chowder

Serves 6–8 • Prep Time: 30 minutes • Total Time: 1 hour

This recipe came from my aunt Caroline Berrett and was shared by my sister Elaine in a Kimball family cookbook. My aunt Caroline was one of the kindest women I have ever known. When my mother was dying, Caroline came once a week to the family home and fixed us delicious food and cheered our spirits. She always had a prayer in her heart and prayed with us before she left. She taught me a great lesson in service: always give more than you are asked. It makes both the receiver and the giver happy. After she left, we would go into the kitchen to find it spotlessly clean with hot cinnamon rolls on the counter.

---

2 cups peeled and diced potatoes

1 cup finely sliced celery

1 cup finely chopped onion

1 cup peeled and finely sliced carrot

13 ounces minced clams

¼ cup butter

½ cup flour

1 cup half-and-half

2 cups milk

1½ teaspoons salt

Dash of pepper

¼ teaspoon thyme

¼ pound bacon, cooked and minced

2 tablespoons fresh parsley, chopped

1. Place the potatoes, celery, onion, and carrot in a large pot. Drain the juice from the clams and pour the juice over the vegetables. Add enough water to cover the vegetables completely. Cover and cook for 15–20 minutes.

2. In the meantime, melt the butter in a medium saucepan. Add the flour. Blend and cook until the flour thickens. Stirring constantly, add the half-and-half and milk. Cook and stir with a whisk until smooth and thick. Season with salt and pepper.

3. Add the flour mixture to the vegetables and cook until the soup thickens.

4. Add the thyme and clams. Cook until the soup is heated through. Do not allow to boil.

5. Garnish with bacon and parsley.

Tasty Tips

- Use a sprig of thyme for garnish instead of the fresh parsley. Also, you can make this soup a main course by serving it in Kneaders freshly baked soup bowls.

French Onion Soup

Serves 6 • Prep Time: 15 minutes • Total Time: 1 hour 40 minutes

This is the best French onion soup I have ever tasted. It was a limited-time offer at Kneaders in 2016. What makes this recipe so great? For sure it's our Kneaders Baguette with three cheeses on it. Our baguettes are made fresh daily in each of our bakeries. It takes a minute for a new baker to get the hang of it, so be a little patient. They are formed, rolled, and cut all by hand and then peeled into our imported Italian ovens. No bread is better; it makes this simple soup taste gourmet.

SOUP

¼ cup butter

3 medium yellow onions, chopped

3 (14-ounce) cans beef broth

1 teaspoon salt

¼ teaspoon garlic powder

3 tablespoons grated Parmesan cheese

TOPPING

1 clove garlic, peeled and halved

1 Kneaders Baguette, cut in 6 slices

6 slices Swiss cheese

6 tablespoons grated mozzarella cheese

6 teaspoons grated Parmesan cheese

1. In a large soup pot over medium heat, melt butter. Sauté onion in the melted butter until brown and slightly transparent, for about 20 minutes.

2. Add the broth, salt, and garlic powder. Bring to a boil, then reduce heat, simmer, and cook uncovered for about 1 hour. In the last 10 minutes of cooking, add the Parmesan cheese.

3. For the topping, preheat the oven to 350 degrees F. Wrap garlic clove in foil cut side up, place on a half-sheet baking pan, and roast 3–4 minutes. Let cool.

4. Place the baguette slices on a half-sheet baking pan and toast about 10 minutes or until brown on both sides. Rub with roasted garlic.

5. Change the oven to broil on high. Divide soup into 6 ovenproof soup bowls. In each bowl, float a toasted slice of baguette on top. Layer baguette with 1 slice Swiss cheese, 1 tablespoon mozzarella, and 1 teaspoon Parmesan on top.

6. Place the soup bowls on a baking sheet and broil for 4 minutes or until the cheese begins to brown. Serve hot and bubbly.

Tasty Tips

- Use a mix of yellow onion, sweet Vidalia onion, red onion, and shallots to produce an even more complex flavor. It makes a difference.

The

HEALER

Dr. Joshua Schiffman

One of the most meaningful connections we have made is with Dr. Joshua Schiffman at Huntsman Cancer Institute at the University of Utah. Dr. Schiffman's groundbreaking research on curing childhood cancer is personal for us. Our grandson Tanner was diagnosed with Stage 4 Hodgkin lymphoma when he was thirteen years old. As we learned more about his cancer and as he underwent treatment at Primary Children's Hospital, we became aware of Dr. Schiffman and wanted to help further his work in any way we could. While he was not Tanner's doctor, his research struck a chord with us because we knew it could help so many others like our grandson.

You might remember seeing our blue elephant cookies in stores and out in the world several years ago during our Hope Fights Childhood Cancer campaign. We made these cookies (and sold other elephant-related items in our stores and online, such as necklaces, T-shirts, and ties) because elephants' DNA makes them cancer-resistant, thanks to their tumor-suppressing protein p53 and its extra copies. Dr. Schiffman and his research team study the elephant p53 and how it works compared to human p53. They also research other animals in nature that have less cancer than expected and try to understand if medicines can one day be made from these discoveries to help treat children with cancer. Our sales of these elephant-related products went toward funding Dr. Schiffman's childhood cancer research. Thanks to our guests' generous donations, we have been able to present the Huntsman Cancer Institute and Dr. Schiffman with hundreds of thousands of dollars for his research. In 2022, we sponsored an elephant cookie decorating class in each location. Living with cancer touches the lives of the entire family. More than the money, we feel like our gift has been letting others know about his research.

Dr. Schiffman had Hodgkin lymphoma when he was

fifteen, so these discoveries and his research are personal to him. He became a pediatric oncologist (childhood cancer doctor) to try to help other children and teenagers with cancer the way the doctors had helped to save his own life. During his training, he learned how discoveries in the lab can lead to new treatment approaches to cancer. Dr. Schiffman moved to Utah to continue his work as a physician-scientist at Huntsman Cancer Institute, and this is where his lab contributed to the discovery of how elephant cancer fighting proteins might be one of the reasons that elephants rarely develop cancer. Dr. Schiffman is dedicated to turning scientific research into new medicines because of his own experience with Hodgkin lymphoma and for the young patients with cancer he has cared for.

Elephant cookies enrobed in chocolate and decorated with sprinkles.

That personal touch has meant the world to us. I consider Dr. Schiffman to be such a dear friend. He has given all of us so much more than his brilliant knowledge and research. He has been a light in our darkest hours. Always encouraging, always a friend, first with Tanner, and then with Gary. When Gary was diagnosed with cancer, we called Dr. Schiffman on the phone and asked if Gary could donate his cancerous tissue to Huntsman Cancer Institute for Dr. Schiffman's research. Dr. Schiffman made the arrangements for the tissue to be transported from Intermountain Medical Center to Huntsman Cancer Institute. On one occasion when we were visiting in Dr. Schiffman's lab, he showed us the results of the elephant protein destroying Gary's cancer. He had one of the lab technicians put the protein into a petri dish before we arrived and, on a powerful microscope, we watched it enter the cells of the cancer and explode them. That's how it looked to us, anyway, and we were blown away by the wonderful implications of Dr. Schiffman's research all over again.

Tanner also loved and appreciated the care Dr. Schiffman showed him. Tanner told me, "It was surreal when I met him because I was aware of his research and of the possibilities of saving so many people as well as children. It meant a lot to know that as a child he'd had exactly what I had. It was great to have someone in my corner who knew exactly what it was like to have cancer as a teenager. He knew my fears and how it is to feel so sick and wonder if this will be your last winter. He always shared hope and a future with me."

Hope and a future. We're grateful to Dr. Schiffman for giving these things to Tanner and to many, many others. These are the kinds of things that you just don't forget.

See GRANDMA GERRI'S CHICKEN SOUP with MATZO BALLS recipe on page 103.

THE HEALER

101

Grandma Gerri's Chicken Soup with Matzo Balls

Serves 8–10 • Prep Time: 35 minutes • Total Time: 2 hours 50 minutes

Grandma Gerri is Dr. Schiffman's mother, and we are so grateful to her for sharing this recipe with us. This amazing soup is made with chicken bone broth and packed with vegetables. If you have someone who is not feeling well, or needs cheering up, you need this soup. Just eating it makes you feel better.

Read Dr. Schiffman's story on pages 100–101.

SOUP

1 (5-pound) chicken, cut into eighths

1 pound carrots, peeled and sliced

3 stalks celery, sliced

3 parsnips, peeled and sliced

1 large sweet onion, coarsely chopped

1 bunch flat parsley, stems removed

1 teaspoon salt

1 teaspoon pepper

MATZO BALLS

4 tablespoons unsalted margarine, melted

4 eggs, slightly beaten

1 cup matzo meal

1 tablespoon salt

Pepper to taste

4 tablespoons chicken broth (from soup)

1. Wash chicken pieces thoroughly. Place in a large stockpot and cover generously with water. Over high heat, bring to a rolling boil. Skim off the fat that comes to the surface.

2. Add all the vegetables. Make sure there is enough water to fully cover the vegetables. Add salt and pepper. Bring back to a rolling boil, then turn the heat down to simmer. Cover pot loosely. Simmer for 2 hours.

3. Prepare the matzo ball mixture by combining margarine, eggs, matzo meal, salt, and pepper in a glass bowl. Then add 4 tablespoons of chicken broth from the top of the simmering soup and mix until combined. Cover the mixture tightly with plastic wrap and cool in the freezer for 20 minutes.

4. Meanwhile, fill another large stockpot with water and bring to a rolling boil. Wet hands with cold water, then form balls from the matzo ball mixture and drop into the boiling water. (Don't make balls too large, as they will double in size.) Cover pot loosely and boil gently for 40 minutes. Drain carefully. Balls are fragile.

5. Back to the soup. Remove all the chicken pieces and set aside for other use, also making sure to discard any bones that might have fallen off the chicken pieces. Remove and discard about half the parsley from the soup. Remove the rest of the vegetables and puree them in a blender. Then add the puree back into the soup and mix until the soup is the consistency of tomato soup.

6. Add the cooked matzo balls to the soup and simmer for 15 minutes. Enjoy!

Irish Stew

Serves 8–10 • Prep Time: 30 minutes • Total Time: 3 hours

My favorite part of having Chef Ryker Brown work for us was his incredible knowledge of sauces. In my mind he was the sauce king. Here Ryker created something truly delicious.

This recipe is not your common Irish stew recipe. Ours is packed with tender beef and fresh vegetables, including potatoes, carrots, and onions, and is enhanced with a bright medley of rosemary, thyme, and Italian parsley. We serve it at Kneaders in January, February, and March.

¼ cup canola or vegetable oil

1 pound beef chuck roast, cubed

1 medium yellow onion, chopped

¼ cup tomato paste

½ cup red wine or apple juice

1 tablespoon kosher salt

¼ teaspoon pepper

1½ cups roughly chopped carrot

⅔ cup roughly chopped celery

3 cups cubed Yukon Gold potatoes

5 cloves garlic, peeled and
 roughly chopped

2½ cups beef broth

¼ cup fresh Italian parsley

1 tablespoon fresh thyme

1 tablespoon fresh rosemary

1. Heat a heavy-bottomed (cast-iron) pot on medium-high and add canola oil. Brown beef for about 15 minutes or until dark brown.

2. Add onion and cook, stirring constantly, until the onion is golden brown and slightly charred, about 8 minutes.

3. Add tomato paste and cook on high, stirring constantly, for 5 minutes.

4. Add red wine or apple juice and cook on medium-high for 3–4 minutes to burn off the alcohol. Reduce heat and continue stirring.

5. Add salt and pepper. Stir. Add carrots, celery, potatoes, and garlic. Brown for about 5 minutes.

6. Add beef broth. Stir to evenly distribute.

7. Prepare the herbs by chopping the parsley leaves and removing the woody stems from the thyme and rosemary. Add to the pot.

8. Cover and simmer for 2 hours. This will give you extra-tender beef. Check and stir occasionally.

9. Remove the lid. Continue to simmer for 30 minutes until thickened. Serve.

Tasty Tips

• Thicken stew or gravy with Cornaby's E-Z Gel instant food thickener, available online.

Italian Wedding Soup

Serves 8 • Prep Time: 25 minutes • Total Time: 45 minutes

Every year we hold a soup festival for a family gathering. We always hope Amy Worthington will bring Italian Wedding Soup. I think Amy knows how much we enjoyed all the taste-testing days.

Since we have never able to source all the ingredients in the stores, we have never able to make it at Kneaders, but it's so good that we still want to share it with you. Savor the superb combination of tiny meatballs and tender greens. You don't need to wait for a special occasion. Serve it tonight.

MEATBALLS

½ cup grated onion

¼ cup fresh Italian parsley, chopped

1 large egg

1 teaspoon minced garlic

1 teaspoon salt

⅓ cup Italian-style panko bread crumbs

½ cup grated Parmesan cheese

8 ounces ground beef

8 ounces ground pork

½ teaspoon ground black pepper

SOUP

2 tablespoons olive oil

1 cup minced yellow onion

1 cup sliced carrots

1 cup diced celery

10 cups chicken stock

1 cup acini di pepe pasta

¼ teaspoon ground black pepper

10 ounces baby spinach,
   finely shredded

Grated Parmesan cheese, for serving

1. In a medium bowl, combine all the meatball ingredients. Mix well using your hands or a fork.

2. Scoop out a heaping teaspoon of the meat, roll it into a meatball, and place it on a half-sheet baking pan. Repeat with remaining meat; this will make about 40 meatballs. They should be very small. Set aside.

3. For the soup, heat the olive oil in a large soup pot over medium heat. Add the onion, carrot, and celery and sauté until the onion is transparent, about 5–7 minutes.

4. Add the chicken stock and bring to a boil.

5. Add the pasta and meatballs. Return the soup to a boil. Cook until the pasta and meatballs are cooked through, about 15–20 minutes.

6. Add the pepper and the spinach. Simmer for 2–3 minutes more, until the spinach is just wilted but still a vibrant green.

7. Ladle the soup into bowls and serve with a little Parmesan cheese.

Tasty Tips

• Teach your children how to form the meatballs. They will have fun, and it will save you lots of time. The meatballs can be made early and stored in the refrigerator until it's time to add them.

Pumpkin Curry Soup

Serves 6 • Prep Time: 15 minutes • Total Time: 35 minutes

In 2013 we kicked off the fall soup season with this pumpkin curry recipe by our contest winner Rachel Von Curren. Curry has a unique flavor that is deep and earthy but has a sweet taste. Curry powder is made from an interesting combination of spices, usually cardamom, coriander, cumin, pepper, saffron, tamarind, and turmeric. Prepare to savor every spicy spoonful of this delicious pumpkin curry soup.

---

2 tablespoons pumpkin seeds

2 tablespoons butter

3 tablespoons flour

2 tablespoons curry powder

4 cups vegetable broth

1 (15-ounce) can pumpkin

1½ cups half-and-half

2 tablespoons soy sauce

1 tablespoon sugar

Salt and pepper to taste

1. Preheat the oven to 375 degrees F.

2. Arrange pumpkin seeds in a single layer on a half-sheet baking pan. Toast in the oven for 10 minutes or until seeds begin to brown.

3. Melt butter in a large pot over medium heat. Stir in flour and curry powder until smooth and mixture begins to boil. Gradually whisk in broth. Cook until thickened.

4. Stir in canned pumpkin and half-and-half. Season with soy sauce, sugar, salt, and pepper. Bring just to a boil, then keep warm on low. Dish into serving bowls and garnish with roasted pumpkin seeds.

Tasty Tips

- A garnish on a soup is easy and makes it feel gourmet, and the pumpkin seeds here are a prime example of this. This soup also pairs well with a loaf of Kneaders Hazelnut 12-Grain Hearth Bread.

The
NEIGHBORS

Amy and Sean's family, left to right:
Zimi, Amy Worthington Peterson, Kimball, Sean Peterson, Andrew.

Amy and Sean Peterson

One of the greatest blessings in life is to have good neighbors. While our children were small, we had some particularly wonderful neighbors, the Peterson family, who lived next door. Their little boy Sean, the fourth of their five children, was often outside on his bicycle, riding around with a big smile on his face.

One night, Gary got a call from Mike Peterson that Sean, age five, and his older brother had gone missing in the foothills near our home. It was February, and it was dark and cold. Gary had a big truck, and they went up on the mountain to find the lost little boys. Sean saw the headlights of the truck and, as he puts it, "I basically threw myself off the mountain, I was so excited to be found." We were all grateful they were safe and sound.

When we started Kneaders, our daughter Amy was a sophomore in high school. Every day, she came home and made three batches of pumpkin bread for us in a small thirty-quart mixer—more than a hundred loaves of bread per day. She has always known how to roll up her sleeves with a smile.

When they were in college, Amy and Sean happened to cross paths in the town where they had both been raised. They each had a moment a bit like my and Gary's "Morning, Sunshine" moment. Amy saw Sean at church and thought, "If he ever asks me on a date, we'll get married." Sean went home after that same brief encounter and said to his brother, "I think I met my wife today." The best part is that neither of them knew at the time that the other was their long-ago neighbor! Once they began dating, they fell in love quickly and knew they were meant to be together.

But life does not always go exactly as planned or along the easiest course. The day after they told both sets of parents that they wanted to get married, Sean and Amy were in a life-altering car accident. Both Sean and Amy were injured. Amy received hundreds of stitches; Sean's jaw was broken, and he was in especially critical condition. He was heavily sedated for two weeks. When he woke up, he couldn't remember much of that time.

During their recovery, Gary and I did our best to help them heal. We made Amy a bed in the bake house building next to our main store so that we could check in on her during the day. Sean's jaw was wired shut, and he couldn't chew, so I made him "French Dip Shakes." I'd blend up beef and a little au jus so that he could drink it through a straw. As Amy and Sean regrouped after their injuries, they knew that life had changed for them—but they were even more convinced that they were each other's person.

While they both still knew they wanted to be married and start a family, other dreams shifted or were put on hold. They began working for us washing dishes and making sandwiches. They scrubbed the floors and worked behind the counters. The next year, they began managing the Provo store, and sales were better than they'd ever been. We also chose them to open our South Jordan store, which was a huge task. Of course, they rose to the occasion.

Eventually, other opportunities came up, and Amy and Sean decided to see where those might lead. They moved to Arizona, and Sean earned his master's degree in business administration. He went into business

David Peterson, Amy and Sean's son, while serving a religious mission in Santiago, Chile.

with his brother, and they moved to Texas. In the meantime, Amy continued to work for the Kneaders home office in Utah. She'd fly in and decorate all the Christmas trees for the store and then fly home, glitter in her hair from handling all those decorations. While they lived in Texas, there were several major storms—Hurricanes Isaac and Harvey and Tropical Storm Cindy—that came through the area, and they were able to step up and help with cleanup and meeting the needs of those who were particularly affected. As with their accident, Sean and Amy found that difficult events could be opportunities for drawing closer, not just to each other, but as a community.

After eight years in Texas, both Gary and Sean's dad, Mike Peterson, were diagnosed with serious medical conditions. Sean and Amy decided it was time to move back. It felt like a true homecoming, and the right thing for all of us. All their experiences—their accident, their moving away—changed who they are, and it changed who we are. When you leave, you realize there is a whole world around you, and you bring that with you wherever you go next. Now, Sean works as our director of supply chain, and Amy is our director of pastry and our director of retail. We don't know what we'd do without them.

And guess where Sean and Amy moved when they came back to Utah?

Right next door to us.

See SAUSAGE LASAGNA SOUP recipe on page 113.

Sausage Lasagna Soup

Serves 8 • Prep Time: 10 minutes • Total Time: 45 minutes

There's nothing like a warm home filled with laughter and comfort. In the South, food is a love language! Amy learned a whole new level of comfort food from her time living among the most amazing people in Buna, Texas. Whether it was a container filled with banana pudding, gumbo, or crawfish étouffée, you knew you were loved. Sausage Lasagna Soup is Amy's family's go-to comfort meal. It warms you right down to your soul.

Read Amy and Sean's story on pages 110–11.

---

2 teaspoons olive oil

1 pound regular sausage

½ pound hot sausage

1 extra-large yellow onion, chopped

4 large garlic cloves, minced

2 teaspoons dried oregano

½ teaspoon kosher salt

¼ teaspoon ground black pepper

¼ teaspoon crushed red pepper flakes

3 tablespoons tomato paste

2 (14.5-ounce) cans fire-roasted diced tomatoes

2 bay leaves

6 cups low-sodium chicken stock

8 ounces mafalda or fusilli pasta

½ cup fresh basil leaves, sliced thinly

PARMESAN RICOTTA MIXTURE

8 ounces ricotta

½ cup grated Parmesan cheese

¼ teaspoon kosher salt

2 cups shredded mozzarella cheese

1. Heat olive oil in a large pot over medium heat. Add both sausages and brown, breaking it up into bite-size pieces with a wooden spoon, about 3 minutes.

2. Add onion, garlic, oregano, salt, pepper, and red pepper flakes, and cook until onion is softened and sausage is browned, about 7 more minutes.

3. Stir in tomato paste and cook for 2 minutes more.

4. Add diced tomatoes, bay leaves, and chicken stock. Bring just to a boil, then reduce heat and simmer for 15 minutes.

5. Add pasta to tomato mixture and cook to al dente.

6. In a medium bowl, combine the ricotta, Parmesan, salt, and pepper to taste. Set aside.

7. Stir fresh basil into soup just before serving.

8. To serve, ladle soup into individual bowls. Serve with dollops of the Parmesan-ricotta mixture and additional shredded mozzarella.

Tasty Tips

• Add more tomato paste for an even deeper tomato flavor.

Sweet Chili

Serves 6 • Prep Time: 15 minutes • Total Time: 1 hour

Thanks for this recipe go to our CFO's sister-in-law Stephanie Vincent. She is such a classy lady. Stephanie was kind enough to let us post this recipe in our monthly newsletter years ago.

This easy recipe can be made quickly but tastes like you spent the day in your kitchen chopping and stirring. The heat and the sweetness are a great combination. It's always a pleasure to share appetizing recipes that can be served with our world-class bread. This recipe goes really well with our Utah Mountain Style Cornbread and Honey Butter (see recipe on page 172).

1½ pounds ground beef

1 large white onion, chopped

2 cloves garlic, minced

1 (16-ounce) can kidney beans, drained

3 (14-ounce) cans Mexican-style stewed tomatoes

1 tablespoon chili powder

½ tablespoon cumin

⅓ cup brown sugar

1. In a large saucepan, add ground beef, onion, and garlic. Cook until beef is browned. Drain fat.

2. Add the beans, tomatoes, chili powder, cumin, and brown sugar. Simmer for 45 minutes.

Tasty Tips

• Serve in our Sourdough Bread Bowls for an easy cleanup.

Turkey Curry Chowder

Serves 6–8 • Prep Time: 20 minutes • Total Time: 45 minutes

At Kneaders we are known for our turkey. All of our turkey is slow roasted and hand pulled using a unique cooking method that adds juiciness instead of leaving it dry. We cook close to a million pounds of fresh turkey a year. We are obsessed with turkey recipes! We hope you find this chowder delightful. It's a great recipe for using up your Thanksgiving leftovers.

2 cups water

½ cup diced green onion

3 cups chopped carrots

3 ribs celery, diced

4 cups cubed potatoes

2½ tablespoons chicken bouillon

1 teaspoon curry powder

½ teaspoon cayenne pepper

2 cups white turkey breast, chopped

ROUX

¼ cup butter

½ cup flour

2 cups heavy cream

Salt and pepper to taste

1. In a stockpot, combine water and veggies. Bring to a boil, then reduce heat to low. Simmer until the veggies are tender, about 20 minutes.

2. Season with chicken bouillon, curry powder, and cayenne pepper. Add the turkey breast meat. Keep warm.

3. To make a roux, melt the butter in a small saucepan. Slowly add the flour, stirring constantly. Slowly add the cream and keep stirring. Heat until thickened, but don't let it boil.

4. Slowly add the roux to the turkey and veggies. Heat through. Salt and pepper to taste.

Three-Cheese Cauliflower Soup

Serves 8 • Prep Time: 30 minutes • Total Time: 1 hour

When I was little, I hated eating cauliflower. I thought it was the worst vegetable on the planet. (Well, maybe Brussels sprouts were worse.) But I had no idea what I was missing out on. The flavor is slightly sweet and creamy, perfect for making soup.

As I worked on this recipe, I thought I would use just yellow cheddar cheese. After several tastings, I realized that it needed a more complex flavor, more of a punch, some heat. So I added the pepper jack. Then it lacked a good creamy texture, so in came Shirley J's white cheddar base. All this sounds so simple, I know, but I probably made it about fifty times before there was something there to love. My college minor in food and nutrition just wasn't enough! In developing recipes, I soon learned to use my imagination, to not be afraid to fail, and that you can always count on friends. Through the years, Shirley J has been one of those friends.

---

1 head cauliflower

¼ cup butter

1 cup chopped green onion,
+ more for garnish

1½ tablespoons minced garlic

2 quarts hot water

2⅓ cups Shirley J White Cheddar
Universal Sauce Cream
Soup and Sauce Mix

2¾ cups grated cheddar cheese,
+ more for garnish

¾ cup crumbled pepper jack cheese

1. Break the head of cauliflower into 2-inch pieces.

2. In a large saucepan, combine the butter, chopped green onion, and cauliflower pieces. Cover and cook for 25 minutes, stirring occasionally, or until the cauliflower starts to become translucent. The cauliflower will be very soft and will break into bite-size pieces.

3. While the veggies cook, roast the garlic in a small saucepan until it is slightly brown. Stir into the veggies.

4. Once the veggies are done cooking, add the hot water. Using a whisk, stir in the white cheddar mix until completely incorporated. Heat to 140 degrees F.

5. Slowly stir in the grated cheddar cheese and crumbled pepper jack cheese, adding slowly so it doesn't clump up. Heat soup to 165 degrees F.

6. Serve garnished with cheddar cheese and green onion.

Tasty Tips

• Shirley J White Cheddar Universal Sauce Cream Soup and Sauce Mix can be purchased at shirleyj.com. Use a cooking thermometer to check the temperature of the soup as you cook.

Turkey Dumpling Soup

Serves 8–10 • Prep Time: 40 minutes • Total Time: 2 hours 15 minutes

Some things just go together, like turkey and Kneaders, turkey and Thanksgiving, and Thanksgiving and leftovers. Thinking of all these winning combinations, we thought we should have a turkey soup recipe on our menu, since we are known for our turkey and because we thought it might be fun to have a variation on some of the traditional dumpling soups you might find.

Nonstick cooking spray

1 pound turkey tenderloin

⅓ cup chicken broth

2 tablespoons butter

¼ cup all-purpose flour

2 ribs celery, chopped

1 medium onion, chopped

½ teaspoon salt

¾ teaspoon poultry seasoning

2 cups water

3 cups chicken broth

1 cup heavy cream

3 medium Yukon Gold potatoes, peeled and cubed

1 (10-ounce) package frozen mixed peas and carrots

1. Preheat the oven to 350 degrees F. Spray a 9x13 baking dish with nonstick cooking spray. Place turkey tenderloin in the dish. Add chicken broth, then cover with aluminum foil. Bake for 45 minutes or until the internal temperature reaches 170 degrees F. Cool and shred turkey. Set aside to be added later.

2. Melt butter in a large saucepan over medium-high heat. Add flour, celery, onion, salt, and poultry seasoning. Cook, stirring constantly, for 10 minutes.

3. Stir in water, broth, cream, and potatoes. Cover and bring to a simmer. Reduce heat to medium and simmer, partially covered, about 10 minutes.

4. Add the peas and carrots and simmer until vegetables are tender, about 15 minutes.

5. Add the turkey to the saucepan and simmer until heated through. Divide among bowls and top with a fresh biscuit (see Best Biscuits recipe on page 148).

SOUPS

Tuscan Tomato Tortellini Soup

Serves 10–12 • Prep Time: 20 minutes • Total Time: 50 minutes

I love this recipe. It is one of the best-flavored soups my daughter-in-law Amy makes. (And she has made a lot of soup while cooking for her husband, James, and their five soccer-playing sons!) She shared this recipe in February 2021 on social media. Ask Siri for "Kneaders Tortellini Soup & Grilled Cheese" and watch the video. It's short and informative.

What to serve with it? Amy's suggestion is to serve Kneaders Baguettes, sliced thin and made into small grilled cheese sandwiches. Nothing says home like a fantastic homemade tomato soup and your favorite grilled cheese.

---

3 tablespoons olive oil

2 medium onions, diced

2½ (14.5-ounce) cans diced tomatoes (undrained) or 5 cups diced fresh tomatoes

3 cups chicken stock

12 ounces roasted red peppers, drained

1 cup basil pesto

1½ cups heavy cream

1 (9-ounce) package refrigerated cheese tortellini, such as Buitoni

Salt and pepper to taste

1. In a soup pot over medium, heat olive oil. Sauté onion in the heated olive oil until the pieces are translucent, about 5 minutes.

2. Add the undrained diced tomatoes to the pot. Warm to a simmer.

3. Add the chicken stock and roasted peppers. Simmer for 20 minutes.

4. Add the basil pesto and cream. Pour the soup into a blender and blend until smooth. Return the soup to the heat.

5. Cook the tortellini according to package instructions and add it to the soup.

6. Salt and pepper to taste. Serve and enjoy!

Tasty Tips

- Cook the tortellini separately while the soup simmers. Want to make it for a larger crowd? Amy says just add another can of diced tomatoes.

White Bean and Chicken Tortilla Soup

Serves 10 • Prep Time: 20 minutes • Total Time: 1 hour

Made with fire-roasted diced green chiles, onion, garlic, and cumin, this tortilla soup is loaded with flavor. It's also packed with protein, thanks to the white beans and chicken. Topped with pepper jack cheese and sour cream and served over tortilla chips, this soup will warm you up on a chilly winter's eve. It makes enough to invite friends, so why not have a party?

1 tablespoon extra-virgin olive oil

1 cup chopped onion

1 clove garlic, minced

3 cups chicken broth

1 teaspoon lemon pepper

1 teaspoon cumin

3 cups cooked chicken, cubed

2 (4-ounce) cans fire-roasted diced green chilies

1 (15-ounce) can corn, drained

2 (15-ounce) cans great northern beans, undrained

⅛ cup sliced green onion

Juice of 1 fresh lime

½ bunch cilantro, chopped

2 cups tortilla chips, for the bottom of the bowls

Shredded pepper jack cheese, for serving

Sour cream, for serving

1. In a large saucepan over medium heat, heat olive oil. Sauté onion until translucent, about 5 minutes. Add minced garlic and continue to cook on medium heat for 2 minutes.

2. Stir in chicken broth, lemon pepper, cumin, and cooked chicken. Simmer on low for 5–10 minutes.

3. Add green chilies, corn, great northern beans, and green onion. Simmer for an additional 5–10 minutes.

4. Stir in lime juice and chopped cilantro. Cook for an additional 2 minutes.

5. Serve warm soup over tortilla chips. Top with pepper jack cheese and sour cream.

Tasty Tips

• In a hurry? Make it with rotisserie chicken.

DRINKS

Blueberry Bliss Smoothie

Makes 1 large (28-ounce) smoothie • Prep Time: 3 minutes • Total Time: 5 minutes

Each of our smoothies is loaded with superfoods. All recipes have at least a full cup of frozen fruit and in this (and others) you will also have a third of a banana. I love the taste of raspberries in anything. They have a tang that is irresistible, while blueberries add sweetness. When I get a smoothie at Kneaders I always add a cup of spinach. Surprisingly, the spinach adds a sweetness to the drink and of course, it is another superfood. Just a note of interest: our smoothies have no added sugar.

DRINKS

1 cup frozen nonfat vanilla yogurt

1½ cup apple juice

½ cup frozen raspberries

½ cup frozen blueberries

⅓ ripe banana

Combine all ingredients in a blender and blend until smooth.

Tasty Tips

- Add 1 cup packed spinach for more nutrition and a little more sweetness.

Boyz & Berries Smoothie

Makes 1 large (28-ounce) smoothie • Prep Time: 3 minutes • Total Time: 5 minutes

I have often thought it would be a great job to name wallpaper or paint colors. Wouldn't that be fun? Yellow is never just "yellow." Instead, it's something like Buttercup, Latte, or Sunny Day.

So with that in mind—and a little creative license—this berry-packed smoothie became Boyz & Berries. My hope was to make the name intriguing so that guests would give it a try. It works for wallpaper, right?

1½ cup apple juice

1 cup raspberry sherbet

½ cup frozen blueberries

½ cup frozen boysenberries

Combine all ingredients in a blender and blend until smooth.

Cranberry Berry Smoothie

Makes 1 large (28-ounce) smoothie • Prep Time: 3 minutes • Total Time: 5 minutes

Picture a sunny day in Alaska on Chichagof Island. My daughter Christy, her husband, Brad, two of our grandsons, Michael and Conner—and Gary and I—were walking through what seemed to be undergrowth. The boys looked closer and found we were walking in wild cranberries and blueberries. Of course we had to stop and eat some. On the island they grew wild everywhere. Later, at a gift shop in the town of Hoonah, I stopped to buy a blueberry and cranberry cookbook. Who would have thought that a cookbook featuring just two berries even existed? This local cookbook gave me ideas for this delicious, tangy, and flavorful smoothie—an Alaskan adventure in a glass.

1½ cups cranberry juice

1 cup raspberry sherbet

1 cup frozen blueberries

Combine all ingredients in a blender and blend until smooth.

Our
LEGACY

Lizzie, Christy Worthington Matthews, and Maddie.

The Children and Grandchildren of Kneaders

My first job, at the age of seven, was to catch grasshoppers for my neighbor who fed them to the lizards at the Brigham Young University Life Science Museum. I received five cents per grasshopper. Gary also learned the value of work at a very young age. When he was nine, he began working for his Uncle Junior at the Junior Mart in Grantsville, Utah. He earned $1.30 an hour for taking groceries to the customers' cars and sweeping the floors. For the time, we were both paid well.

Both of us learned some great principles: First, lizards die if you don't feed them; second, if you really want something, you can work hard and get it; third, the world needs productive people; fourth, when problems arise, don't quit—think of a hundred possible solutions and *something* will work; and fifth, you are happiest when you help others.

Why am I telling you all this? To share why we started Kneaders. Even though there are plenty of jobs and chores at home, it's a different dynamic when you're working together to run a business. Our older children worked for us when we owned Subway sandwich shops, but we saw our younger children missing those lessons and opportunities to be out in the world, interacting with people they didn't know. Now those children of ours have moved on to run the company, and their children are learning the same lessons by working at Kneaders.

Our oldest daughter, Laura Worthington Smith, and her husband, Curtis, helped us out from the very beginning. Even though Curtis was a dentist and Laura had four small children at home when we opened that first Orem store, they were right there to make sure that Kneaders took flight. The day we opened Kneaders was Curtis's day off. The night before, I called him and asked if he could possibly set up our cash register. The menu was pretty simple at that time. He got our cash register ready and volunteered to run it for us the next day. During the weeks to come, all the customers asked about our dentist-turned-cashier for the day. Curtis and Laura later joined with his brother and mother to open the Lehi Kneaders, which they owned for years.

Each of Laura and Curtis's children have been employed at Kneaders in different ways. Austin worked at our warehouse in Orem for a time, and Katelyn spent hours making bows and baskets and enjoyed going to retail markets with us. Conner worked in the Lehi Kneaders—as their fastest sandwich maker ever—and is now the warehouse manager for our company. It's a huge job that supports our stores in all the states we're in. Laura and Curtis's younger son, Tanner, works with his brother Conor in the warehouse. Tanner's experience with cancer was one of the main reasons we've supported the cancer research efforts of Dr. Joshua Schiffman at the Huntsman Cancer Institute (you can read more about Dr. Schiffman on page 100). We are pleased to report that Tanner is healthy and doing well, and just got married in December 2022. His wife, Maddie, has also joined our warehouse crew.

Our second daughter, Angie Worthington Bishop, and her husband, Scott, were also right there for us as we launched Kneaders. Even when Scott was serving in the Air Force as a doctor, Angie and her children folded our customer newsletters every month and shipped them out to our guests. Their children helped in any way they could and were always on the lookout for ideas for the bakery as they moved from Washington, DC, to California to Nebraska. When they made their final move to Kaysville, Utah, they came to help us box pies and rolls and carry them to cars at Thanksgiving and Christmastime. Some people have temp workers for the holidays—we have family.

Angie and Scott's daughter Erika worked for us while she was in college, and what became this cookbook was one of her projects. Their son, Matthew, came and lived with us before his church mission and worked at the warehouse organizing and sorting. Their second son, Ben, also lived with us before his mission and has recently been a driver for Kneaders, often making the long trip to Logan. The youngest in their family, Emily, began designing special occasion cards for us to sell with our gift baskets this past year. We've loved having the chance to be around them as they grow and enjoy seeing them develop their own talents and skills.

Our third daughter, Christy Worthington Matthews, says that she is married to Kneaders's biggest fan: her husband, Brad. As always, family and Kneaders were intertwined right from the beginning—we delayed the opening of our first store because Christy's oldest boy, Michael, was born four weeks early, and I needed to rush out there to be with Christy and that new baby.

Christy wrote and compiled the first newsletters that we sent to customers. Even though she was living in Maryland, we'd have her send them to Angie in California, who would print and label the newsletters and ship them to Utah. It might not have been the most cost-effective way to do it, but we wanted everyone to feel included in helping with our family business. Christy also worked for many years as our director of retail, going to markets and purchasing retail as well as managing retail managers in the stores. She's currently our imports manager. She and our son, James, decided they could save a great deal of money on our Christmas baskets, boxes, and tins if they went overseas to skip the middleman. So Christy taught herself the importing process, and she and James have traveled overseas many times to source and negotiate with factories. Christy says that if you drive by her house in July or August and see the lights on at 2 a.m., it's because of the time difference in working with countries in Asia. She is often doing change orders and negotiations with our overseas manufacturers into the wee hours of the night. It's always been important to her to give our customers the best product for the lowest possible price.

Christy and Brad's children have all worked for Kneaders. Their oldest son, Michael, spent a summer working with Kneaders's resident handyman/electrician, and he was able to learn a few tips and tricks about electrical work. He also helped with odd jobs whenever needed. Their two girls, Lizzie and Maddie, have worked countless Thanksgivings with cousins, delivering pies to customers. They've also helped during Christmas seasons by making baskets and putting cookies and breads in bags for our basket makers. Many times, we've ended up in laughing fits at 2:00 a.m. As young girls, Lizzie and Maddie often created designs and pretended they were entering the Kneaders Design-a-Basket contests. Christy says they are both "super creative like their grandma," which makes me smile. One year, we all loved their Mother's Day design so much we printed it and sold it that year, which was fun for everyone.

Our three younger children and their families are featured in other essays throughout this book, and you'll get to know their stories, recipes, and memories, too. This family endeavor has tried and tested us to the limit, and also made us laugh until we've cried, given us the chance to have plenty of flour fights and conversations over chocolate milk and pastries, and brought the cousins and generations together in ways that wouldn't have otherwise been possible.

Recently, Angie wrote the following to me in a note: "At the end of the day, the most important thing that the grandkids have learned is that each one of them has unique talents and abilities. That each is loved by Grandma and Grandpa, and that everyone's talents are important and have a place to help move things forward at Kneaders and in the world. We are better as a family because of the times we've been able to work together."

And Christy told me, "Mom, we love everything about Kneaders and are so proud of what this little family business has become."

These things warm my heart to hear, because it's exactly what Gary and I hoped to give our children and grandchildren when we opened Kneaders over twenty-five years ago. Our family is our dearest legacy, and we're so grateful for the times we've been able to share with them through serving our guests.

See BLUEBERRY #5 SMOOTHIE recipe on the next page.

Blueberry #5 Smoothie

Makes 1 large (28-ounce) smoothie • Prep Time: 3 minutes • Total Time: 5 minutes

I can't say enough about our smoothies at Kneaders. So much fruit is packed in each one, and they are just cool and refreshing. Summer is a great time for smoothies, but surprisingly we also sell a ton on snowy or rainy days. I think it might remind people of summer days during gloomier times.

To judge our recipe contests on a chainwide level, we always need great judges. Our idea was that if all ages liked the recipe, we had a winner. Luckily, we have a big family that encompasses all ages for taste-tasting!

Smoothies were often a wonderful source for competitions. One year we asked employees to submit recipes for a smoothie that contained blueberries. Before our family arrived for taste-testing, we made all the smoothies and gave each of them a number from 1 to 22. Each member of the family tasted each smoothie and wrote the number down to vote for their favorite. All the votes were counted and we had an overwhelming winner: #5. I spent hours trying to come up with a great name. I think I named it "Blueberry the Berriest." Conner, my young grandson, came to Kneaders for lunch just after and wanted a Blueberry #5 smoothie. The cashier was baffled, but Conner insisted it was named Blueberry #5, and was disappointed with Grandma for not having it on the menu. The name was later changed permanently to Blueberry #5.

Read the grandchildren's story on pages 128–30.

1½ cups guava juice

½ cup pineapple sherbet

½ cup nonfat vanilla yogurt

½ cup frozen blueberries

½ cup frozen strawberries

⅓ ripe banana

Combine all ingredients in a blender and blend until smooth.

Goin' Guava Smoothie

Makes 1 large (28-ounce) smoothie • Prep Time: 3 minutes • Total Time: 5 minutes

I love the exceptional flavors blended into this popular smoothie that we serve at Kneaders. It was named by Dave, our CFO and son-in-law, who hails from southern California. It reminds us all of happy days at the beach, far away from the snow. If you haven't tried it yet, here is the recipe for you to enjoy at home. These flavors blend together so naturally, they are the perfect tropical combination.

DRINKS

1½ cups guava juice

1 cup pineapple sherbet

½ cup frozen mango

½ cup frozen strawberries

⅓ ripe banana

Combine all ingredients in a blender and blend until smooth.

Planet Peaches Smoothie

Makes 1 large (28-ounce) smoothie • Prep Time: 3 minutes • Total Time: 5 minutes

Creamy and thick, this recipe is absolutely delicious. At the drive-through window, I often help customers with teenagers who have just been to the orthodontist. Peaches have a very tangy but sweet taste depending on the variety of the peach. To me this smoothie calms the soul. It's the best smoothie to help you feel better and improve your day. So I understand why these particular customers love them, and we love sharing in those moments—and, I hope, helping you feel a bit better.

---

1 cup frozen nonfat vanilla yogurt

1½ cups peach juice

½ cup frozen peaches

½ cup frozen mango

Combine all ingredients in a blender and blend until smooth.

Rockin' Red Smoothie

Makes 1 large (28-ounce) smoothie • Prep Time: 3 minutes • Total Time: 5 minutes

About every three years or so, we have a chainwide contest to develop a new smoothie. Nearly twenty years ago, this was the winner. We had three beautiful redheaded girls who worked for us at the bakery, and they came up with this recipe together. I named it Rockin' Red after those energetic, intelligent, fun-loving teenagers.

1½ cup peach juice

½ cup pineapple sherbet

½ cup raspberry sherbet

½ cup frozen peaches

½ cup frozen strawberries

Combine all ingredients in a blender and blend until smooth.

Tasty Tips

• If using fresh fruit, add 1 cup of ice cubes and blend.

Strawberry Swing Smoothie

Makes 1 large (28-ounce) smoothie • Prep Time: 3 minutes • Total Time: 5 minutes

Named by the Pleasant Grove High School Ballroom dance team while on a California tour, this smoothie is made with yogurt, strawberry, and banana. The recipe is easy and straightforward and an all-time favorite of young and old alike. It always reminds me of Strawberry Days in Pleasant Grove with all my girls in their handmade strawberry dresses watching the local parade. I love being taken back to simpler times, and this smoothie does the trick.

1½ cups apple juice

1 cup nonfat frozen vanilla yogurt

1 cup frozen strawberries

⅓ ripe banana

Combine all ingredients in a blender and blend until smooth.

Tasty Tips

• Garnish with fresh strawberries and banana slices.

Strawberry Tsunami Smoothie

Makes 1 large (28-ounce) smoothie • Prep Time: 3 minutes • Total Time: 5 minutes

The Strawberry Tsunami Smoothie is another chainwide winner. Filled with so many flavors, this smoothie is definitely one of our best sellers. Amber, a longtime employee, was the originator of this recipe and the winner of that year's smoothie contest. She started as an expeditor (our term for the employee who takes food to customers in the restaurant after it has been prepared) and went on to become a cashier, then a night manager, and finally a pastry chef. Amber worked for Kneaders for eighteen years and had five children with her husband during the time she was with us. I asked her recently which of her Kneaders jobs had been her favorite. Without hesitation she replied, "pastries." We are so fortunate to have such dedicated and talented employees and love thinking of them when we make their recipes. Thanks to Amber and all the other employees who have become such an important part of the Kneaders family.

1½ cup cranberry juice

½ cup pineapple sherbet

½ cup nonfat frozen vanilla yogurt

½ cup frozen strawberries

½ cup frozen peaches

Combine all ingredients in a blender and blend until smooth.

Mexican Spice Hot Chocolate

Makes 4 cups • Prep Time: 5 minutes • Total Time: 15 minutes

I grew up drinking hot chocolate with marshmallows. One of my favorite memories is of my dad telling me bedtime stories while I sipped hot chocolate. He would sing to me, "Every cloud must have a silver lining, Cuddle up and don't feel blue," then kiss me goodnight and tuck me into bed. That's why hot chocolate has a special place in my heart. This spiced version was one of the first hot drinks to make the menu at Kneaders. Mexican Spice is definitely a grownup version of hot chocolate—it's both warm in temperature and a little spicy. I hope you love it, too.

¼ cup unsweetened cocoa powder

⅓ cup sugar

½ teaspoon ground cinnamon,
 + more for garnish

½ teaspoon ground nutmeg

⅛ teaspoon salt

Dash cayenne pepper

½ cup hot water

3½ cups milk

1 teaspoon vanilla

Cinnamon sticks for garnish

Whipped Cream Topping (see
 recipe on page 227)

1. In a saucepan, over medium heat, combine cocoa powder, sugar, cinnamon, nutmeg, salt, and cayenne pepper.

2. Stir in hot water and mix to combine.

3. Bring to a boil and stir for 2 minutes. Add milk and stir. Heat thoroughly.

4. Remove the pan from the heat. Stir in vanilla and beat with a whisk until foamy.

5. Pour into cups and garnish with Whipped Cream Topping, cinnamon sticks, and a sprinkle of cinnamon.

BREADS

Apricot Almond Wreaths

Serves 10–12 • Prep Time: 20 minutes • Total Time: 3 hours

Apricot Almond Wreaths were part of our Easter tradition at Kneaders. The last time we sold them was in 2016, but now you can make them on your own, perhaps as part of an Easter tradition to share with friends and neighbors. This traditional German bread is called *Osterkranz*. Instead of filling it with the traditional marzipan, we have added dried apricots to the dough. The wreath is symbolic of life and resurrection and reminds us of everlasting life through Christ.

---

1 cup warm water (90–100 degrees F.)

2½ cups all-purpose flour

3 tablespoons honey

1 teaspoon salt

1½ teaspoons instant yeast

½ teaspoon almond extract

¼ cup dried apricots, coarsely chopped

1 egg

2 tablespoons water

½ cup confectioners' sugar

2 teaspoons milk

¼ teaspoon vanilla

1 tablespoon toasted sliced almonds

2½ cups bread flour

1. Using a stand mixer, combine the water, flour, honey, salt, yeast, and almond extract together. Mix on low speed for 6–8 minutes. Dough should feel soft and stretch easily. Add the apricots and mix for 1 minute on low speed. Transfer the dough to a lightly oiled bowl. Cover and let rest until the dough has doubled in size, about 1 hour.

2. Transfer the dough to a lightly floured surface. Divide into 3 equal pieces.

3. Roll out each piece into an 8 to 10 inch long strand. Cover and let rest for 5 minutes.

4. Roll out each piece until they are all approximately 20 inches long. Line the 3 strands up side by side, about 5 inches apart from each other. Slide the top edge of each strand together, keeping the rest of the strands spaced apart. Do not pinch the top edges together. Start braiding the strands together about 2 inches down from the top edges of each strand, starting with the right strand. Bring the right strand over the middle strand so that it is now in between the middle strand and the left strand. Keep them spaced apart. Bring the left strand over the middle strand so that it is now in the middle. Repeat this pattern until all strands are braided together, leaving about 2 inches unbraided at the top and bottom of each strand. Now bend the top strands down and braid them with the bottom strands, forming a circle. Place onto a half-sheet pan lined with greased parchment paper. Cover and let proof until the strands have almost doubled in size and the dough leaves a slight indentation after being pressed gently, approximately 30–45 minutes.

5. Preheat the oven to 335 degrees F. while the dough is proofing.

6. Make an egg wash by whisking the egg and 2 tablespoons water together until well combined. Brush the top of the wreath with egg wash and place into the preheated oven. Bake for 15–20 minutes or until the wreath is golden brown and the internal temperature is at least 190 degrees.

7. Remove the half-sheet pan from the oven and carefully place the hot wreath onto a cooling rack.

8. Prepare the topping by mixing together the confectioners' sugar, milk, and vanilla. Drizzle over the wreath while it is still warm. Then sprinkle sliced almonds across the top.

The
MILLERS

*Former Utah governor Jon Huntsman
honoring Sherm and Barbara Robinson.*

Sherm and Barbara Robinson

If you've ever seen the movie *Footloose,* you likely recognize the famous Lehi Mills (formerly Lehi Roller Mills) in the movie. The mills have been one of Utah's landmarks since 1906, when they were first founded by the Robinson family. Sherm Robinson was the third generation of Robinsons to own and operate the mills. He and his wife, Barbara, are also dear friends of ours and our relationship with them and with Lehi Mills has been critical to Kneaders' success from the very beginning.

To bake wonderful bread, you need wonderful flour. Sherm's flour was derived from a specialty grain grown in Idaho and milled to perfect specifications for making hearth bread. In order to have such quality ingredients for your flour, you must have a great relationship with your growers. And Sherm was the kind of person you met and instantly felt like was your best friend.

Gary remembers that Sherm always checked with us to make sure we weren't having any problems with the flour we bought from him. He cared about every detail of the process. Sherm would come by the store himself to see how his product was performing. He was continually interested in the ovens we used and wanted to make sure that the flour was the right specification for the hearth breads we were trying to make. Sherm even wanted to make sure that the flour was working well with the Italian mixers we had purchased to mix our dough.

Sherm's wife, Barbara, was as good a friend to us as Sherm. She worked closely with her husband. Without a doubt, she is the best baker I know. She was in charge of all the research and development at the mill. Every packaged mix they sell, such as the pancake mix, are Barbara's recipe. Of course, she worked with food scientists to prepare the recipes for sale, but they were *her* recipes. I love the bread recipe she has shared with us, and I especially love her banana bread. One of the best parts of our relationship was attending baking classes at the American Institute of Baking (AIB) in Kansas with her. Lehi Mills had a longtime relationship with AIB. It was at those classes that I fell in love with hearth breads. Barbara and I would attend week-long courses in commercial baking, with classes for eight hours each day, but at night we would go shopping, try different restaurants, and just enjoy each other's company. I probably learned more about baking from her than I learned from the classes!

Before we opened our first store, Sherm asked Gary to go to the San Francisco Baking Institute to have the flour he had developed for hearth breads tested. He wanted to know how they compared with French, Italian, and other European flours. Érik Kayser—known as one of the best bakers in France—was the guest baker at that conference. He was baking with various flours from mills in Europe as well as the United States. He rated Sherm's flour as one of the best flours, as good as the European flours. We were all so pleased. At our Kneaders twentieth birthday celebration at Disneyland in California, Sherm was awarded our Vendor of the Year Award for his service to Kneaders. Barbara was there to support him as she always was.

We loved our long association with this family, and we discovered that relationship went back even farther than we'd thought!

Sherm's office in Lehi was lined with shelves containing small milling ledgers, where he and his family had kept track of all the customers' information—orders, notes, etc.—through the years. He had one book for each customer. One day, Gary was in Sherm's office and pulled down one of the ledgers at random. As he leafed through it, he saw his Grandfather Worthington's name. He had delivered a wagon of wheat to be milled into flour. He returned a week later to pick up his order. This was a two-day wagon trip each way. It was at that moment Gary realized that the Robinsons and the Worthingtons had trusted each other for more than one hundred years.

Sherm eventually sold the mill, but I was able to speak with its current manager, Brock Knight, as I was gathering memories of Sherm and Barb. (Sherm passed away in 2021.) Brock told me that they had stopped selling bread mixes for a time and had concentrated on muffin, pancake, cake, and brownie recipes. I was so delighted to hear that this year they are bringing out both a white bread and a sourdough bread mix. I was also delighted to learn that Brock had married one of Barbara's nieces, so they call Sherm and Barbara *uncle* and *aunt*. Family and friendship associations sometimes begin before we even imagine and continue long into the future. Gary and I are so grateful for our relationship with the Robinsons. We think of them often—of all the ways they helped us to be better at Kneaders, and of all the ways they helped us as friends.

Two constants at Kneaders over the past twenty-five years have been that we have always used Lehi Mills flour, and that we've valued our relationship with the Robinson family.

> See BARBARA'S LEHI MILLS BASIC BREAD recipe on page 145.

Barbara's Lehi Mills Basic Bread

Makes 4 large loaves • Prep Time: 20 minutes • Total Time: 2 hours 35 minutes

Barbara is a master bread baker. When she touches flour something special happens. She made this bread and sold it at the mill for a time. Looking at this beautiful loaf of bread made by Barbara makes my mouth water.

Read the Robinsons' story on pages 142–43.

8 cups Lehi Mills whole wheat flour

8 cups Lehi Mills white flour

½ to ¾ cups sugar or honey

¼ cup butter or margarine, melted or ¼ cup vegetable oil

2 tablespoons salt, or to taste

2 eggs (optional)

3–4 tablespoons active dry yeast or 2 tablespoons instant yeast*

6½–7½ cups lukewarm water

*If using *active dry* yeast, stir the yeast into the water. Let stand for 3–5 minutes to soften. If using *instant* yeast, it can be mixed directly into the flour.

1. Using a stand mixer, attach the dough hook and flour shield. Mix flour, sugar, butter, salt, and eggs together until mixture is crumbly. If using active dry yeast, in another bowl, sprinkle yeast over warm water and stir, then set aside. Add water and yeast mixture to dry mixture and mix on low speed for 10–15 minutes, or until dough is developed. Add additional water or flour as needed, 1 tablespoon at a time. Keep dough slightly sticky to the touch.

2. Place dough in a large oiled bowl, cover with plastic, and let rise until doubled, 30–40 minutes. Punch down.

3. Lightly flour your hands and counter surface. Place dough on counter and divide into four equal portions. Dough should feel slightly sticky and soft and will stretch without tearing. Roll each portion into individual loaves and place in greased bread pans. Preheat the oven to 350 degrees F. Cover loaves with plastic and allow to rise until top of dough is approximately 1–2 inches above the sides of the pans.

4. Bake for 30–35 minutes, covering with foil the last 10 minutes if the tops are getting too brown. Remove from pans and cool on rack before slicing and storing.

Chocolate Hearth Bread

Makes 1 loaf • Prep Time: 20 minutes • Total Time: 4 hours

On December 2, 1997, Kneaders first opened its doors in Orem, Utah. The smell of our Chocolate Hearth Bread and cinnamon loaves filled every corner of the bakery and greeted each customer. We were happy and tired, but mostly we were thankful for all of the people who helped us get to that moment. We loved sharing this bread with our guests that first day, and we are delighted to share it with you again now.

1 cup warm water (90–100 degrees F.)

2 cups bread flour

2 tablespoons Dutch cocoa powder

1 teaspoon salt

2 tablespoons sugar

1 teaspoon instant dry yeast

1 teaspoon vanilla

¼ cup semisweet chocolate chips

Nonstick baking spray

1. Using a stand mixer, combine the water, flour, cocoa powder, salt, sugar, yeast, and vanilla together. Mix on low speed for 6–8 minutes. Dough should feel soft and stretch easily. Add the chocolate chips and mix for 1 minute on low speed.

2. Transfer the dough to an oiled bowl. Cover and let rest until the dough has doubled in size, about 1 hour.

3. Transfer dough to a lightly floured surface and gently flatten the dough into a rectangle shape approximately 8 inches wide. Fold both sides to the middle. Then fold the top and bottom to the middle. Flip over and place back into the oiled bowl. Cover and let rest for 20–30 minutes.

4. Transfer dough to a lightly floured surface and shape into a round ball. Place seam side down onto a lightly floured surface.

5. Cover and let rise until it is almost double in size and leaves a slight indentation after being pressed gently, approximately 45–60 minutes.

6. While the dough is rising, place a pizza stone or Dutch oven into a cold oven and preheat to 450 degrees F.

7. If baking on a preheated pizza stone: Gently transfer the loaf to a lightly floured cutting board or pizza peel. Slide the loaf onto the hot pizza stone. Bake for 20–25 minutes until desired color is reached, and the internal temperature is at least 190 degrees F.

8. If baking in a preheated Dutch oven: Use oven mitts to remove the hot Dutch oven and lid. Spray with nonstick baking spray and gently place the dough into the Dutch oven with the seam side up. Replace

the lid and place back into the oven. Bake for 20 minutes, then carefully remove the hot lid. Bake for 15–20 minutes, or until the desired color has been reached and the internal temperature is at least 190 degrees.

9. Remove from the oven and carefully place hot bread onto a cooling rack.

Tasty Tips

- To help the loaves have a nice shine and a better rise, place an empty steam pan in the bottom of the oven while it is preheating. When you've put the loaf in the oven, pour 1 cup of hot water into the steam pan and close the oven door. You are looking for lots of steam.

Best Biscuits

Makes 18 (2-inch) biscuits or 8 (3-inch) biscuits • Prep Time: 10 minutes • Total Time: 30 minutes

I knew we'd need the perfect biscuit recipe for our Turkey Dumpling Soup (see recipe on page 118), so I looked online and tried all the ones in my cookbooks. The ones I found were okay, but I was looking for something outstanding. I finally called our good friend Sherm Robinson at Lehi Mills. In the next ten minutes, Sherm solved all of my problems. I was using the wrong flour.

I grew up thinking flour is flour, and boy was I wrong. I can't thank the Robinsons enough for sharing hundreds of years of milling expertise with us. They blessed our lives. Here is the recipe Sherm shared for biscuits. As I mentioned earlier, some things just go together—like Lehi Mills flour and Kneaders Bakery.

---

2 cups Lehi Mills Turkey Unbleached Enriched Bread Flour or other high-quality all-purpose flour

4 teaspoons baking powder

¼ teaspoon baking soda

¾ teaspoon salt

3 tablespoons unsalted butter

1 tablespoon high ratio shortening, such as Sweetex

1 cup buttermilk

1. Preheat the oven to 450 degrees F. Line a baking sheet with parchment paper. Set aside.

2. In a large mixing bowl, combine flour, baking powder, baking soda, and salt. Using a pastry cutter, cut the butter and shortening into the dry ingredients. Mixture will look like crumbs.

3. Make a well in the crumbs and pour in the buttermilk. Stir just until the dough comes together. Dough will be very sticky.

4. Dust a surface with flour. Turn dough onto floured surface, then dust the dough with flour. Fold dough over on itself 4 times, rotating 90 degrees after every fold.

5. Press dough down so it is 1 inch thick. Cut out biscuits with a 2-inch biscuit cutter (for dumplings) or a 3-inch cutter (for larger biscuits). Place biscuits on prepared half-sheet baking pan, almost touching. Bake until biscuits are light golden on top, 15–20 minutes.

Tasty Tips

- Don't twist the cutter when cutting the dough. It will pinch the sides and prevent them from rising.

Diné Frybread

Serves 8 • Prep Time: 20 minutes • Total Time: 1 hour 15 minutes

Gladeeh is a kind person who loves her Diné heritage. We are grateful that she would share her recipe with us.

Read Gladeeh Begaye's story on pages 184–85.

3 handfuls (about 1½ cups) flour

1 palm (about 1½ teaspoons) baking powder

½ palm (about ½ teaspoon) salt

1 handful (about ½ cup) powdered milk (optional)

2½ cups warm water

1 large spoonful (about 3 cups) lard or shortening

1. Mix to soft dough and let rise, then break off a small, baseball-sized piece of dough and flatten it with your hands, or use a rolling pin to make a roughly 8-inch round, no less than ¼-inch thick.

2. In a skillet (cast iron preferred) over medium-high heat, melt the lard or shortening until it is 1 inch deep, adding more if needed. Deep-fry dough until it rises or bubbles up and is golden brown. Drain oil on paper towel–lined plate. Repeat flattening and frying until the dough is gone.

3. Serve warm with Honey Butter (see recipe on page 173) and dusted with powdered sugar for a sweet treat. For a savory meal, top with taco meat, pinto beans, lettuce, salsa, and sour cream.

Ciabatta Bread Pizza

Serves 8 • Prep Time: 10 minutes • Total Time: 20 minutes

If you're in need of a quick and easy dinner, pick up two loaves of our ciabatta bread and try one of these four recipes or use them as inspiration to create your own. This is a fun dinner for kids to help with, and a great way to use leftovers from the week. Let Mom or Dad be the judge of this at-home version of *Chopped*.

This might just become a Saturday night tradition. Pass the leftovers, please!

Classic Pepperoni

2 loaves Kneaders Ciabatta Bread

2 cups pizza sauce

2 cups shredded mozzarella

1 (5-ounce) package pepperoni

BBQ Chicken

2 loaves Kneaders Ciabatta Bread

2 cups barbecue sauce, such
as Sweet Baby Ray's

2 cups shredded mozzarella

1 red onion, diced

Cilantro, stems removed
and chopped fine

2 cups rotisserie chicken,
coated in barbecue sauce

Pesto Chicken

2 loaves Kneaders Ciabatta Bread

2 cups pesto sauce

2 cups shredded mozzarella

2 cups rotisserie chicken

8 basil leaves, sliced chiffonade

Alfredo Bacon

2 loaves Kneaders Ciabatta Bread

2 cups alfredo sauce

2 cups shredded mozzarella

8 slices precooked bacon

1 cup rotisserie chicken

Fresh parsley, chopped

1. Preheat the oven to 500 degrees F. Cut ciabatta loaves in half lengthwise and place on baking sheets cut side up.

2. Evenly divide sauce between the four halves and spread an even layer on top of bread. Top each half with desired toppings. Evenly divide the mozzarella cheese and sprinkle on each half.

3. Bake for 5–7 minutes until the cheese is bubbly and golden brown. Let cool slightly, cut into triangles, and serve immediately.

Hot Cross Buns

Makes 12 rolls • Prep Time: 15 minutes • Total Time: 2 hours

These rolls have a long history—they've been part of Easter celebrations since the twelfth century. Justin, our executive baker, spent hours testing them before he came up with this final recipe. Raisins or currants are traditional in the dough but you can use any dried fruit. The buns are marked on the top with a cross piped in icing. We're so glad that we get to share this Easter tradition with you.

¾ cups warm water (90–100 degrees F.)

½ cup whole milk

2 tablespoons honey

2 tablespoons butter, softened

2 eggs, divided

3¼ cups all-purpose flour

1½ teaspoon instant yeast

1 teaspoon salt

¾ cup raisins or currants

½ teaspoon ground cinnamon

1 cup confectioners' sugar

½ teaspoon vanilla

5 teaspoons milk

1. Using a stand mixer, combine water, whole milk, honey, butter, 1 egg, flour, yeast, salt, and raisins or currants in the mixing bowl. Mix on low speed for 6–8 minutes. Dough should feel soft and stretch easily. Transfer the dough to a lightly oiled bowl. Cover and let rest until the dough has doubled in size, about 1 hour.

2. Transfer the dough to a lightly floured surface. Divide the dough into 12 equal pieces. Shape each piece into a round ball. Place each piece seam side down onto a half-sheet pan lined with lightly greased parchment paper, keeping the pieces spaced about 2 inches apart. Cover and let set until they are almost double in size and leave a slight indentation after being pressed gently, approximately 45–60 minutes. Preheat the oven to 350 degrees F.

3. Whisk together 1 egg and 2 tablespoons of water to make an egg wash. Gently brush each roll with the egg wash, then place the half-sheet pan in the oven on the center rack and bake for 20 to 25 minutes, or until the buns are golden brown.

4. Remove from the oven and allow to cool.

5. Prepare the icing by combining the confectioners' sugar, vanilla, and whole milk into a small bowl. Use a fork or whisk and mix until smooth. Using a piping bag with a ⅛-inch tip, pipe an X on the top of each bun. You can also make a temporary piping bag by spooning the icing into a gallon ziptop bag, squeezing the icing to one corner of the bag, and snipping off a small corner of the bag.

Irish Soda Bread

Makes 1 loaf • Prep Time: 15 minutes • Total Time: 1 hour

Each March, we enjoy celebrating Pi Day on the 14th and St. Patrick's Day on the 17th with our customers. Some of our favorites that month are Irish Stew (see recipe on page 104) and Irish Soda Bread. What exactly *is* Irish Soda Bread? You can think of it as just a big biscuit. This bread doesn't keep long because of the high soda content, but your family will likely eat it up in no time. It's especially good with homemade jam—or feel free to try one of ours (I especially like our Pleasant Grove Strawberry Jam on it).

---

3 cups high-quality all-purpose flour, such as Lehi Mills

2½ teaspoons sugar

1 teaspoon salt

1 teaspoon baking soda

3 tablespoons softened butter

1 egg

1¼ cups buttermilk

1. Preheat oven to 375 degrees F.

2. Combine all ingredients together in a mixing bowl. Mix on low speed just until everything starts to come together into a dough, approximately 1 minute. Finish mixing by hand until all flour is absorbed into the dough.

3. Transfer dough to a lightly floured surface and loosely shape into a round ball. Place onto a greased half-sheet baking pan.

4. Slightly flatten the top by gently patting it down. Use a serrated knife to score an X across the top center of the loaf. Transfer back to the half-sheet pan and immediately place in the oven. Bake for 35–40 minutes, or until the internal temperature reaches 190 degrees. Best when served while still warm.

Tasty Tips

- Check the expiration date on your baking soda. Fresh soda yields the best results.

Jacob's Loaf

Serves 8 • Prep Time: 25 minutes • Total Time: 2 hours 10 minutes

Read Jacob Hutchings's story on pages 46–47.

1¼ cups warm water (90–100 degrees F.)

2½ cups all-purpose flour, such as Lehi Mills

1 teaspoon salt

1 teaspoon instant yeast

1 egg

Flax seeds

Sunflower seeds

Sesame seeds

Poppy seeds

1. Combine water, flour, salt, and instant yeast together in a mixing bowl. Mix on low speed for 6–8 minutes. Dough should feel soft and stretch easily. Transfer to an oiled bowl, cover, and let rest until the dough has doubled in size, about 1 hour.

2. Transfer dough to a lightly floured surface and gently flatten into a rectangle shape, approximately 8 inches wide. Fold both sides to the middle. Then fold the top and bottom to the middle. Flip over and place back into the oiled bowl. Cover and let rest for 20–30 minutes.

3. Place a pizza stone in the oven and preheat to 450 degrees F.

4. Transfer dough to lightly floured surface and gently flatten into a rectangle, approximately 10 inches long, 3–4 inches wide. Fold in half so the top of the rectangle lines up with the bottom, making a thinner rectangle 2–3 inches wide. Transfer to a clean surface with no flour, placing it so that the seam side is down on the bottom center of the dough. Gently roll the dough out until it reaches 20 inches in length. The outer skin of the dough should be nice and smooth. Using a ruler and a knife, make a mark every 2½ inches until there are 8 equal pieces. Cut out and gently shape into round balls.

5. Dip each ball into a bowl of water and place onto a greased parchment paper, making a circle with 7 of the dough balls, and placing the eighth one in the middle. They should be close enough so that all of the rolls are touching each other. Sprinkle one type of seed on the top of two rolls each (see picture). Cover and let proof until they are almost double in size and leave a slight indentation after being pressed gently.

6. Prepare egg wash. Crack the egg into a small bowl. Lightly beat with a fork or whisk. Brush the egg onto each of the rolls.

BREADS

7. Place the rolls with their parchment paper on a cutting board or pizza peel. Slide off onto the hot pizza stone in the preheated oven.

8. Bake for 10–15 minutes until golden brown and internal temperature has reached 190 degrees. Remove from oven, allow to cool, and serve warm.

The
BREAD
WHISPERER

Justin Alcorn

When we have our Kneaders Halloween parties, our corporate executive baker, Justin Alcorn, often dresses up as a superhero. I love this because I actually do believe he has a superpower—I always think of him as the Bread Whisperer. He can coax miracles out of dough.

Justin first learned how to make bread when he worked at his family's bagel shop, Homeport Bagels and Sandwiches, in Brookings, Oregon. When Justin was thirteen and living in Utah, his family had a yard sale at their home—and Justin's father sold the house! It wasn't even up for sale. Justin's dad had grown up in Brookings and had always wanted to go back. They didn't know what they were going to do for work, only that they wanted to live in Brookings. They spent the first two weeks there living in a tent trailer. They heard that the local bagel shop was owned by a husband and wife. The husband had recently passed away and the wife had decided to sell, so Justin's parents decided to buy the shop and bakery. They came up with their own bagel recipes (flavors like cinnamello, cookie crunch, and bubble gum bagels) and things took off from there.

Justin worked at Homeport from the very start—waking at 1:30 every morning to begin mixing the dough. They hand-shaped, boiled, and baked each bagel by 8:00 a.m. and then began making their famous clam chowder, chili, and potato soups. Justin helped all through the lunch rush and then clocked out for the day, more than twelve hours after he'd clocked in.

Justin has many fun memories of his family's bakery. His younger brother Travis went in with him to help in the summers. When Travis fell asleep during breaks, Justin would pull pranks on him. One time, Travis fell asleep sitting in front of a fan in the back. Just before they opened, Justin sprinkled some flour in front of the fan so it blew all over Travis's face. Then Justin woke Travis up so that he could be the one to greet the customers with his unknowingly floured face. Justin also remembers making funny faces at his younger sister as she was ringing up customers to make her laugh. Homeport Bagels and Sandwiches was one of the only places in town to go in high school for lunch breaks, so it was always busy and well-known throughout Brookings. The bakery was open Monday through Friday and closed on the weekends so that Justin's family could enjoy their weekends on the Oregon coast.

We were thrilled when Justin joined Kneaders in 2006. Right away, we knew that he understood what the job required. Baking bread is challenging, exacting, and complex. Justin has continued to go above and beyond, bringing ideas, recipes, and excellence to the table. He's always interested in learning more and has completed baking schools in Kansas and San Francisco since coming to work with us. He has been a critical ingredient in the success of Kneaders for the past sixteen years because of his genius in creating recipes, managing difficult situations, and dealing with unexpected circumstances.

So much research and development is involved when we invent our recipes, and Justin has helped develop many of our favorite breads—Rosemary Focaccia, Cranberry Pistachio, Potato Rosemary, Raisin Walnut, Cheddar Garlic, Jalapeno Cheddar, Challah, Chocolate Babka, hamburger buns, Churro Sweet Bread, Triple Chocolate Sweet Bread, Zucchini Pecan Sweet Bread, Banana Sweet Bread, and more. He's always stepped forward when needed. There have been times when he's flown to an out-of-state store to bake all night when an entire bake team called in sick, or stayed all night baking baguettes by himself so that everything would be ready for the opening day of a new store. We know we can count on Justin without reservation.

Justin has said that walking into Kneaders for the first time felt like home, and that working with James, Dave, and Gary was like working with family. I tell Justin that's because he *is* family.

See JALAPEÑO CHEDDAR BAGEL recipe on page 161.

THE BREAD WHISPERER

Jalapeño Cheddar Bagels

Makes 12 bagels • Prep Time: 35 minutes • Total Time: 2 hours 20 minutes

Read Justin Alcorn's story on pages 158–59.

2½ cups (594 grams) water

6¼ cups (998 grams) bread flour, such as Lehi Mills Unbleached Bread Flour

1 tablespoon (18 grams) salt

2¾ teaspoons (9 grams) instant dry yeast

2 tablespoons (27 grams) sugar

1 cup (108 grams) sliced jalapeños, chopped

¾ cup (64 grams) finely shredded Parmesan

1 cup (96 grams) finely shredded mild cheddar

Note: For precise baking, use the weight measurements; volume measurements have been provided for comparison and are not as precise.

1. Using an instant-read thermometer, run hot water from the faucet until the thermometer reads 85–90 degrees F. Then, weigh out 594 grams and pour into the bottom of the mixer bowl.

2. Weigh out the flour and place it on top of the water in the mixer bowl.

3. Weigh out the salt, yeast, and sugar. Place these ingredients on top of the flour in the mixer bowl.

4. Using the dough hook attachment, mix all ingredients on the lowest speed for 5 minutes.

5. Weigh out the jalapenos. Set aside.

6. Weigh out the cheeses and set aside.

7. After 5 minutes, stop the mixer and add the jalapenos and Parmesan cheese to the mixer bowl. Mix on the lowest speed until all ingredients are well incorporated throughout the dough, approximately 2 minutes. If needed, stop the mixer and push the dough down to the bottom of the mixer bowl to help it mix in more evenly. Or you may finish folding everything in by hand.

8. When done mixing, the dough temperature should be around 78–80 degrees F. The dough should feel wet and slightly stick to your hand. Add a little more flour or water if the dough is too tacky or dry.

9. Place the dough in an oiled bowl large enough to hold it. Cover with plastic wrap or a clean towel. Allow to rise for 30 minutes.

10. After 30 minutes, fold the dough by removing the cover from the bowl and punching the dough down with both hands, degassing it. Then fold the sides and ends of the dough to the center, overlapping them. Cover and let rest for an additional 30 minutes.

11. Remove the dough from the bowl and place onto a cutting board or clean surface.

Continued on next page.

Continued from previous page.

12. Divide the dough into 12 equal pieces, approximately 156 grams each.

13. Roll each piece out into a 7- to 8-inch strand. Keep the dough strands an even thickness throughout. Cover the strands and let them rest for 5 minutes.

14. Preheat the oven to 415 degrees F.

15. Spray two 13x18 half-sheet pans with nonstick baking spray.

16. After 5 minutes, shape the bagels. Take a strand and roll it between your hands until it is approximately 10 to 11 inches long, keeping the strand an even thickness throughout. Then overlap one end of the strand about 1 to 1½ inches over the other end. Connect these two ends by stretching the ends of the top strand over the bottom strand and pinching the dough together underneath the bottom strand, keeping the dough an even thickness throughout. The center hole should measure approximately 1½ to 2 inches wide.

17. Place 6 shaped bagels on each pan, spaced evenly apart. Cover and let rest until the bagels have almost doubled in size, approximately 20–30 minutes.

18. Fill a large stockpot halfway with hot water. Place on the stovetop over high heat and bring the water to a boil.

19. When the bagels are ready, place 2 to 3 bagels into the boiling water at a time. If they've rested enough, they will float.

20. Blanch each bagel for 30 seconds. Using a large slotted spoon or skimmer, remove the blanched bagels from the boiling water. Respray the pan with nonstick baking spray before placing the blanched bagels back onto it. Do not blanch the second pan of bagels until you are ready to bake them.

21. Sprinkle a small handful of the shredded cheddar cheese along the top of each bagel.

22. Place the bagels into the preheated oven on the center rack. Bake for approximately 15 minutes or until the bagels are a light golden brown on top and bottom.

23. You may need to rotate the pan during baking to help the bagels brown evenly.

24. Using a wooden or plastic spatula, remove the bagels from the half-sheet pan and place onto a cooling rack. If the bagels stick to the pan, apply more nonstick baking spray next time.

25. Allow to cool and enjoy!

Phyllis's Homemade Whole Wheat Bread

Makes 2 loaves • Prep Time: 20 minutes • Total Time: 2 hours 30 minutes

If I had only one home baker recipe for bread, this would be it. You can make it from ingredients you may have in your food storage or pantry. Phyllis Peterson, my son-in-law Sean's mother—and my next-door neighbor—made this several times a week while Sean was growing up. Whenever I visited Sean and Amy in Arizona or Texas, Sean baked this bread for me. I loved the gesture. Fresh-baked bread makes you feel welcomed and at home.

3½ cups warm water (90–100 degrees F.)

2 tablespoons instant yeast

½ cup honey

½ cup vegetable oil

7 cups wheat flour, divided

4 tablespoons powdered milk

4 teaspoons salt

1. Preheat oven to 400 degrees F.

2. In a medium bowl, combine the water, yeast, honey, and oil.

3. In a larger bowl, combine 5 cups flour, powdered milk, and salt.

4. Using a stand mixer with dough hook attachment, mix together the wet and dry ingredients.

5. Slowly add another 2 cups of flour or more until the dough is smooth and supple.

6. Place in a lightly oiled bowl and allow to rest until doubled.

7. Punch down and flatten the dough, then form it into 2 loaves and put in greased bread pans. Let double in size.

8. Bake 5 minutes, then turn the oven down to 350 degrees F. and bake for 30 minutes more.

9. Turn out of the pan, slice, and serve warm.

Kaiser Rolls

Makes 12 rolls • Prep Time: 20 minutes • Total Time: 3 hours

In the early 2000s we made these kaiser rolls at Kneaders. Some of our sandwiches were made on them, but we soon found that our Ciabatta and Focaccia Breads worked better. I know customers loved these and were sad to see them leave the menu. They're really good for a breakfast sandwich or as a hamburger bun. We are sharing for all our loyal and longtime kaiser roll fans.

2¼ cups warm water (90–100 degrees)

1 tablespoon instant dry yeast

1 tablespoon sugar

3 tablespoons softened butter

3 eggs, divided

1 tablespoon salt

5–6 cups high-quality all-purpose flour, such as Lehi Mills

Poppy seeds

1. Using a stand mixer with a dough hook attachment, add water, yeast, sugar, butter, eggs, salt, and flour. Mix together for 6–8 minutes on low speed. Dough should feel soft and stretch easily. You may need to adjust the amount of flour you add to help produce a soft, supple dough.

2. Once the dough is mixed, transfer it to a lightly oiled bowl. Cover with plastic wrap and let rest for 1 hour.

3. Transfer the dough to a clean, lightly floured surface. Gently flatten into a rectangle shape and divide into 12 equal pieces. Loosely round each piece by pulling and stretching the ends and tucking them underneath. Cover and let rest for 5 minutes.

4. Gently flatten each roll so they are approximately 3½-inch circles. Place a 3-inch kaiser stamp on top center of each roll and press down firmly until the stamp reaches the bottom of the roll but does not cut all the way through.

5. Place rolls onto a greased or parchment-lined half-sheet baking pan at least 2 inches apart. Cover with plastic wrap and let rest until they leave a slight indentation after being gently pressed, approximately 30–45 minutes. Rolls will have almost doubled in size.

6. Preheat the oven to 425 degrees.

7. Make an egg wash by whisking 1 egg with 2 tablespoons of water. Lightly brush the top of each roll with the egg wash. Sprinkle with poppy seeds.

8. Bake for 10–15 minutes, or until golden brown.

9. Transfer to a wire rack and allow to cool before eating.

Tasty Tips

- Wheat crops vary, so flour can absorb water differently from season to season. You may have to adjust the amount of flour in the recipe.
- To help the rolls rise taller in the oven, bake them on a preheated pizza stone.

Olive Bread

Makes 1 loaf • Prep Time: 15 minutes • Total Time: 5 hours

Olive bread was one of our original hearth breads. It's delightfully savory. We make it with our famous levain yeast, but we're sharing it here with dry yeast as a substitution, making it easier for the home baker. Serve with Italian Wedding Soup (see recipe on page 107) or your favorite Mediterranean meal. Olive bread is another flavorful bread for dipping. If you like olives, you will love this bread.

---

1 cup warm water (90–100 degrees F.)

1¾ cups bread flour

¼ cup whole wheat flour

1 teaspoon salt

1 teaspoon instant dry yeast

½ teaspoon whole dried thyme leaves

¼ cup kalamata olives, coarsely chopped

Nonstick baking spray

1. Using a stand mixer with a dough hook attachment, add water, bread flour, whole wheat flour, salt, and yeast. Mix on low speed for 6–8 minutes. Dough should feel soft and stretch easily. Add the thyme and mix for 1 minute on low speed. Add the kalamata olives and fold in by hand. Transfer the dough to a lightly oiled bowl. Cover and let rest until the dough has doubled in size, about 1 hour.

2. Transfer the dough to a lightly floured surface and gently flatten into a rectangle shape approximately 8 inches wide. Fold both sides to the middle. Then fold the top and bottom to the middle. Flip over and place back into the oiled bowl. Cover and let rest for 20–30 minutes.

3. Place a pizza stone or Dutch oven into a cold oven and preheat to 450 degrees F.

4. Transfer the dough to a lightly floured surface and shape into a round ball. Put dough back on the lightly floured surface seam side down. Cover and let proof until almost double in size and leaves a slight indentation after being pressed gently, approximately 45–60 minutes.

IF BAKING ON A PREHEATED PIZZA STONE

1. Gently transfer the loaf to a lightly floured cutting board or pizza peel. Slide loaf onto the hot pizza stone. Bake for 20–25 minutes until desired color is reached and the internal temperature is at least 190 degrees F.

2. Remove from oven and carefully place hot bread on a cooling rack.

IF BAKING IN PREHEATED DUTCH OVEN

1. Use oven mitts to remove hot Dutch oven and lid. Spray with nonstick baking spray and gently place into the Dutch oven seam side up. Replace the lid and place in the oven. Bake for 20 minutes, then carefully remove the hot lid. Bake for 15–20 more minutes or until the desired color has been reached and the internal temperature is at least 190 degrees F.

2. Remove from oven and carefully place hot bread on a cooling rack.

Tasty Tips

- To help the loaves have a nice shine and better rise, place an empty steam pan in the bottom of the oven while it is preheating. When ready to bake, pour 1 cup of hot water into the pan and close the oven door.

Rosemary Focaccia Bread

Makes 2 loaves • Prep Time: 25 minutes • Total Time: 4 hours

Rosemary Focaccia Bread is such a flavorful bread. It's the best bread for dipping I can think of. We still make this loaf at Kneaders today. The most amazing part of it is the fresh rosemary that we chop every single day. We don't know anyone else who puts fresh rosemary in their bread. So bake your loaf, serve it warm from the oven, pour some oil and balsamic vinegar into a flat dish, grind a little salt and pepper on top—and enjoy.

---

1 tablespoon active dry yeast

1 tablespoon sugar

1 cup warm water (90–100 degrees F.)

1 teaspoon salt

2 tablespoons melted butter, divided

2 tablespoons chopped fresh rosemary, divided

3 cups flour, divided

¼ teaspoon sea salt, for garnish

Nonstick baking spray

1. Place the yeast, sugar, and water in a large bowl and let it rest until mixture becomes bubbly, approximately 10 minutes.

2. Mix in 1 tablespoon of butter, salt, 1 tablespoon of rosemary, and 2 cups of flour.

3. Knead for 10 minutes by hand on a lightly floured surface or for 5 minutes in a stand mixer with a dough hook attachment. Add the remaining 1 cup of flour little by little as needed.

4. Place the kneaded dough in an oiled bowl. Cover with a towel and let it rise in a warm place until doubled, approximately 1 hour.

5. Punch down the dough and divide in half. Shape the dough into 2 small rounded loaves and place on a half-sheet baking pan sprayed with nonstick baking spray.

6. Sprinkle the remaining tablespoon of rosemary over the loaves and press it lightly into the surface of the dough. Cover and let rise again until it doubles in size, approximately 45 minutes.

7. Preheat the oven to 375 degrees F. Bake the loaves for 15–20 minutes until they are lightly browned. Remove from the oven, brush with remaining butter, and sprinkle with sea salt.

Sesame Semolina Bread

Makes 3 loaves • Prep Time: 20 minutes • Total Time: 4 hours

In 2003 we started a Bread of the Month campaign. We wanted to introduce our customers to exciting breads that are made around the world. This was our first official Bread of the Month. It's made with semolina flour, honey, and olive oil. Our first recipe used black sesame seeds, but since they're harder to find, we make this recipe with white ones. The sweetness of the dough comes from semolina flour, which is softer and has less bran than regular wheat flour. It's delicious served with spaghetti or lasagna—make it a meal with a fresh green salad, and dinner's done.

1 cup warm water (90–100 degrees F.)

1½ cups bread flour

1 cup semolina flour

2 tablespoons olive oil

2 tablespoons honey

1¼ teaspoons salt

1¼ teaspoons instant yeast

Sesame seeds for topping

Nonstick baking spray

1. Using a stand mixer with dough hook attachment, combine water, bread flour, semolina flour, olive oil, honey, salt, and yeast. Mix together for 7 minutes on low speed. Place the dough in a lightly oiled bowl, cover, and let rest for 1 hour.

2. Fold the dough and let it rest for 30 minutes. Divide the dough into 3 equal pieces. Roll out each piece to a 21-inch rope. Working from each end simultaneously, coil the dough toward the center, forming an *S* shape.

3. Place the loaves onto a half-sheet baking pan lined with parchment paper and dusted with semolina flour. Mist the tops of the loaves with water and sprinkle with sesame seeds. Then mist the tops of the loaves with vegetable oil spray. Let the loaves rise for 30–60 minutes.

4. Preheat the oven to 450 degrees F. Bake on the center rack for 15–20 minutes.

Tasty Tips

- To help the loaves have a nice shine and better rise, place an empty steam pan on the bottom rack of the oven while preheating. Then, when ready to bake, pour 1 cup of hot water into the pan and close the oven door.

Utah Mountain Style Cornbread and Honey Butter

Serves 12 • Prep Time: 20 minutes • Total Time: 1 hour

About a year after we opened, we started making bread for the Sundance Ski Resort. Our driver always loved the trip up the snowy canyon to deliver the orders. We made several hearth breads for them (Asiago Cheese, French Country Sourdough, and Focaccia). We also made this cornbread, which was served at the top of the lift to help warm up cold skiers. The smoothness of the honey butter is a perfect complement to the sweet fluffy texture of the cornbread. Serve with Sweet Chili (see recipe on page 114).

½ cup melted butter

⅔ cup granulated sugar

2 eggs

1 cup buttermilk

½ teaspoon baking soda

1 cup cornmeal

1 cup all-purpose flour

½ teaspoon salt

1. Preheat the oven to 375 degrees. Butter an 8-inch square baking pan.

2. Combine melted butter and sugar in a mixing bowl.

3. Add eggs and beat until incorporated.

4. Combine buttermilk with baking soda in another bowl. Stir this mixture into the egg mixture.

5. Add cornmeal, flour and salt. Stir until well blended and just a few lumps remain.

6. Pour batter into the baking pan. Bake for 30 minutes or until a toothpick inserted in the center comes out clean.

Tasty Tips

• If you don't have buttermilk, use 1 cup (minus 2 tablespoons) whole milk and add 2 tablespoons of lemon juice.

VARIATIONS

• For corn muffins, grease a muffin tin with butter. Fill each cup about halfway with batter. Bake for 15 minutes.

• For a savory taste, add a small can of diced jalapenos at the end of the mix and stir until incorporated.

• For added texture and yumminess, stir in 1 (11-ounce) can canned corn to the already-mixed batter. My favorite is Steam Crisp White Shoepeg Corn.

Honey Butter

Makes 2 cups • Prep Time: 10 minutes • Total Time: 20 minutes

1 cup (2 sticks) butter, room temperature

¾ cup honey

½ cup powdered sugar

1 teaspoon cinnamon

½ teaspoon vanilla

¼ teaspoon salt

1. Cream together the butter and honey in a medium mixing bowl.

2. Add the powdered sugar ¼ cup at a time and mix until incorporated.

3. Add the cinnamon, vanilla, and salt and mix until incorporated.

4. Whip for about 10 minutes until the butter is light and fluffy.

Tasty Tips
- The butter can be stored in the refrigerator for up to 2 weeks.

DIPS *and* SPREADS

Asiago Cheese Dip

Makes 7 cups • Prep Time: 15 minutes • Total Time: 4–5 hours

What is the difference between Asiago and Parmesan cheese? Both are made from cow's milk. Asiago has a nutty, creamy, sweet taste depending how long it has been aged (3 to 9 months). Parmesan cheese has a nutty, flaky texture with a sharper taste because it has been aged from 1 to 2 years. Either cheese can be used in this recipe.

CHEESE BREAD

1 Kneaders Baguette or bread of choice, sliced in 20 pieces

½ cup grated Parmesan cheese

Salt and pepper to taste

CHEESE DIP

1 cup chicken or vegetable broth

4 ounces sun-dried tomatoes (not oil-packed)

1½ cups shredded Asiago cheese

32 ounces (2 pounds) sour cream

1¼ cups mayonnaise

4 ounces cream cheese, softened

1 cup fresh mushrooms, sliced

1 cup green onion, thinly sliced, + more for garnish

1. For the cheese bread, set the oven to broil on high. Place baguettes on a baking sheet and sprinkle with Parmesan cheese and salt and pepper to taste. Broil until bread is golden brown. Set aside to cool completely.

2. For the cheese dip, in a small saucepan, bring broth to a boil, then remove from heat. Add tomatoes, cover, and set aside for 5 minutes, until tomatoes are plump. Drain and chop tomatoes.

3. In a 3.5- or 4-quart slow cooker, mix Asiago cheese with sour cream, mayonnaise, cream cheese, mushrooms, and green onion. Add chopped tomatoes and stir until incorporated.

4. Cover and cook on high for 1½–2 hours or on low for 3–4 hours. Stir well before serving and garnish with green onion. Serve warm with toasted baguette slices.

Tasty Tips

- Dip can be kept warm in a slow cooker turned to low for up to 2 hours.

Fast and Fabulous Dipping Oil

Serves 6–8 • Prep Time: 5 minutes

You know how it is when they bring warm bread and dipping oil to your table at an Italian restaurant? You can hardly wait to start eating. Now you can replicate that experience at home. Paesano bread is a peasant sourdough bread made with a thin cornmeal crust. Use this flavored dipping oil to complete your Italian meal.

¼ cup olive oil

2 cloves garlic, pressed

¼ teaspoon Italian seasoning

Sweet balsamic vinegar

1 tablespoon grated Parmesan cheese

In a small bowl, combine oil, garlic, and Italian seasoning. Stir, then transfer to a low-sided dipping dish or plate to serve. Add a few drops of balsamic vinegar. Sprinkle with grated Parmesan cheese.

Chunky Pesto

Makes 2 cups • Prep Time: 15 minutes • Total Time: 30 minutes

Pesto is a traditional Italian sauce. Usually it is made with basil, garlic, pine nuts, Parmesan cheese, and olive oil. As you can see, this pesto recipe is anything but traditional. We think you will enjoy this recipe. It pairs perfectly with our Italian breads.

½ cup pine nuts

1¼ cups crumbled feta

10 sun-dried tomatoes, roughly chopped

1 handful parsley, roughly chopped

3 tablespoons extra-virgin olive oil

½ clove garlic, minced

Juice and zest of ½ a lemon

Salt and pepper, to taste

1. Preheat oven to 350 degrees F. Spread pine nuts on a baking sheet. Bake for 10 minutes, until toasted. Check frequently to make sure they don't burn. Allow to cool completely.

2. In a medium bowl, stir together feta, tomatoes, parsley, olive oil, garlic, and lemon. Season with salt and pepper.

3. Stir warm toasted nuts into the pesto. Let rest for 5 minutes. Adjust seasonings to taste.

Tasty Tips

- Serve with warm Kneaders Paesano Bread. To reheat, mist bread with water and bake, directly on the rack, at 375 degrees F. for 10–15 minutes. Cut and serve.

Spinach Artichoke Dip

Makes 4 cups (not nearly enough—it's so good!) • Prep Time: 15 minutes • Total Time: 45 minutes

This recipe is my favorite. My niece Jenny Runyan Farris shared it with me years ago. Her parents, Linda and Don Runyan, and their son Todd opened the first Kneaders store in Arizona in Yuma. Jenny would travel from St. George, Utah, to Yuma, Arizona, to help them with retail displays and baskets. We've always enjoyed her energy and talents. Thanks to all the Runyan family.

2 cups grated Parmesan cheese

1 (10-ounce) package frozen chopped spinach, thawed

1 (14-ounce) can artichoke hearts, drained and chopped

⅔ cup sour cream

8 ounces cream cheese

⅓ cup mayonnaise

2 teaspoons minced garlic

1. Preheat the oven to 375 degrees F.

2. In a bowl, mix together Parmesan cheese, spinach, and artichoke hearts.

3. In a separate bowl, combine sour cream, cream cheese, mayonnaise, and garlic. Mix well, then combine with artichoke mixture.

4. Bake in a glass baking dish for 20–30 minutes.

Tasty Tips

• Serve warm with toasted Kneaders Baguette slices.

Hot Artichoke Crabmeat Dip

Serves 16 • Prep Time: 20 minutes • Total Time: 50 minutes

When you have knock-your-socks-off bread, you need a mouthwatering dip to go with it. Artichoke dips are plentiful, crab dips abundant—but put them together and you have something extraordinary. Serve at a special occasion. Yes, the "big game" counts.

---

8 ounces cream cheese, softened

1 cup mayonnaise

1 garlic clove, pressed

14 ounces artichoke hearts in water, drained and chopped

1 pound lump crab

¾ cup grated fresh Parmesan cheese

⅓ cup green onion, thinly sliced, + more for garnish

Zest of 1 lemon

⅛ teaspoon ground black pepper

⅓ cup chopped red bell pepper

1. Preheat the oven to 350 degrees F.

2. In a large bowl, combine cream cheese and mayonnaise. Add pressed garlic to the bowl. Mix well.

3. Add artichokes, crabmeat, Parmesan cheese, green onion, lemon zest, and black pepper. Mix well.

4. Spoon mixture into a 9x13 baking dish. Bake 25–30 minutes or until golden brown around the edges.

5. Sprinkle with red bell pepper and additional green onion.

Layered Sun-Dried Tomato and Basil Dip

Serves 12 • Prep Time: 25 minutes • Total Time: 8 hours 25 minutes

This Mediterranean dip can be made long before the party begins. It is a work of art. Serve it at your next party and you will impress everyone, including yourself.

---

22 ounces cream cheese, softened, divided

¾ cup butter, softened

1 teaspoon salt, divided

¼ teaspoon pepper

1⅓ cups sun-dried tomatoes in oil, drained, + more for garnish

⅓ cup (about half a 6-ounce can) tomato paste

4 garlic cloves

1½ cups fresh basil, firmly packed

¼ cup pine nuts

2 tablespoons extra-virgin olive oil

2 tablespoons fresh lemon juice

¼ cup grated Parmesan cheese

Fresh rosemary sprigs, for garnish

1. In a medium bowl, beat 16 ounces cream cheese, butter, ½ teaspoon salt, and pepper with an electric mixer on medium until creamy. Set aside. This is the butter mixture.

2. In a food processor, chop sun-dried tomatoes. Add tomato paste, 3 ounces cream cheese, and ¼ teaspoon salt. Process until smooth, stopping to scrape down sides. Spoon into a bowl and set aside. This is the tomato mixture.

3. In the food processor, chop garlic, basil, pine nuts, olive oil, and lemon juice. Add Parmesan cheese, remaining 3 ounces cream cheese, and remaining ¼ teaspoon salt. Pulse until just blended, stopping to scrape down sides. This is the basil mixture.

4. Spray a 6-inch springform pan with nonstick cooking spray. Layer evenly ½ cup butter mixture, half of the tomato mixture, ½ cup butter mixture, half of the basil mixture, then the remaining tomato mixture, ½ cup butter mixture, remaining basil mixture, then the remaining butter mixture. Cover with plastic wrap. Chill for at least 8 hours.

5. To serve, run a knife gently around the edge of the pan to loosen the sides. Carefully remove sides and bottom of pan. Place layered spread on a serving tray. Garnish with fresh rosemary sprigs and sun-dried tomatoes.

Tasty Tips

- As you assemble the dip, you may need to place it in the freezer for 5–10 minutes after each layer to help the layer solidify.
- Serve with toasted Kneaders Baguette slices. Also, if you're buying cream cheese in 8-ounce packages, you'll need 3 of those to have enough for 22 ounces.

DIPS AND SPREADS

The
TEACHER

Gladeeh Begaye

We first heard about Gladeeh Begaye twenty-three years ago, when we were still a new business. One of her friends frequented our Provo store and came in to ask us if we would consider donating our day-old bread to charity. They knew about all the work Gladeeh does in bringing food, clothing, and other necessities to those who are in need on the reservation where she grew up. The moment we met Gladeeh, we knew this was something we wanted to do. Her enthusiasm, energy, and spirit are absolutely irresistible.

Gladeeh is a member of the Diné Nation. Her father died when her mother was expecting Gladeeh, and then at age nine, Gladeeh also lost her mother. She went on to graduate from Brigham Young University and to receive her master's degree from Utah State University in Logan, Utah. She has been giving back to her people for decades through her non-profit organization Reservations Bound.

At first, Gladeeh picked up the bread herself every day. Right from the beginning, we learned so much from her. We learned that the preferred name of her tribe, rather than Navajo, is Diné, which means *The People.* We also discovered that our round loaves were especially cherished because the round shape is significant in Diné culture.

We have so many great memories with Gladeeh across the years, from putting together red boxes full of necessities to send down to the reservation to laughing when things didn't go exactly as expected. One of our favorite memories together is the time we sent extra Thanksgiving pies down to the reservation. I love the way Gladeeh tells the story:

Colleen and Gary called and said, "Would you like some of our extra pies?" I said, "Sure, we'll take some." My kids were so excited to help out— we love pumpkin pie. When we went to pick them up, I thought we'd be getting half a dozen pies. But when I arrived, there was Gary with an entire truckload of pumpkin and cream pies! Gary laughed and told me, "I hope you make it down there with all this." I thought to myself, "We are probably going to be leaving a trail of cream all the way there!"

But it worked. Most of the pies made it down there just fine. When we arrived at the reservation, the community was ready and waiting for us. That's when I realized something that made me laugh. We were in such haste that we'd loaded the pies upside down! As they opened the boxes, the people would ask, "What is it?" because the pies were so unrecognizable.

"It's a pie!" I'd tell them. And then they'd turn it right side up and dig in. The kids were having such a great time. It was the first time they'd ever had a cream pie. The grandmas would kind of test it and try it out. Pretty soon, they were in there scooping up the pie and everyone else was following their lead. We had such a great time.

Because of Gladeeh, we've been able to give to many other people. After we started donating the day-old bread from our Provo store to her, we decided to have each of our locations decide where they want to donate their day-old bread. Those donations have gone to organizations such as City Hope Center, Tabitha's Way, The Church of Jesus Christ of Latter-day Saints, and Matthew's Crossing Food Bank. She made us have more room in our hearts, and she made us want to give more to our communities and the people around us. We're lucky to have her as our friend.

See DINÉ FRYBREAD recipe on page 149.

Warm Bacon Cheese Spread

Serves 6 • Prep Time: 10 minutes • Total Time: 1 hour 10 minutes

We are so blessed to have such amazing bread, made fresh every day. One year our slogan was "It's all about the bread." That same year we had several contests involving our media friends. We were in search of the best dips and spreads to serve with our breads. This spread and others in this section are some of those recipes.

---

1 Kneaders Sourdough Bread Bowl

1 (8-ounce) package cream cheese, softened

1½ cups sour cream

2 cups shredded cheddar cheese

1½ teaspoons Worcestershire sauce

12 ounces sliced bacon, cooked and crumbled

½ cup green onion, chopped

1. Preheat the oven to 325 degrees F.

2. Cut the top fourth off the bread bowl. Carefully hollow out the bowl, leaving a 1-inch shell. Cut the removed bread and top of loaf into cubes. Set aside.

3. In a large bowl, beat cream cheese until fluffy. Add sour cream, cheddar cheese, and Worcestershire sauce. Mix thoroughly. Stir in bacon and green onion.

4. Spoon mixture into the bread bowl. Wrap in a piece of aluminum foil and place on a baking sheet.

5. Bake for 1 hour or until heated through. Serve with the cut bread cubes and your favorite Kneaders bread.

Reuben Dip

Makes 3 cups • Prep Time: 15 minutes • Total Time: 30 minutes

Some say a Lithuanian grocer created the Reuben sandwich for his weekly poker buddies. Other stories suggest that Reuben's Delicatessen first created it for a famous actress in 1914. The origin may be mysterious, but the flavor is well known. We think you'll enjoy the way this recipe turns this classic into a hearty dip. This recipe was submitted by Jody Sears and printed in our June 2013 newsletter.

Nonstick cooking spray

8 ounces cream cheese, softened

1½ cups shredded Swiss cheese, divided

½ cup Thousand Island dressing

4 ounces corned beef, chopped

½ cup sauerkraut, drained

1. Preheat the oven to 400 degrees F. Spray a 9-inch pie plate with nonstick cooking spray.

2. Mix together cream cheese, 1 cup Swiss cheese, Thousand Island dressing, and corned beef. Spread on pie plate. Top with sauerkraut and remaining ½ cup Swiss cheese.

3. Bake for 15 minutes or until bubbly around the edges.

4. Serve with Kneaders Rustic Rye Bread.

Sweet Toffee Dip

Makes 1¼ cups • Prep Time: 10 minutes • Total Time: 1 hour 10 minutes (if you can wait)

I know what you are thinking: Can anything make pumpkin bread better? Yes. This is it. My friend Jean Walton brought this creamy dip to a church meeting to be served with Kneaders Pumpkin Sweet Bread. All the girls loved it. Thank you, Jean, for sharing this wonderful recipe with us.

---

8 ounces cream cheese, softened

½ cup sugar

¾ cup brown sugar

1 teaspoon vanilla

1½ (1.4-ounce) toffee candy bars, finely chopped

1. In a medium bowl, mix together cream cheese, sugar, brown sugar, and vanilla until smooth. Chill for at least 1 hour.

2. Just before serving, stir in chopped toffee bars.

Sweet Pumpkin Spread

Makes 4 cups • Prep Time: 10 minutes • Total Time: 1 hour 10 minutes

You are right—at Kneaders we can't get enough pumpkin. Pumpkin has a special place in our hearts. And for sure there are never enough ways to serve it. This dip is good enough to just eat by itself as a dessert pudding.

---

1 (5-ounce) package instant vanilla pudding mix

1 (15-ounce) can pumpkin puree, such as Libby's 100% Pumpkin

1 teaspoon pumpkin pie spice

1 (16-ounce) container frozen whipped topping, thawed

1. In a large bowl, mix together pudding mix, canned pumpkin, and pumpkin pie spice. Fold in whipped topping.

2. Chill for 1 hour. Serve.

Tasty Tips
- Serve with Kneaders Pumpkin Sweet Bread.

Bloomin' Jack Bread

Makes 1 loaf • Prep Time: 15 minutes • Total Time: 40 minutes

This recipe comes from our April 2013 newsletter. Carol Hansen, my daughter-in-law's mother, was one of our customer recipe contest winners. We love the Hansen family and all of the contributions their family has made to Kneaders.

All you have to do to make this recipe is pick up a freshly baked loaf of Kneaders French Country Sourdough Bread and put on some tasty finishing touches. This recipe makes the most beautiful appetizer for any event.

---

1 loaf Kneaders French Country Sourdough Bread, unsliced

16 ounces Monterey Jack cheese, thinly sliced

½ cup butter, melted

½ cup green onion, finely diced

2 tablespoons poppy seeds

1. Preheat oven to 350 degrees F. Line a baking sheet with aluminum foil.

2. Using a sharp serrated-edge bread knife, and making sure you end your cuts about ¾-inch from the bottom, cut the top of the bread lengthwise about 4–6 times, about ½-inch apart, then cut the top of the bread widthwise 12–15 times, also about ½-inch apart. This will make a "bloomin' onion" effect; you want the top of the bread to look like a grid of ½-inch squares.

3. Insert cheese slices between cuts. In a small bowl, combine butter, green onion, and poppy seeds. Drizzle over bread.

4. Wrap bread in foil. Bake for 15–20 minutes. Unwrap and bake for an additional 10 minutes or until cheese is melted.

Tomato Bruschetta with Olive and Feta

Makes 12 slices • Prep Time: 20 minutes • Total Time: 30 minutes

The tomato, olives, and feta cheese combo is Greek in origin but is enjoyed by all the world. At Kneaders we made a wonderful side salad out of this tasty combination. Serve it on a slice of ciabatta bread.

---

1 clove garlic, peeled and halved

1 pint grape tomatoes, quartered

1 teaspoon salt, divided,
  + more for sprinkling

¼ teaspoon sugar

3 tablespoons olive oil,
  + more for brushing

1 tablespoon red wine vinegar

½ teaspoon black pepper, divided,
  + more for sprinkling

1 loaf Kneaders Ciabatta Bread

1½ cups pitted kalamata olives

½ cup crumbled feta cheese

2 teaspoons chopped oregano

1. Preheat the oven to 375 degrees F.

2. Wrap garlic clove in foil cut side up, place on a half-sheet baking pan, and roast 3–4 minutes. Let cool.

3. In a medium bowl, combine tomatoes, ½ teaspoon salt, and sugar. Let the mixture sit for 30 minutes.

4. After 30 minutes, spin tomatoes in a salad spinner for 45–60 seconds to remove any excess liquid. Return tomatoes to the bowl and add olive oil, vinegar, and ¼ teaspoon pepper. Toss and set aside. This is the tomato mixture.

5. Position oven rack 6 inches away from broiler element and preheat broiler on high. Slice ends off the ciabatta and discard. Slice bread into 12 (½-inch) slices. Place on a baking sheet and broil for 1–2 minutes per side, until deep golden brown. Let cool slightly.

6. In a food processor, pulse olives, remaining ½ teaspoon salt, and remaining ¼ teaspoon pepper until smooth. This is the olive mixture.

7. On each ciabatta slice, rub one side with roasted garlic and brush with olive oil. Sprinkle with salt and pepper. Spread an even layer of the olive mixture on each slice. Top with tomato mixture and feta. Sprinkle with oregano and serve.

Garlic Mushroom Bruschetta

Serves 8 • Prep Time: 5 minutes • Total Time: 25 minutes

Shiitake mushrooms have a woodsy, earthy taste when eaten raw, but when cooked, they take on a rich umami flavor. Umami is known as the fifth taste; it has a deep meaty, savory flavor. These mushrooms are a good substitute for meat when sautéed in olive oil. Enjoy this vegetarian treat on our Kneaders Ciabatta Bread. This bread is made with flour, water, salt, and a touch of oil for ease of handling.

3 tablespoons olive oil, divided

½ pound shiitake mushrooms, thinly sliced

2 cloves garlic, roughly chopped

Salt and pepper

1 loaf Kneaders Ciabatta Bread, sliced

1. Preheat oven to 400 degrees F.

2. In a large sauté pan over medium heat, heat 1 tablespoon olive oil. Add mushrooms and cook until soft, about 5 minutes. Stir in garlic and cook 1 minute more, until garlic is fragrant. Season with generous pinches of salt and pepper to taste. Keep warm.

3. Place sliced ciabatta bread on a half-sheet baking pan and drizzle with remaining 2 tablespoons olive oil. Toast in the oven until golden, about 10–15 minutes. Top toasted ciabatta slices with warm garlic-mushroom mixture.

Low-Fat Onion Spread

Makes enough for 20 baguette toasts • Prep Time: 10 minutes • Total Time: 1 hour 10 minutes

This onion spread is an instant winner. Who doesn't want to save a few calories?

The creamy cottage cheese serves as the base for spicy red peppers and milder green onions. With a slight lemony taste, it's the perfect spread for any Kneaders bread.

---

1 cup low-fat cottage cheese

4 ounces light cream cheese

2 teaspoons lemon juice

Chopped roasted red peppers, to taste

Garlic salt, to taste

Freshly cracked black pepper, to taste

¼ cup green onion, chopped

1. In a blender, combine all ingredients except the green onion. Pulse until smooth.

2. Pour mixture into a medium bowl and stir in onions. Refrigerate for at least 1 hour before serving.

Tasty Tips

- Serve the dip cold in a bowl with a basket of hot bread. A Kneaders Baguette goes great with this dip. Slice into 20 round pieces and broil on high for 7 minutes on one side and 4 minutes on the other, or until the bread turns golden brown.

Baked Brie with Cranberry Sauce and Walnuts

Serves 10 • Prep Time: 7 minutes • Total Time: 25 minutes

Easy but impressive. In this day of charcuterie boards, can you imagine how classy a board would look with toasted bread and baked Brie on one end and fruits and chocolate on the other? This is party worthy.

---

1 (16-ounce) round Brie cheese

¾ cup prepared cranberry sauce

⅔ cup walnuts, chopped

Zest of 1 orange

1. Preheat oven to 350 degrees F.

2. Using a serrated knife, remove rind from the top of the Brie and discard. Place cheese cut side up on a large ovenproof plate. Bake for 10 minutes.

3. Top Brie with cranberry sauce. Bake for an additional 5 minutes.

4. Scatter walnuts and orange zest over top of softened, bubbly Brie.

5. Serve warm with toasted Kneaders Baguette slices.

STUFFINGS and CROUTONS

Artichoke Garlic Stuffing

Serves 10 • Prep Time: 25 minutes • Total Time: 55 minutes

Ryker Brown put together this amazing artichoke stuffing. It's packed with flavor and full of onion, garlic, sun-dried tomatoes, artichoke hearts, basil, and parsley. When you add Italian sausage or leftover turkey, it becomes a meal.

---

2 bags Kneaders Garlic Croutons or 1 recipe French Country Garlic Croutons (see recipe on page 205)

¼ cup pine nuts

3 tablespoons extra-virgin olive oil, divided

1½ cups onion, chopped

2 cloves garlic, minced

¼ cup sun-dried tomatoes

1 cup artichoke hearts, chopped

3 tablespoons fresh basil, chopped

3½ cups vegetable stock

1 teaspoon salt

½ teaspoon black pepper

1 teaspoon parsley, chopped

1. Preheat the oven to 350 degrees F. Spray a 9x13 baking dish with nonstick cooking spray. Set aside.

2. Place croutons in a large mixing bowl and set aside. In a dry skillet, toast pine nuts over medium heat, stirring constantly, until golden brown, about 4 minutes. Add pine nuts to croutons.

3. Heat 2 tablespoons oil in the same skillet over medium heat. Add onion and sauté for 5 minutes. Add garlic and cook for an additional 2 minutes, stirring constantly. Transfer sautéed onion and garlic to the bowl of croutons and pine nuts. Add sun-dried tomatoes, artichokes, basil, vegetable stock, salt, and pepper. Stir until combined.

4. Transfer stuffing mixture to prepared baking dish. Drizzle remaining tablespoon oil over the stuffing. Cover with aluminum foil. Bake for 30 minutes. Remove from the oven and top with parsley.

Tasty Tips

- Artichoke garlic stuffing tastes great with Italian sausage mixed in. Sauté 1 pound Italian sausage in medium skillet, drain, and add with the other mix-ins.

"To Die For" Stuffing

Serves 12 • Prep Time: 10 minutes • Total Time: 1 hour 5 minutes

My daughter Angie Bishop surprised us with this great stuffing for Thanksgiving in 2022. Made from the ends of Kneaders bread (also called the "heels"), it was so delicious that I asked if I could share this updated "To Die For" stuffing with you. The sacks of bread ends are one of the best deals at the bakery. If you don't see them, just ask. Tell them Colleen sent you.

Your ends bag should include Asiago Cheese, French Country Sourdough, Hazelnut 12-Grain, Country White, Honey Wheat, and Rustic Rye. Use all the breads in the ends bag except for the rye (the dark-brown one).

---

8 cups cubed Kneaders bread ends

½ cup butter

1 cup onion, chopped

2 cups celery, chopped

2 (14.5-ounce) cans chicken broth

1. Preheat the oven to 350 degrees F. Spread cubed bread on a half-sheet baking pan. Bake 20 minutes, stirring halfway. The bread should be browned and dry all the way through. Remove from the oven.

2. Turn the oven up to 375 degrees F. In a large saucepan, melt the butter. Add the onion and celery and stir until browned. Remove from heat.

3. In a large bowl, combine the chicken broth, melted butter mixture, and toasted bread. Stir until all parts are moistened. If the mixture needs more liquid, add extra chicken broth as needed.

4. Spread the mixture in a 9x13 baking dish and cover with aluminum foil. Bake for 25 minutes. Remove the aluminum foil and cook for an additional 10 minutes or until the top is crusty.

Tasty Tips

- For added flavor, you can add any of the following: 1 pound sausage, cooked and drained; 1 cup chopped roasted chestnuts; giblets, chopped and cooked; 1 medium Granny Smith apple, peeled and chopped; or ¾ cup craisins. Add mix-ins when you stir in the bread before baking.

Asiago Caesar
Croutons

Hazelnut 12-Grain Ranch
Croutons and Stuffing

French Country Garlic Croutons

Hazelnut 12-Grain Ranch Croutons and Stuffing

Serves 12 • Prep Time: 25 minutes • Total Time: 1 hour 20 minutes

Nothing is better than toasted hearth bread. It's amazing that such simple breads can be so flavorful. My husband, Gary, created Hazelnut 12-Grain Hearth Bread after visiting a store in El Paso, Texas. This on-the-border bakery, recommended to us by one of our children, had our exact Italian oven. They made a 7-grain bread with no nuts; Gary wanted 12 grains plus nuts.

I love Hazelnut 12-Grain as toast, but the rich nutty taste of the bread combined with the flavor of ranch dressing in this recipe is addicting. The whole hazelnuts are the best part. The first half of this recipe explains how to turn the bread into croutons. Follow the whole recipe to get a flavorful stuffing.

---

2 loaves Kneaders Hazelnut 12-Grain Hearth Bread, sliced and cubed

¾ cup butter, melted

¼ cup dry ranch dressing mix (usually in a 1-ounce packet)

2 (14.5-ounce) cans chicken broth

2 cups celery, chopped

1 cup onion, chopped

1. Place bread cubes on a half-sheet baking pan to dry out for at least 24 hours.

2. Preheat the oven to 350 degrees F.

3. Place the bread cubes on a baking sheet. Mix together the melted butter and the dry ranch dressing mix. Toss the bread with the butter and ranch mix. Bake for 20 minutes, stirring halfway. The bread should be browned on all sides and dry all the way through. Set aside to cool.

4. Turn the oven up to 375 degrees F. In a large bowl, combine the chicken broth, celery, onions, and any other add-ins you desire (see "To Die For" Stuffing recipe on page 200 for ideas). Add croutons and stir until moistened throughout. If the mixture needs more liquid, add extra chicken broth.

5. Spread the mixture in a 9x13 baking dish and cover with aluminum foil. Bake for 25 minutes. Remove the aluminum foil and cook for an additional 10 minutes or until the top is crusty.

Asiago Caesar Croutons

Makes enough for 20 salads or 1 batch stuffing • Prep Time: 10 minutes • Total Time: 35 minutes

At Kneaders, we have been baking Asiago Cheese Bread since the beginning. These cheesy, crunchy croutons are amazing on any green salad. You can also use them in our "To Die For" Stuffing (see recipe on page 200).

---

2 loaves Kneaders Asiago Cheese Bread, sliced and cubed

¾ cup butter, melted

3 tablespoons grated Parmesan cheese

½ tablespoon sugar

½ tablespoon garlic powder

½ teaspoon onion powder

½ teaspoon salt

½ teaspoon white pepper

½ teaspoon dry mustard

2 tablespoons lemon juice

1. Place bread cubes on a half-sheet baking pan to dry out for at least 24 hours.

2. Preheat the oven to 350 degrees F.

3. Mix together everything but the bread. Place the bread pieces on a half-sheet baking pan and toss with spice mix.

4. Bake for 25 minutes, stirring halfway. The bread should be browned and dry all the way through.

5. Remove from the oven and let cool to room temperature.

Tasty Tips

• Be sure to get your loaves sliced at the store—it will make prep much faster.

French Country Garlic Croutons

Makes enough for 20 salads or 1 batch stuffing • Prep Time: 5 minutes • Total Time: 40 minutes

French Country Sourdough Bread is a simple bread, made with flour, water, salt, and a sourdough start. Each of our locations grows a start in their store that must be fed twice a day. Maintaining a sourdough start is like feeding a baby—you can't miss a feeding. Lots of work? Yes, but we think it's worth it!

---

2 loaves Kneaders French Country Sourdough Bread, sliced and cubed

¾ cup Kneaders Extra Virgin Olive Oil

1 tablespoon garlic powder

1 cup grated Parmesan cheese

1. Place bread cubes on a half-sheet baking pan to dry out for at least 24 hours.

2. Preheat the oven to 250 degrees F. In a small bowl add olive oil and garlic powder and whisk until combined. Pour the garlic oil over the croutons and toss to evenly coat the bread.

3. Spread the croutons on two half-sheet baking pans. Sprinkle cheese evenly over the croutons.

4. Bake for 25 minutes. Toss croutons and bake for another 10 minutes. Croutons should be browned and dry all the way through.

Tasty Tips

- These croutons may be stored for up to 1 week in a sealed container. However, they must be completely dry inside to be stored.

CAKES *and* TRIFLES

Chocolate Cakes

We love chocolate here at Kneaders. Here are a few cakes we've found that satisfy our cravings—we hope you enjoy baking them too. We've tried to include recipes for all levels of baking experience. Many thanks to a former bakery executive chef, Julia Sharp, for working on these recipes for Kneaders. She makes the most beautiful and meaningful special cakes for family and friends.

Easy Chocolate Cake Box Mix Hacks

Makes 2 (8-inch round) cakes or 1 (9x13) cake • Prep Time: 5 minutes • Total Time: 35 minutes

To a favorite chocolate cake box mix, add or substitute one or two of the following ingredients, not all. If you only have time for one, make it mayo.

1 teaspoon vanilla or preferred flavor

Substitute whole milk or soda for water

Substitute melted butter
   for vegetable oil

Add an extra egg yolk

Add 2 tablespoons sour cream

Add ½ cup mayo

1. Preheat the oven to 350 degrees F. Line the bottom of 1 (9x13) or 2 (8-inch round) cake pans with parchment paper.

2. Mix according to package directions, making substitutions or additions as desired.

3. Bake for 28–33 minutes or until cake springs back. Allow to cool 10 minutes before removing from the pan.

4. Run a knife along the outside edge of the pan before tipping it out, then peel off parchment. Allow to cool completely before frosting.

Tasty Tips

- There are some advantages to using a box mix: Softer texture, more consistency (science is on its side), saves time, and keeps longer.

Basic Chocolate Cake from Scratch

Makes 2 (8-inch round) cakes or 1 (9x13) cake • Prep Time: 10 minutes • Total Time: 40 minutes

2 cups granulated sugar

1¾ cups all-purpose flour

¾ cups unsweetened cocoa

1½ teaspoons baking powder

1½ teaspoons baking soda

1 teaspoon salt

2 eggs

1 cup whole milk

½ cup vegetable oil

2 teaspoons vanilla

1 cup boiling water

1. Preheat the oven to 350 degrees F. Line the bottom of 1 (9x13) or 2 (8-inch round) cake pans with parchment paper.

2. In a large mixing bowl, stir together sugar, flour, cocoa, baking powder, baking soda, and salt.

3. Add eggs, milk, oil, and vanilla. Beat on medium speed for one minute. Stir in boiling water. The batter will be thin.

4. Bake for 28–33 minutes, or until cake springs back. Cool 10 minutes before removing from the pan.

5. Run a knife along the outside edge of the pan before tipping it out, then peel off parchment. Allow to cool completely before frosting.

Master Chocolate Cake from Scratch

Makes 2 (8-inch round) cakes or 1 (9x13) cake • Prep Time: 20 minutes • Total Time: 50 minutes

1 cup water

⅓ cup Dutch process extra dark cocoa

2 ounces semisweet chocolate chips

¾ cup butter

2 cups cake flour

1½ cups granulated sugar

½ teaspoon baking powder

¾ teaspoon baking soda

¼ teaspoon salt

3 eggs, whisked together

2 teaspoons vanilla

¼ cup buttermilk

1. Preheat the oven to 350 degrees F. Line the bottom of 1 (9x13) or 2 (8-inch round) cake pans with parchment paper.

2. In a small saucepan over medium heat, whisk water and cocoa powder together until it comes to a boil. Let boil for 30 seconds. Turn off heat and let cool a little.

3. In a microwave-safe bowl, melt butter and chocolate chips together in 30-second increments until well combined. Add to mixing bowl and sift dry ingredients into the melted butter and chocolate chips, taking care not to overmix.

4. Add eggs, vanilla, buttermilk, and cocoa powder liquid. Stir until combined. (Mixing in a stand mixer works just as well.)

5. Bake for 28–33 minutes, or until cake springs back. Cool 10 minutes before removing from the pan.

6. Run a knife along the outside edge of the pan before tipping it out, then peel off parchment. Allow to cool completely before frosting.

Black Forest Cake

Makes 1 (8-inch) double-layered cake • Prep and Assembly Time: 20 minutes • Total Time: 55–60 minutes

The Black Forest cake was named for the region in Germany where it originated. It's a chocolate sponge cake with a rich cherry filling. It was one of the first cakes we made in the bakery and a favorite of many. We no longer serve it in our stores, but we know you love it, so we want to share the recipe with you. For those of you who bought it yearly for a birthday celebration, we are sharing this recipe so the tradition can continue on. Happy baking!

1 (2- to 3-ounce) milk, semisweet, or dark chocolate bar, as desired

1 dark chocolate cake box mix, or 1 recipe Basic Chocolate Cake from Scratch or 1 recipe Master Chocolate Cake from Scratch (see recipes on pages 209–11)

1 pound milk chocolate ganache (see recipe on page 225)

1 (20-ounce) can cherry pie filling, such as Duncan Hines Wilderness

1 batch Whipped Cream Topping (see recipe on page 227)

6 maraschino cherries

CHOCOLATE CURLS

1. Microwave the chocolate bar for 10 seconds; this will help it shave into curls.

2. Set a piece of parchment paper on your work surface, then, holding the top of the chocolate bar with one hand and resting the bottom on the parchment paper, use a vegetable peeler to make the curls, starting at the top and sliding the peeler to the bottom. Continue until you have the desired amount of curls.

3. Transfer the curls to a container with a lid and place them in the freezer until needed. This makes them easier to work with and less likely to melt.

CAKE

1. Spray 2 (8-inch round) cake pans evenly with cooking spray.

2. Follow the baking instructions for the recipe you are making.

3. Once the cake has been baked and cooled, place a round of parchment between the two layers, wrap in plastic wrap, and freeze for 1–2 hours.

ASSEMBLY

1. Remove the cake from the freezer and place one layer on a cake board. Spread a thin layer of melted ganache on top.

2. Using a piping bag, pipe a ½-inch Whipped Cream Topping border around the top of the cake.

3. Add ½-inch-deep layer of cherry filling to the center of the cake layer.

4. Carefully place the second layer on top of the layer you've completed.

5. Ice the sides of the cake with Whipped Cream Topping.

6. Remove the chocolate curls from the freezer and sprinkle the bottom half of the cake with the frozen chocolate curls.

7. Spread cherry filling over the top of the cake, leaving a ½-inch space around the rim of the cake. If the cherry filling is too close to the side of the cake, it may slide off.

8. Using a piping bag, pipe a border of Whipped Cream Topping around the top edge of the cake.

9. In the center of the cake, pipe 6 rosettes.

10. Top each rosette or circle with a maraschino cherry.

11. Use a fork to drizzle melted chocolate ganache over the rosettes and cherries. Refrigerate until ready to eat.

Chocolate Drizzle Cake

Serves 12 • Assembly Time: 30 minutes • Total Time: 65–70 minutes

In almost every culture, cakes are part of special occasions. Several years ago while delivering a wedding cake, we had a long climb up a hill to get to the venue. We had three layers of cake, so each one of us carried one layer. One of the layers was accidentally dropped. Oh no! Immediately we called the store, and another cake top was ready to go when the manager went back to pick it up. It was placed on top of the cake long before any of the family arrived for pictures. They never knew—but the three of us will never be the same again.

Chocolate ganache is a luscious combination of cream and melted chocolate. It has a gorgeous shine and a rich chocolate taste—so velvety and beautiful for any of your special occasions.

---

1 dark chocolate cake box mix, or 1 recipe Basic Chocolate Cake from Scratch or 1 recipe Master Chocolate Cake from Scratch (see recipes on pages 209–11)

4 cups Chocolate Buttercream icing (see recipe on page 225)

2 cups Chocolate Ganache (see recipe on page 225)

1. Spray 2 (8-inch round) cake pans evenly with cooking spray.

2. Follow the baking instructions for the recipe you are making.

3. Let the cake cool in the pan for 10 minutes. Remove onto cooling racks.

4. Using a serrated knife, cut each cake into two even layers.

ASSEMBLY

1. Place the first layer of cake on a cake stand.

2. Using a spatula, rubber scraper, or butter knife, spread a ¼-inch-thick layer of buttercream over the first cake layer. Add the second layer and repeat the buttercream layer. Add the third layer and repeat the buttercream layer.

3. Place the last layer of cake on the top, bottom side up.

4. Make sure the whole cake is level and well-rounded. Trim off any excess cake or icing.

5. Coat the sides and top of the cake with chocolate buttercream using a cake icer, spatula, rubber scraper, or butter knife until the cake is smooth.

6. Melt the chocolate ganache to 120 degrees F. and pour over the top of the cake, tilting the cake or spreading the ganache so it drips over the sides.

7. Using a piping bag with a star tip (such as #846), pipe rosettes around the top of the cake close to the outside edge.

The MOTHER WARRIOR

Yermonia Balasanyan in the pastry kitchen.

Yermonia, Armen, and Anait Balasanyan

One day, years ago, a young man named Armen came into the store and asked for the owner. The crew came and got me and I went out to meet him. With no introduction, he said, "You need to hire my mom." I asked, "Where is your mom?" We walked out the front door and there was Yermonia, waiting patiently. She was a beautiful woman, her hair and makeup arranged perfectly, and I could see the great love she and her son shared. She'd brought me a book with her beautiful pastries pictured in it.

My first attraction was not to the pastries (although they were wonderful) but to the pride her son had in her and the pride she had in him. At that time, he was twenty years old. He always seemed older and wiser than his age.

This was my introduction to the Balasanyan family. I could tell they were special, but I had no idea that they would change Kneaders forever.

The Balasanyans were Armenian refugees. Because of the war in Armenia, they had to leave their country, moving from place to place. They ended up in Russia, where Armen was conscripted into the Russian Army at age seventeen. Yermonia did not want her son to be a part of that, so they left to have a better life in the United States. Her children say that everything she did was guided by faith.

Yermonia and Armen traveled to Brooklyn, New York, where they knew absolutely no one. Yermonia found a job in a Russian bakery, and Armen began working at an Italian restaurant. Yermonia had a hard time feeling like she was in the United States because she was always interacting with Russian speakers. She decided the family needed to come to Utah. When they arrived in Provo, Yermonia found a job at the Marriott hotel in downtown Provo as a pastry chef, and Armen began working there as a morning cook so he could translate for Yermonia. When the Marriott decided to close its bakery, Yermonia got a job at a different bakery. She always poured herself into her work, but Armen could tell that she wasn't happy. He began going around to other bakeries, and that's how we found one another.

Yermonia was a determined mother first and foremost, and she was also an absolute artist. She didn't follow a recipe. To her, a recipe was just a suggestion. Baking brought her joy, and food was her love language. She never made a mistake because baking was intuitive to her. It was a part of who she was.

Yermonia made her pastries by hand. Her baklava, eclairs, Napoleons, and fruit tarts were exquisite. Customers still remember and ask about her chocolate torte. She had no template and no machine, and everything she made turned out consistent and beautiful. Once, for the opening of Brigham Young University's fine arts building, Yermonia made three thousand fruit tarts by hand.

A few years after Armen and Yermonia came to the United States, Yermonia's daughter Anait was able to join them in Provo. The moment Anait arrived, she was ready for her new life. She was seventeen and wanted to get a driver's license and study English. Armen hadn't yet started school, because, as Anait says, "As an immigrant, you just start working. You get the family on its feet." She also wanted to spend as much time with her mother as she could, since they'd been apart for many years. So Anait began working at Kneaders as well. I remember her meticulously cleaning the pastry case every morning. She remembers working at the drive-through while she was still learning English, figuring out a clever way to learn while still helping customers. Someone would come through and order a blueberry muffin, for example, and Anait would ask the other workers, "Where are the blueberry muffins?" They'd show her, and so she learned the menu without having to reveal that she didn't know the names.

Armen, Anait, and Yermonia at Anait's graduation from Brigham Young University.

Armen remembers Gary listening to Yermonia when she became emotional because she was passionate about her work and was sometimes unable to explain what she meant due to the language barrier. He says Gary always listened and helped bridge the gap. Armen thought Gary brought constant calm to the organization and said, "Colleen, you were everywhere doing everything all the time! I don't think you've ever taken a break." I love that he said this about Gary because I feel that has been the whole of my life! Me being all over the place, full of ideas and energy, and Gary being the constant. Anait loved that we were such a family business. She said they felt like they were an extension of our family. I felt—and feel—the same way.

Yermonia valued education deeply. She told her children, "It doesn't matter what you choose to do, but you need to get an education." Armen wasn't sure what he wanted to do at first—would he also run a bakery?—but eventually he decided he wanted to become a dentist. Even when he was working thirty hours per week, he worked on his bachelor's degree at the University of Utah. After graduation, he attended the University of Indiana Dental School, and now he owns five dental practices in Charlotte, North Carolina. Anait studied finance at Brigham Young University and worked in that field for several years, taking a job with Wachovia in Charlotte.

In the spring of 2005, Yermonia was diagnosed with cancer. It was the same year Anait graduated from Brigham Young University. A day before Anait's graduation, Yermonia was admitted to the hospital. She missed the graduation, but she gathered her strength and came to Anait's graduation party that night, even after being in the hospital on IVs all day. The summer before she passed away in 2008, they all traveled to Armenia for Armen's marriage, and Yermonia was able to dance at his wedding. Armen and Anait had the phrase *mother warrior* inscribed on her gravestone in Armenian. "We lived through a war," Armen and Anait said, "but losing her was the most difficult thing. She always fought for our place under the sun and for a good life for us."

After losing her mother, Anait began reflecting on her own work. She decided that life was too short and that she needed to do something she loved. She followed in Armen's footsteps and attended the Indiana School of Dentistry and became a dentist. Last year Anait and Armen partnered together and opened their own practice. She loves coming in to work, where no day is the same as another. She loves seeing her patients and knows that they can tell that she cares for them and that she loves her job.

I was touched when Anait told me recently, "We're in a different business with our dental office, but business rules still apply. I'm like you, Colleen. I'm the first one to say yes when someone comes into the practice needing something right away. I always find a way to fit them in because that's the example we saw at Kneaders." We learned so much from Yermonia and her children as well. They showed us every day what it meant to work hard and to support one another. They are some of the very best people I know, and they helped make us who we are today.

See FLOURLESS CHOCOLATE TORTE
recipe on page 219.

Flourless Chocolate Torte

Serves 12 • Prep Time: 15 minutes • Total Time: 50 minutes

Read the Balasanyans' story on pages 216–18.

6 eggs at room temperature

½ cup granulated sugar

1 pound semisweet chocolate wafers (55–65% dark, such as Guittard Prestige 57%)

½ pound (2 sticks) butter, diced

1 batch Chocolate Ganache (see recipe on page 225), optional

Fresh fruit, for garnish, optional

1. Preheat oven to 375 degrees F, and grease and line a 9-inch springform pan with parchment paper.

2. Using a stand mixer with whisk attachment, beat eggs and sugar until thick and pale yellow, about 5–8 minutes.

3. In a small saucepan over low heat, melt butter. Add chocolate in small increments to the saucepan and stir until chocolate is melted. Let cool for 15 minutes.

4. Pour half the chocolate mixture into egg mixture and fold in gently; add remaining chocolate and fold in.

5. Pour the batter into the prepared pan and bake for 27–35 minutes, until the top is no longer shiny and the center barely jiggles. A toothpick inserted into the center should come out with only a few crumbs attached.

6. Let the torte cool completely, then run a sharp, thin knife around the inside of the pan and remove the springform ring.

7. You can garnish the torte with powdered sugar or cocoa powder and/or fresh berries and Whipped Cream Topping (see recipe on page 227).

8. If desired, cover the torte with Chocolate Ganache, letting it drip down the sideds. When dry, add fresh fruit of your choice (see picture).

Vanilla Cakes

With a few delicious vanilla cake recipes in your repertoire, you can use them as a canvas for creativity—or they're absolutely delightful as-is.

Easy Vanilla Cake Box Mix Hacks

Makes 2 (8-inch round) cakes or 1 (9x13) cake • Prep Time: 5 minutes • Total Time: 35 minutes

To a favorite vanilla (or other flavor) cake box mix, add or substitute one or two of the following ingredients, not all. If you only have time for one, make it mayo.

1 teaspoon vanilla or preferred flavor

Substitute whole milk for water

Substitute melted butter
　for vegetable oil

Add an extra egg yolk

Add 2 tablespoons sour cream

Add ½ cup mayo

1. Preheat the oven to 350 degrees F. Line the bottom of 1 (9x13) or 2 (8-inch round) cake pans with parchment paper.

2. Mix according to package directions, making substitutions or additions as desired.

3. Bake for 28–33 minutes or until cake springs back. Allow to cool 10 minutes before removing from the pan.

4. Run a knife along the outside edge of the pan before tipping it out, then peel off parchment. Allow to cool completely before frosting.

Tasty Tips

- For a lemon or lime cake, add 1 (3.4-ounce) box lemon instant pudding (such as Jell-O), 1 teaspoon zest of 1 lemon or 1 lime, 1 extra egg yolk, and substitute melted butter for oil.
- For a strawberry or raspberry cake, add 1 (3-ounce) box raspberry or strawberry gelatin dessert (such as Jell-O); 1 cup of fresh raspberries or strawberries, chopped; 1 extra egg yolk; and substitute melted butter for oil.

Basic Vanilla Cake from Scratch

Makes 2 (8-inch round) cakes or 1 (9x13) cake • Prep Time: 10 minutes • Total Time: 50 minutes

¾ cup butter, softened

1½ cups granulated sugar

2 teaspoons vanilla

3 eggs

2½ cups all-purpose flour

2 teaspoons baking powder

½ teaspoon salt

1 cup whole milk

1. Preheat the oven to 350 degrees F. Line the bottom of 1 (9x13) or 2 (8-inch round or 6-inch round) cake pans with parchment paper.

2. Using a stand mixer with paddle attachment on medium speed, whip butter, sugar, and vanilla until light and fluffy, about 3 minutes.

3. Add the eggs one at a time, mixing at medium speed. When fully incorporated, beat mixture about 4 minutes until mixture is aerated and light. In a medium bowl, whisk the flour, baking powder, and salt together. Alternate adding the dry ingredients and the milk to the butter mixture on medium speed. Don't overmix.

4. Bake for 28–33 minutes, or until cake springs back. Cool 10 minutes before removing from the pan.

5. Run a knife along the outside edge of the pan before tipping it out, then peel off parchment. Allow to cool completely before frosting.

Master Vanilla Cake from Scratch

Makes 2 (8-inch round) cakes or 1 (9x13) cake • Prep Time: 20 minutes • Total Time: 55 minutes

2½ cups cake flour

2½ teaspoons baking powder

1 teaspoon baking soda

1 teaspoon salt

4 eggs

1½ cups granulated sugar

3 teaspoons vanilla

1 cup canola oil

1 cup buttermilk

1. Preheat the oven to 350 degrees F. Line the bottom of 1 (9x13) or 2 (8-inch round) cake pans with parchment paper.

2. In a medium bowl, combine cake flour, baking powder, baking soda, and salt. Whisk ingredients together and set aside.

3. Using a stand mixer with paddle attachment, beat eggs for 10–20 seconds. Add sugar and continue to beat on medium speed for about 30 seconds. Add vanilla and oil, then beat.

4. Reduce speed to low and slowly add half of the dry ingredients and half of the milk, then add the rest of the flour and the rest of the milk. Beat just until combined. Scrape down the sides of the bowl. The batter will be thin.

5. Bake for 28–33 minutes, or until cake springs back. Cool 10 minutes before removing from the pan.

6. Run a knife along the outside edge of the pan before tipping it out, then peel off parchment. Allow to cool completely before frosting.

Tasty Tips

- Cake flour has a lower protein content than traditional all-purpose flour, which results in a more tender, delicate crumb in the finished product. If you do not have access to cake flour, feel free to substitute as necessary, but your results will vary from the original recipe.

Icings

Chocolate Buttercream

1 cup butter, softened

3½ cups powdered sugar

½ cup cocoa powder

½ teaspoon salt

2 tablespoons pure vanilla

4 tablespoons whole milk
or heavy cream

1. In a stand mixer with a paddle attachment, beat butter until smooth on medium speed. Sift sugar and cocoa into the mixing bowl. Mix at the lowest speed until powdered sugar and cocoa are incorporated into the butter.

2. Increase mixer speed to medium and add salt, vanilla, and milk or cream and beat for 3 minutes. If the frosting needs to be thicker, add more powdered sugar. If the frosting needs to be thinner, add more milk or cream 1 teaspoon at a time.

Chocolate Ganache

12 ounces semisweet or bittersweet
chocolate, finely chopped

1 cup heavy whipping cream

2 tablespoons butter

¼ teaspoon pure vanilla

1. Pour chocolate into a metal mixing bowl.

2. Stirring constantly, heat the whipping cream, butter, and vanilla in a small saucepan to just about boiling, but don't let it actually come to a boil. You should see bubbles forming around the edges of the pot. Heat to about 180 degrees.

3. Immediately pour the hot cream mixture over the chocolate and use a small whisk to mix until smooth.

Classic American Buttercream

1 cup unsalted butter, softened

4 cups powdered sugar,
  sifted and divided

¼ teaspoon salt

1 tablespoon pure vanilla extract

4 tablespoons milk or heavy cream,
  divided

1. In a stand mixer with the paddle attachment, beat butter on medium speed for a few minutes.

2. Sift sugar into the mixing bowl. Mix at the lowest speed until powdered sugar is incorporated into the butter. Increase mixer speed to medium, add vanilla, salt, and 2 tablespoons of milk or cream. Beat for 3 minutes.

3. If the frosting needs to be thicker, add more powdered sugar in ¼-cup increments. If the frosting needs to be thinner, add more milk or cream 1 teaspoon at a time.

Cream Cheese Frosting

16 ounces cream cheese,
  room temperature

1½ cups powdered sugar

1 teaspoon pure vanilla

1 cup heavy cream, cold (the
  higher the fat content, the
  better, 40% ultra preferred)

1. In a medium bowl with an electric hand mixer, beat the cream cheese, sugar, and vanilla until smooth and fluffy.

2. In a separate bowl, beat the heavy cream to nearly stiff peaks, then add the whipped cream into the cheese mixture and quickly and briefly beat to combine. Do not over beat.

German Chocolate Frosting

1 cup granulated sugar

1 (12-ounce) can evaporated milk

½ cup unsalted butter

3 egg yolks

1 teaspoon pure vanilla

1 (7-ounce) package flaked coconut

1½ cups pecans, chopped

1. In a medium saucepan over medium heat, combine sugar, milk, butter, egg yolks, and vanilla. Cook, stirring constantly, until thickened, about 10 minutes.

2. Stir in coconut and pecans. Transfer to a bowl and, stirring occasionally, allow to cool to room temperature before frosting the cake.

Whipped Cream Topping

1 quart heavy cream

1 cup granulated sugar or powdered sugar

1½ teaspoons vanilla extract

1 tablespoon cream of tartar (if using powdered sugar, you can skip this ingredient)

1. Place the mixing bowl of a stand mixer in the freezer for 10 minutes.

2. In a small bowl, mix the granulated sugar and cream of tartar until completely combined. Set aside.

3. Attach the whisk attachment to the stand mixer. Take the mixing bowl out of the freezer and add the heavy cream and vanilla extract.

4. Start the mixer on low speed, slowly adding the granulated sugar mix (or powdered sugar) into the heavy cream mix. Whisk for 5 minutes.

5. Slowly raise the speed to medium and whisk for another 5 minutes. The heavy cream will start to thicken.

6. Slowly raise the speed of the mixer to high and whisk for about 5 minutes or until the whipping cream has come to a stiff peak. (You can check by lightly pressing down a spatula then pulling up and away from the whipped cream. You will see a peak and it will hold its shape.) Do not overmix—if the whipped cream is overmixed, it will look flat and dense and will be grainy.

7. Remove the bowl from the mixer, place plastic wrap over the bowl, then cool in the refrigerator.

Tasty Tips

- If you want to make chocolate whipped cream, add ½ cup cocoa powder to this recipe.

Fresh Fruit Charlotte

Serves 14 • Prep Time: 10 minutes • Total Time: 65–95 minutes

The first time I saw a fruit charlotte I was mesmerized. Could we possibly make this beauty at Kneaders? Our research and development chefs worked hard to develop a recipe simple enough that all our chefs in our various stores would be able to reproduce it. For years we made it every summer and tied a red, white and blue ribbon around the middle. Here is that recipe for you. After this simple recipe you'll want to try making your own ladyfingers and berry filling for the cake. Be sure to post pictures on social media. We'd love to see them!

1 vanilla cake box mix, or 1 recipe Basic Vanilla Cake from Scratch or 1 recipe Master Vanilla Cake from Scratch (see recipes on page 221–23)

About 24 (4.25-inch) Italian Ladyfingers (such as Savoiardi)

2 cups strawberries, halved

1 cup blueberries

½ cup blackberries

½ cup raspberries

1 jar Kneaders Raspberry Jam

½ cup Classic American Buttercream Icing (see recipe on page 226)

1 batch Whipped Cream Topping (see recipe on page 227)

1. Spray 2 (8-inch round) cake pans evenly with cooking spray.

2. Follow the baking instructions for the recipe you are making.

3. Let the cake cool in the pan for 10 minutes. Remove onto cooling racks.

ASSEMBLY

1. Level the tops of both cakes. Place the first layer on a cake stand.

2. Using a piping bag, pipe a buttercream border around the top of the first layer, then fill the inside with Kneaders Raspberry Jam.

3. Place the second layer of the cake on top of the first layer.

4. Spread a thin layer of Kneaders Raspberry Jam over the top of the cake.

5. Ice the sides of the cake with Whipped Cream Topping.

6. Place ladyfingers around the outside of the cake, using the whipped cream to hold them in place. Repeat until all sides of the cake are covered.

7. Place strawberries cut side down, filling the top surface of the cake. Fill in empty spaces with fresh raspberries, blueberries, and blackberries.

Tasty Tips

• Try a combination of tropical fruits like mango, oranges, pineapple, green grapes, and pomegranate seeds, substituting Kneaders Apricot Pineapple Jam for the raspberry jam.

Vanilla Fresh Fruit Cake

Serves 12 • Prep Time: 30 minutes • Total Time: 65–70 minutes

Kaycie McDonald came to us as a pastry chef by way of Disney. She is a talented decorator. Her ideas are innovative and refreshing. She certainly is helping us to move to the next level in our pastries here at Kneaders. If you are lucky enough to live in Utah Valley, I hope you saw the beautiful gingerbread houses she made for the Orem and Lehi stores. I know you are thinking *I can't make a cake like this.* Yes, you can. Kaycie has broken it down for you step by step by step. You've got this!

---

1 vanilla cake box mix, or 1 recipe Basic Vanilla Cake from Scratch or 1 recipe Master Vanilla Cake from Scratch (see recipes on page 221–23)

2 cups Whipped Cream Topping (see recipe on page 227)

2 kiwis, peeled and sliced

1 pint fresh strawberries, washed, divided

1 pint fresh blueberries

1 (15-ounce) can mandarin orange slices, drained

Powdered sugar, for garnish

1. Spray 2 (6-inch round) cake pans evenly with cooking spray.

2. Follow the baking instructions for the recipe you are making.

3. Let the cake cool in the pan for 10 minutes. Remove onto cooling racks.

ASSEMBLY

1. When cakes are completely cooled, divide each cake into two layers using a long serrated knife. You should have four layers in total. Wrap each layer of cake in plastic wrap and place in the refrigerator until ready to use.

2. Prepare a large piping bag with Whipped Cream Topping and cut a hole approximately an inch in diameter at the tip of the piping bag.

3. Place the first layer of vanilla cake on the center of a cake plate.

4. Using a spatula or piping bag, spread an even layer of Whipped Cream Topping directly on top of the first layer of the cake, all the way to the edge.

5. Pit and slice half the strawberries thinly. Halve the remaining strawberries with their greens still attached.

6. Arrange ¼ of the sliced strawberries, sliced kiwis, fresh blueberries, and mandarin slices directly on top of the whipped cream on the first layer.

7. Place the next layer of vanilla cake on top of the fruits and whipped cream layer. Adjust the cake until it is centered on the first layer of cake and press slightly.

8. Pipe another layer of Whipped Cream Topping on the second layer of cake, then arrange the next ¼ of the fruit on the topping.

9. Place the third layer of vanilla cake on top of the fruits and whipped cream layer. Adjust the cake until it is centered on the first layer of cake and press slightly.

10. Pipe another layer of Whipped Cream Topping on the third layer of cake, then arrange the next ¼ of the fruit on the topping.

11. Place the fourth layer of cake bottom side up on top of the third layer.

12. Pipe about ½-inch-thick layer of Whipped Cream Topping on the fourth layer of cake.

13. Arrange various remaining fruits, including the halved strawberries, on top of the cake (see photo).

14. Using a sifter, dust the cake lightly with powdered sugar.

15. Serve immediately, or store in the refrigerator until ready to serve.

Tres Leches Cake

Serves 12 • Prep Time: 45 minutes • Total Time: 80–85 minutes

During my years at Kneaders, I have had the opportunity to work with such kind, knowledgeable, energetic, and willing pastry chefs. Cristina Castro is certainly one of those people. She has worked so hard to develop her craft and continues to learn and search for additional insights and ways to improve, something I admire very much. This is my favorite of all the recipes she developed for Kneaders. Cristina helped us with this cookbook by using her talent to bake several of the recipes to be photographed.

Nonstick baking spray

1 vanilla cake box mix, or 1 recipe Basic Vanilla Cake from Scratch or 1 recipe Master Vanilla Cake from Scratch (see recipes on page 221–23)

⅔ cup heavy cream

1 (5-ounce) can evaporated milk

1 (14-ounce) can condensed milk

½ teaspoon vanilla extract

2 cups strawberries

2 tablespoons strawberry jam

Whipped Cream Topping (see recipe on page 227), refrigerated

1. Spray 1 (9x13) cake pan evenly with baking spray.

2. Follow the baking instructions for the recipe you are making.

3. Let the cake cool in the pan for 10 minutes. Remove onto cooling rack.

4. Add cream, evaporated milk, condensed milk, and vanilla extract into a bowl or liquid measuring cup. Whisk together until combined. Makes 2 cups.

5. Refrigerate until ready to use.

TOPPING

1. Wash and dry the strawberries.

2. Using a cutting board and knife, remove the strawberry stems and slice them into circles. (The thicker the strawberry slices are, the longer they will last.)

3. Add the sliced strawberries and jam to a bowl. Stir the strawberries and jam together until they are fully combined and set aside. The jam will coat and protect the strawberries from wilting and allow them to stay fresh longer.

ASSEMBLY

1. Using a fork, poke holes all over the cake in the pan.

2. Pour 1 cup of the liquid mixture over the cake, starting on the edges and working your way to the center. Let the cake sit for about 5 minutes. Add the remaining cup of the mixture, working outward from

the center of the cake. Let the cake sit for about 5 minutes.

3. Add about ½ the Whipped Cream Topping to the center of the cake. Use an offset spatula to spread it evenly over the cake.

4. Pour the strawberry topping onto the center of the cake. Use an offset or rubber spatula to spread the strawberries evenly over the cake.

5. Fill a piping bag with the remaining Whipped Cream Topping and pipe a border around the edge of the cake.

6. Chill the cake in the refrigerator until ready to eat. Enjoy!

Red Velvet Cake
with Chocolate and Strawberries

Makes 1 (6-inch) four-layer cake • Prep Time: 20 minutes • Total Time: 1 hour 5 minutes

I can't stop looking at this beautiful cake, with its chocolate ganache and fresh strawberries. Designed by Kaycie McDonald, it looks too good to eat (but don't let that stop you).

Nonstick baking spray

2½ cups cake flour

1 teaspoon baking powder

1 teaspoon salt

2 tablespoons unsweetened cocoa powder (not Dutch process)

1 tablespoon liquid red food coloring (add up to 1 more tablespoon for a brighter color)

½ cup unsalted butter, softened to room temperature

1½ cups granulated sugar

2 eggs, room temperature

1 teaspoon vanilla extract

1 cup buttermilk, room temperature

1 tablespoon distilled vinegar

1 teaspoon baking soda

1 batch Cream Cheese Frosting (see recipe on page 226)

1 recipe Chocolate Curls (see below)

1 batch Drip Ganache (see below)

1 pint strawberries, washed

CAKE

1. Preheat the oven to 350 degrees F. Spray 2 (6-inch) cake pans with nonstick baking spray.

2. In a medium bowl, sift together the cake flour, baking powder, and salt. (Sifting is important to the finished texture.)

3. In a small bowl, mix the food coloring (the more you use, the brighter the color) and cocoa powder together to form a thin paste without lumps. Set aside.

4. Using a stand mixer with paddle attachment, beat the butter and sugar together until light and fluffy, about 3 minutes. Add eggs one at a time, beating after each addition, and scraping the sides of the bowl down. Beat in the vanilla and the red cocoa paste, then scrape down the bowl.

5. In a medium bowl, mix together the buttermilk, vinegar, and baking soda. Yes, it will fizz!

6. With the mixer on low, add half of the flour mixture, beating until combined. Add half of the buttermilk mixture and beat on low until combined. Repeat with the second half of the flour mixture, then the second half of the buttermilk mixture.

7. Divide the batter evenly between the prepared cake pans.

8. Bake for approximately 30–35 minutes. Start checking for doneness when you can smell the flavor of the cake. When done, the cake should pull away from the outside edges and will spring back when lightly touched in the middle.

Continued on next page.

Continued from previous page.

9. Cool the cakes in their pans on a wire rack for 10 minutes. Remove from pans and allow them to cool completely before frosting.

10. When cooled, use a serrated knife to cut each cake into two even layers and level the cake top. Wrap the four layers of cake in plastic wrap and refrigerate until ready to use.

CHOCOLATE CURLS

1 (2- to 3-ounce) milk, semisweet, or dark chocolate bar, as desired

1. Microwave the chocolate bar for 10 seconds; this will help it shave into curls.

2. Set a piece of parchment paper on your work surface, then, holding the top of the chocolate bar with one hand and resting the bottom on the parchment paper, use a vegetable peeler to make the curls, starting at the top and sliding the peeler to the bottom. Continue until you have the desired amount of curls.

3. Transfer the curls to a container with a lid and place them in the freezer until needed. This makes them easier to work with and less likely to melt.

DRIP GANACHE

1 (8-ounce) bar dark baking chocolate (60% dark or greater), chopped until the size of chocolate chips

2 tablespoons vegetable oil

1. Place the chocolate and oil in a microwaveable bowl.

2. Microwave the chocolate and oil mixture in 30-second increments, stirring between each interval.

3. Microwave until ganache is smooth and no lumps are present.

4. Set bowl aside and allow ganache to cool slightly before using.

CAKES AND TRIFLES

ASSEMBLY

1. Fill a large piping bag with Cream Cheese Frosting, and cut a ½-inch opening at the tip.

2. Center the first layer of cake on a cake plate.

3. Pipe a layer of Cream Cheese Frosting on top of the first layer, and, using a small spatula, spread evenly.

4. Place the next layer of cake on top of the cream cheese layer. Keep the outside edge of the cake clean; the layers of cake should be visible.

5. Repeat placing and frosting the remaining 2 layers of cake, then place the top layer without frosting it.

6. Place the assembled cake in the refrigerator until the Cream Cheese Frosting is firm.

7. After removing the cake from the refrigerator, pipe a small amount of cream cheese between each cake layer and smooth with a spatula. Cake layers should still be visible.

8. Pipe Cream Cheese Frosting on the top, smoothing out the top and sides with a spatula.

9. Return the cake to the refrigerator until Cream Cheese Frosting is firm to the touch.

DECORATION

1. Using a squeeze bottle or piping bag, pour the warm drip ganache on top of the refrigerated cake, allowing the ganache to pour over the edge and drip down the sides. Use a spatula to help it along.

2. Arrange strawberries, covering a crescent-shaped space along one side of the cake top. It's best to arrange the strawberries before the ganache sets. Dip strawberries lightly in warm ganache before placing on the top of the cake. When the ganache has set, sprinkle lightly with chocolate curls.

3. Serve immediately or store in the refrigerator until ready to serve.

Southern Banana Nut Bundt Cake

Makes 12 mini Bundt cakes • Prep Time: 20 minutes • Total Time: 45 minutes

In the South, this popular cake is called a hummingbird cake. One of our executive pastry chefs, Jessica McGuire Daly, brought a sample of it for us to taste. We loved the unique flavor of this dense, moist cake with bananas, pineapple, and cinnamon, covered in a rich cream cheese frosting and topped with pecans. We just *had* to put it on the menu.

2½ cups T55 flour, such as Francine Farine de Blé Bio (available online)

1½ cups sugar

¾ teaspoon salt

¾ teaspoon baking soda

¾ teaspoon cinnamon

3 medium eggs, beaten

1 cup oil

1 teaspoon vanilla

¾ cup crushed pineapple with juice

1½ cups coarsely mashed banana

1 cup chopped pecans, divided

Nonstick baking spray

1. Preheat the oven to 350 degrees F.

2. In a large bowl, whisk together flour, sugar, salt, baking soda, and cinnamon. In another bowl, combine eggs, oil, and vanilla. Add wet ingredients to dry ingredients and stir until dry ingredients are just moistened. Stir in crushed pineapple, banana, and ¾ cup pecans.

3. Spray 2 (6-cavity) mini Bundt pans with baking spray, making sure to coat each individual cavity well. Spoon batter into prepared pans, filling each cake mold cavity half full.

4. Bake for 20–22 minutes or until a wooden toothpick comes out clean. Allow cakes to cool slightly, about 5 minutes. Remove cakes from pans by inverting the pan onto a cooling rack.

5. If you are not going to serve the cakes right away, you can brush or spray them with pineapple simple syrup (see next page) to keep them from drying out.

Continued on page 240.

PINEAPPLE SIMPLE SYRUP

⅓ cup boiling water

½ cup granulated sugar

1 tablespoon crushed
pineapple with juice

Continued from page 238.

1. Whisk together water and sugar. Add pineapple and let sit for 10 minutes.

2. Strain out the pineapple chunks. Pour syrup into a spray bottle and spray lightly on each cake, or use a pastry brush to apply the syrup.

CREAM CHEESE GLAZE

½ cup butter, softened

8 ounces cream cheese, softened

4 cups powdered sugar

1½ teaspoons vanilla extract

1. Combine all ingredients and heat cream cheese glaze over medium heat until thin but not transparent.

2. Pour cream cheese glaze in a circle over the top of each cake, allowing it to run partway down the sides.

3. Garnish immediately with small chopped pecan pieces.

CAKES AND TRIFLES

Spice Cake

Makes 1 (8-inch) cake • Prep Time: 30 minutes • Total Time: 1 hour 5 minutes

Whenever I visit a store, I like to visit with each one of the guests. I want to hear their story. I love talking to them about their Kneaders experience, and I always ask what products they would like us to sell in the bakery. It's amazing what you can learn when you allow people to speak freely and say what they really feel. I'm so grateful to so many of our Kneaders friends who have taken the time to give us ideas, feedback, and recipes for their bakery favorites. Here is one of those recipes. We made it years ago in the bakery. The penuche frosting adds a caramel flavor and a fudge-like texture. Your kids will want to lick the bowl, but save the spoon for yourself.

Nonstick baking spray

2½ cups all-purpose flour

2 teaspoons baking powder

1 teaspoon baking soda

½ teaspoon salt

1½ teaspoons ground cinnamon

1 teaspoon ground ginger

½ teaspoon ground nutmeg

½ teaspoon ground cloves

1 cup vegetable oil

1¾ cup dark brown sugar, packed

1 cup unsweetened applesauce

4 large eggs, slightly beaten

2 teaspoons vanilla extract

1. Preheat oven to 350 degrees F. Spray 2 (6-inch) round cake pans with baking spray.

2. In a medium bowl, whisk the flour, baking powder, baking soda, and all spices together.

3. In another bowl, whisk the brown sugar, applesauce, eggs, vanilla, and oil until combined.

4. Pour the wet ingredients into the dry ingredients. Mix until ingredients are just incorporated.

5. Spread into the prepared cake pans. Bake for 28–33 minutes. Cake is done when the cake springs back when it is touched in the middle. Cool the pans on a rack for 10 minutes and then invert to release the cakes. Cool completely or wrap in plastic wrap and freeze before frosting.

Continued on page 243.

PENUCHE FROSTING

1 cup unsalted butter

2 cups brown sugar, packed

½ cup milk

Hot water (optional)

2 cups confectioners' sugar
(more or less as needed)

Continued from page 241.

1. In a saucepan, over medium heat, melt butter and add brown sugar. Bring to a boil. Boil for 2 minutes, stirring constantly. Add milk and bring back to a boil, stirring constantly.

2. Remove from heat and allow the mixture to cool to room temperature.

3. Gradually sift confectioners' sugar into the mixture while beating. Stir until well incorporated. Stop adding sugar when the frosting is thick enough to spread. If you need to thin it out a little, add some hot water.

ASSEMBLY

1. After cooling, level the top of each cake, saving cake scraps for decoration. Divide each cake into 2 even layers. You should have 4 level layers in total.

2. Place one level on your serving plate.

3. Using a piping bag, pipe an even layer of penuche on top of the cake.

4. Place the next layer on top. Repeat frosting process, then place the next layer on top. Repeat frosting process.

5. Place the last layer of cake bottom side up (the bottom will be easier to frost).

6. Pipe frosting over the top of the cake. Make a swirl with a small offset spatula.

7. Refrigerate until the penuche frosting is firm to the touch.

FINISH

1. Break up cake scraps until they resemble a crumb topping.

2. Establish the front of the cake. Sprinkle cake crumbs in a crescent shape around the top left side of the cake. Add sugared pecans if desired. Store in the refrigerator until ready to serve.

Tasty Tips
- Add 1 cup shredded apple, carrot, or zucchini to the cake mix with the wet ingredients.

Fast Triple-Chocolate Peppermint Trifle

Serves 16 • Prep Time: 25 minutes • Total Time: 2 hours 25 minutes

It's been exciting to appear on television lifestyle shows. We've had the opportunity to be on TV in all six states where we have stores. That said, live TV is challenging—the world gets to see every mistake you make. This is one of the beautiful trifles we've shared on TV. Kneaders Triple Chocolate Bread and red-and-white peppermint candies are two Christmas flavors that were meant to be together. Special thanks to Amy Peterson, Tamara Vincent, Ryker Brown, and Jessica Daly for sharing Kneaders with the TV world.

¼ cup peppermint candies, such as Starlight Mints, divided

2 (3.4-ounce) packages instant white chocolate pudding mix, such as Hershey's

3 cups heavy cream

5 cups milk, divided

2 loaves Kneaders Triple Chocolate Bread, cut into bite-size pieces

2 (5-ounce) packages chocolate pudding mix, such as Jell-O Cook and Serve

1 (16-ounce) bottle premium chocolate sauce, such as Ghirardelli

1. Add the peppermint candies to a gallon ziptop bag, then insert that bag into another gallon ziptop bag. Using a rolling pin, crush the candies into small pieces. Set aside.

2. Pour the heavy cream and 1 cup milk into a large bowl and beat with a hand mixer until soft peaks form. Add the dry instant white chocolate pudding mix to the whipped cream and beat until firm peaks form. Add all but 1 tablespoon of the crushed peppermint, and stir until well incorporated. Chill for 1 hour.

3. Cook the chocolate pudding mix according to package directions. Remove from heat and cover with waxed paper to prevent skin from forming. Put in an ice water bath to cool.

4. Spread ⅓ of the peppermint white chocolate pudding into the bottom of an (8–9 inch) glass trifle bowl.

5. Top with half of the Kneaders Chocolate Bread pieces, and drizzle 1 cup of the chocolate syrup over the bread pieces.

6. Add half of the chocolate pudding and spread evenly. Add ⅓ of the peppermint white chocolate pudding.

7. Add the second half of the bread pieces. Drizzle another cup of chocolate syrup over the bread pieces, and spread the rest of the chocolate pudding on top. Cover with plastic wrap and refrigerate for 2 hours.

8. Sprinkle the rest of the crushed peppermint over the top, then serve.

Tasty Tips

- Use Kneaders Peppermint Bark (page 321) broken into small chunks on the top of the trifle for an extra flavor kick.

Pumpkin Trifle

Serves 10 • Prep Time: 15 minutes • Total Time: 8 hours 15 minutes

Pumpkin Bread was the first sweet bread we ever made at the bakery. I know, I know—some of you really want us to add chocolate chips. One year, two of our stores did. What were the results? Drumroll . . . The truth is, our customers only purchased it once and then they went back to the original. I never heard the word *nasty*, but I did hear it ruined the flavor. We agree. If you're looking for a fall showstopper, buy three loaves of pumpkin bread (two for the recipe and one to eat on the way home) and get started on this yummy treat!

---

2 loaves Kneaders Pumpkin Bread, cut into 1-inch cubes

1 (4.6-ounce) package vanilla pudding mix, such as Jell-O Cook and Serve

2 cups milk

½ cup brown sugar, packed

⅓ teaspoon ground cinnamon

1 (16-ounce) tub frozen whipped topping, such as Cool Whip, thawed

½ cup chocolate toffee bits or 5 (1.4-ounce) toffee candy bars, such as Skor, chopped

1. Prepare pudding according to package directions. While hot, stir brown sugar and cinnamon into the pudding. Then allow to cool to room temperature.

2. Place half the pumpkin bread cubes in the bottom of an 8-inch trifle bowl.

3. Pour half the pudding over the cubed bread. Spread evenly to the edges.

4. Spread half the whipped topping over the pudding layer evenly to the edge.

5. Place the remaining bread cubes on the whipped topping, then pour the remaining pudding over the cubed bread and spread evenly to the edges. Spread the remaining whipped topping over the pudding and spread evenly to the edges.

6. Sprinkle chocolate toffee bits on top. Refrigerate overnight.

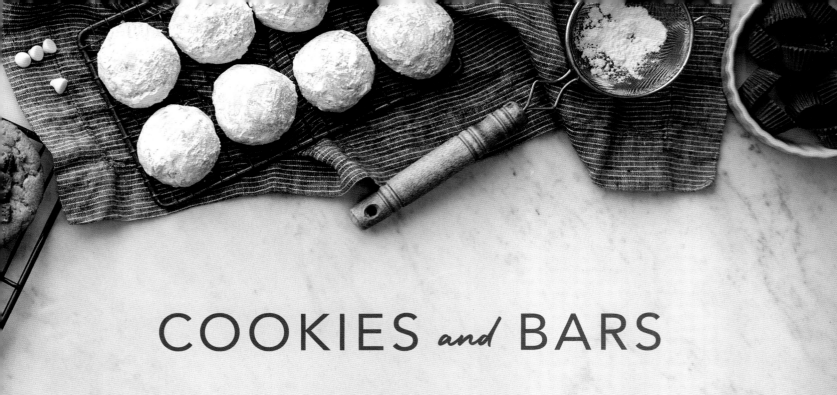

COOKIES and BARS

Baklava

Makes 30–40 pieces • Prep Time: 35 minutes • Total Time: 2 hours 30 minutes

Read Sam Delis's story on pages 252–53.

PASTRY

1 pound (4 cups) blanched almonds, walnuts, or a combination of both, chopped

¼ cup sugar

1 tablespoon ground cinnamon

1 (1-pound) package phyllo pastry dough

¾ pound (3 sticks) unsalted butter, melted

1. Preheat oven to 300 degrees F. In a medium bowl, combine blanched nuts, sugar, and cinnamon. Follow directions on phyllo dough package to keep layers from drying out. Brush the bottom of a 9x13 pan with butter, place one sheet of dough on top, then brush with butter. Repeat 7 more times for 8 layers. Sprinkle nut mixture over the layers and cover with 2 more buttered layers. Repeat the layering method until all the nut mixture is used. Finish by covering with the rest of the buttered dough sheets. Note: Be sure to butter and fold over all the dough edges around the edge of the pan to prevent drying out.

2. Cut baklava into small diamond shapes with a sharp knife. Place the pan in the center of the oven, with another pan on the bottom shelf filled with water. Check the water pan frequently during baking and add water as needed. This prevents the pastry from drying out while baking.

3. Bake 2 to 2½ hours or until top is a golden brown.

SYRUP

2 cups water

¾ cup sugar

1 tablespoon lemon juice

¾ cup honey

1. While the baklava is baking, combine all syrup ingredients except honey in a saucepan over medium-high heat. Bring to a boil, then simmer for 15 minutes to reduce. Add the honey and simmer for 10 more minutes. Place in refrigerator to cool.

2. After the baklava is golden brown, place it on a counter and pour the cooled syrup over the hot pastry. Allow to cool, then serve by placing each piece on a paper baking cup.

The
PROBLEM
SOLVER

Sam Delis

You can tell a lot about a person by what they choose to have on their walls. We put a great deal of thought into deciding how we would decorate our restaurants—the part of our "home" we invite customers to share. Sam Delis, our supply chain vice president, has a picture on his office wall that draws my eye every time I visit. It's a print of the smokestacks that were once a dominant part of the skyline in Murray, Utah. In the picture, the smokestacks are drawn in black and accented with orange and red. It's a striking piece, and one that resonates with Sam.

Sam's family immigrated from Greece, and his grandfather, Constantine Delis, worked at the Murray stacks. Constantine never drove a car, instead riding his bike to work every day. Sam remembers that Constantine was always coughing because of the vapors he breathed working at the smelter at the stacks, and how hard he'd worked to give his family a good life. Sam keeps the print on his wall to remind himself that he's here because of what his grandfather and other family members sacrificed.

Sam's grandmother, Katharine, made baklava for his family during the holidays. She couldn't read or write, so whenever she shared a recipe with Sam and his wife, Laura, she would say, "you need a small handful of this" or "a large handful of that" when specifying how much to use of each ingredient. Katharine would also say to use a "teacup or a coffee cup" for measuring things out. It was very hard to get exact measurements out of her, but Laura says the recipes always turned out terrific. To carry on the family tradition, Laura still makes Katharine's baklava every Christmas to remind their children of their Greek heritage.

Sam was a mentor and friend to our son James and our son-in-law Dave, both at church and when he was the director of national and chain accounts at Nicholas and Company. After twenty-five years at Nicholas, Sam was ready for a change, and Kneaders was growing and looking to hire someone like him. We were all delighted when it worked out for Sam to make the move to Kneaders.

And what a welcome he had. His first week at work coincided with an unexpected and unprecedented nationwide poultry shortage. Fresh turkey is the foundation of our business. Most of us—including Gary and me, James, Dave, and their families—were on a long-planned family vacation in Hawaii. Sam was left on the ground in Utah, and he had to handle everything without us there. James called Sam every day at 4:00 a.m. Hawaii time (7:00 a.m. in Utah) to find out what was going on. Sam kept calm and handled the crisis, and that was a perfect signifier of how he'd handle similar situations in the future. He was the hero through all of that.

Sam has also been the hero in helping us make it through the COVID-19 pandemic, which has hit small businesses and restaurants particularly hard. Everything shut down across the world in those early days, and we had to figure out different ways to get what we needed to keep the stores open. But Sam got us through. He has a *don't- take-no-for-an-answer* mentality. He stays realistic and realizes that we might have to do something different than we'd originally intended, but he always finds a solution. Even before the pandemic, Sam had helped us source our ingredients from family-owned, local companies as much as possible. When supply chains were interrupted with the pandemic, we were still able to get much of what we needed from our local companies.

Sam has a lot of contacts and connections, but it's not just that. Sam also has a lot of friends. He has an incredible ability to make every single person his friend and to treat each person fairly. He has a great ability to calm a situation.

Sam's attitude has mentored us all. Sometimes I go in his office upset, but I know that by the time I leave, I will be calm. Sam sees the truth in things and makes sure we're always playing to that truth. We look to him the way he looks to the picture that reminds him of his grandfather, and we know we will find a way.

See BAKLAVA recipe on page 251.

Chocolate Dipped Italian Cookies

Makes 18–20 cookies • Prep Time: 30 minutes • Total Time: 1 hour 10 minutes

Our very first pastry chef was Yermonia Balasanyan. You can read more of the Balasanyan family's amazing story on pages 216–18. Yermonia made these Chocolate Dipped Italian Cookies for us with raspberry jam in the middle—everyone craved them.

1 cup butter, softened

¾ cup granulated sugar

2 eggs, at room temperature

1 teaspoon vanilla

½ teaspoon pure almond extract

½ teaspoon baking powder

1/8 teaspoon salt

2½ cups flour

2 teaspoons citrus zest of
   choice (optional)

Raspberry jam

Semisweet chocolate chips or dark
   chocolate candy melts for dipping.

1. Preheat the oven to 350 degrees F. Line a half-sheet baking pan with parchment paper.

2. Using a stand mixer with paddle attachment, cream together butter and sugar for about 2 minutes on medium speed until the mixture is pale and fluffy.

3. Add the egg, vanilla, and almond and mix until completely combined. Sift together the baking powder, salt, and flour. Add the dry ingredients (including the citrus zest, if desired) to the mixer and mix on low speed until they are just combined. Dough will appear a bit crumbly—do not overmix or the cookies will be dense and hard.

4. Place a medium star tip (we like the Ateco #846) in a piping bag. Spoon the dough into the bag and pipe the desired shapes onto the parchment immediately. The dough can also be spread between two sheets of parchment or waxed paper, chilled, unrolled, and cut out using a cookie cutter.

5. Bake cookies for 10–12 minutes. Allow to cool completely.

6. Place a small amount of jam in the center of 1 cookie and press another cookie to it lightly until the filling reaches the outside edges.

7. In a small microwave-safe bowl, melt the chocolate chips or candy melts, heating in 30-second increments until completely melted. Use enough chocolate so a cookie can be dipped halfway easily.

8. Dip a cookie halfway into the melted chocolate and place on a parchment-lined half-sheet baking pan. Repeat until all cookies are dipped.

9. Refrigerate for 10 minutes to allow the chocolate to set.

Gingerbread Mummy Cookies

Makes 20 large cookies • Prep Time: 35 minutes • Total Time: 3 hours

In 2009, all the girls in the family went on a trip to New York City to do some shopping and go to Broadway plays. While we were there, we found a candy shop with the cutest gingerbread mummy cookies. My first thought was that we had to make them at Kneaders. We now serve our own mummy cookies every October. The gingerbread recipe was shared by my dear friend Sue Speed.

---

1 cup butter

1 teaspoon ground cinnamon

1 teaspoon ground nutmeg

1 teaspoon ground cloves

1 teaspoon ground ginger

1 cup sugar

1 teaspoon dark molasses

2 eggs, well beaten

1 teaspoon white vinegar

5 cups all-purpose flour

1 teaspoon baking soda

Classic American Buttercream Frosting (see recipe on page 226)

Red and yellow food coloring or gel

White chocolate melting discs

1. In a large saucepan over high heat, bring butter, spices, sugar, and molasses to a boil, stirring constantly. Let cool until lukewarm.

2. Whisk in eggs and white vinegar.

3. Sift flour and baking soda together, then add to mixture, mixing the flour in with your hands. Keep mixing until the dough is very smooth.

4. Chill covered for 2 hours or overnight.

5. Preheat the oven to 350 degrees F.

6. Divide dough into 6 portions. Roll out each portion on a piece of aluminum foil large enough to cover a half-sheet baking pan. Cut out gingerbread shapes. Remove excess dough. Place foil and cutouts onto baking sheets. Repeat for each portion of dough.

7. Bake for 9–10 minutes. Let cool for 10 minutes on half-sheet pan, then move to cooling rack.

8. Tint Classic American Buttercream Frosting orange with food coloring or gel. Fill a piping bag with orange buttercream and a #6 round tip and make one eye on the right side. On the opposite side with a #4 round tip, pipe stitches over the heart area.

9. Using a medium microwave-safe bowl, melt white chocolate in the microwave in 30-second increments, stirring until completely melted. Allow to cool until slightly stiff. Fill a piping bag with the chocolate, and using a #47 basket weave tip, zigzag down the mummy, missing the eye and the stitches. Let the cookie dry for 15 minutes in a cool place.

Tasty Tips

• This recipe can also be used for gingerbread houses and Christmas tree ornaments.

Grandma's Cookies

Makes 36 cookies • Prep Time: 40 minutes • Total Time: 1 hour 20 minutes

When I was a little girl—about seven years old—my mother would make these raisin and nut–filled cookies. I would sit on the counter in her green kitchen and watch her roll out the dough into strips and then carefully fill it with this heavenly filling. She would always slice off the ends to tidy them up a bit. Every time, she gave those ends to me to eat. Just thinking about those warm moments brings happiness. We've tried to develop a procedure to make these cookies at the bakery, but the truth is they would take far too long to make. When our family made a Kimball family cookbook, all three of the sisters included a recipe for these cookies—and each was a little different. Here are the best of all three rolled into one for you to try.

1½ cups raisins

1 cup white sugar

1 cup water

2½ teaspoons cornstarch

1 cup chopped walnuts

1 cup shortening

2 cups brown sugar, packed

3 eggs, well beaten

4 cups flour

1 teaspoon baking soda

½ teaspoon baking powder

1 teaspoon cinnamon

⅛ teaspoon salt

1. In a saucepan over medium heat, combine raisins, white sugar, water, and cornstarch. Cook for about 10 minutes or until the filling turns clear. Stir in nuts. Cool for about 30 minutes or until it thickens.

2. In a large mixing bowl, cream shortening and brown sugar together. Add eggs, mixing well. Scrape the sides of the bowl.

3. In a medium bowl, whisk together flour, baking soda, baking powder, cinnamon, and salt. Add to the large mixing bowl and mix until all ingredients are incorporated.

4. Divide dough into 3 equal sections.

5. Preheat oven to 350 degrees F. and grease three baking pans.

6. Roll out first section into a strip about 5x14 inches and ¼-inch thick.

7. Spread a third of the filling down the middle of the strip, leaving a space on the top and bottom. Fold the top and bottom sides onto the filling, overlapping on top. Cut 1-inch slices off each end. Cut 12 equal pieces, putting each seam side down on the pan. Repeat two more times.

8. Bake for 10 minutes or until puffy and brown on the edges.

9. Remove from oven and leave on the cookie sheet for 10 minutes, then transfer to a cooling rack.

Tasty Tips

• Mom handing out raw dough was long before we knew not to eat raw flour or raw eggs. Bake the ends and then give them to your kids.

Mexican Wedding Cookies

Makes 36 cookies • Prep Time: 35 minutes • Total Time: 1 hour 30 minutes

Almost every nation has their version of these cookies. We wanted to make these to complement our Christmas baskets. They look like little snowballs and add such a pretty and delicious touch to any basket—or cookie plate! One day we were in the bakery trying to decide which country to attribute the cookies to. We had the sweetest and most wonderful Mexican bakers working for us at the time. One of them said, "Oh my heck, just call them Mexican Wedding Cookies." And, to honor their request, we did.

---

2 (2.25-ounce) packages diced pecans

1 cup butter, softened

½ cup confectioners' sugar,
   + more for coating cookies

1½ teaspoon vanilla

1¾ cups all-purpose flour

1. Preheat oven to 325 degrees F. Spread diced pecans on a half-sheet baking pan and toast for 15 minutes, stirring once or twice to avoid burning. Remove from oven and allow to cool. Spoon diced pecans into a large ziptop bag. Using a rolling pin, crush the pecans until they resemble coarse flour.

2. Turn oven up to 350 degrees F. Line a half-sheet baking pan with parchment paper.

3. Using a stand mixer with paddle attachment, cream butter and sugar at low speed until smooth.

4. Add vanilla and combine. On low speed, gradually add flour until dough is combined. Fold in pecans with a spatula. Chill the dough in the refrigerator for 30 minutes.

5. With floured hands, shape 1 rounded tablespoon of dough into a ball and place on prepared half-sheet pan.

6. Continue to dust hands with flour and place dough balls on half-sheet pan.

7. Bake for 15–20 minutes. When the cookies are cool enough to handle but still warm, roll in confectioners' sugar. Allow to cool on cooling rack.

Tasty Tips

• It's fun to try different nuts for a different flavor, but they're always better if they're roasted.

The CHAMPION

Kirk Weisler performing with the Blue Man Group.

Kirk Weisler

Have you ever seen someone directing traffic with a baguette? Better yet, have you ever seen someone directing traffic with a baguette *while wearing a Grinch costume?* Neither had I, until our friend Kirk Weisler did just that one holiday season. Can you imagine—a six-foot-something man in green tights with a huge grin on his face, standing on a busy street and waving surprised motorists into our Kneaders parking lot.

To get to the baguette/Grinch moment, we have to go back a few years to when Kneaders first opened. Kirk was our champion and hype man from the very beginning. He came into our Orem store during the first week we were in business to buy a cinnamon roll as a bribe for a coworker. He was immediately delighted by our bakery and cafe. "It feels like it smells," he told me later. "The cinnamon rolls looked as big as a plate, and so of course I had to get myself one, too." And he kept coming back. One day, while standing in line, he said out loud, "I love Kneaders!" Soon, he had the whole line chanting along with him. *"I love Kneaders! I love Kneaders!"*

I came out from the back to see what was going on. Kirk had everyone talking about what fans of Kneaders they were. His enthusiasm was contagious, and he added such warmth and camaraderie to our store from those very first visits. Sometimes he would talk to people through our drive-through window and tell them how good our bread was. And now and then he would buy people a loaf of bread through our drive-through window so they could try it out. It was always so much fun when Kirk came into Kneaders.

"Kneaders just became this thing," Kirk said. "People would go again and again. It was a great product, and a good feeling. Even if you didn't know people in the line, you had something in common with them, which was that you wanted to be in that line. It felt *good* to be in that line."

Kirk used our products in such fun and innovative ways. He did story time with his work crew on Fridays and served them cookies and milk. He'd buy a hundred cookies from us for those story times. I loved seeing how he connected with people and the way he made them feel. Kirk especially loves our Ginger Bob cookies (the gingerbread men we sell at Christmastime and other times of the year). So I think it's only fitting that he's sharing with us a similar-tasting recipe from his mother. According to Kirk, you didn't want to be slow to the cookie jar when his mom made these cookies.

Recently, I was delighted when Kirk began calling us to offer training to our employees. And he wanted to be paid in brownies and Asiago cheese bread! I'd close the story an hour early and gather the workers to come and learn from Kirk. I felt like he was not only helping them become better employees, he was also helping them become better at the way they lived their lives. He talked about how they could become great at something. That resonated with them and with me.

Because I'd seen how wonderful Kirk was with people, I decided to ask him to come in and tell a story to our guests at Christmastime. He chose the story of the Grinch, and he dressed to fit the part. He decided there should be a big crowd, so he went right out to the road with a baguette and started waving down cars. Before long, we had a full store of smiling people. Kirk's enthusiasm is contagious, even (and maybe especially!) when he's wearing a Grinch costume.

During the past few years, Kirk has spoken to conferences and district leader meetings for us. During the COVID-19 pandemic, he helped us by going to every store in the chain, cheering the employees on, talking to the customers, and spreading Kneaders love to everyone he met. That brought smiles to the faces of employees and guests alike.

We have made many friends along the way, but few have been our friends for all twenty-five years. Kirk is our champion.

See MOLASSES COOKIES recipe on page 264.

Molasses Cookies

Makes 72 cookies • Prep Time: 15 minutes • Total Time: 1 hour 20 minutes

Read Kirk Weisler's story on pages 262–63.

2 cups sugar

1 cup shortening

2 eggs, beaten

1 cup molasses

1 teaspoon vanilla extract

6 cups all-purpose flour

3 teaspoons baking soda

1 teaspoon salt

3 teaspoons ground cinnamon

2 teaspoons ground ginger

2 cups buttermilk

1. Preheat oven to 375 degrees F.

2. Line half-sheet baking pans with parchment paper or lightly grease them.

3. In a large bowl, beat together the sugar and shortening until creamy.

4. Add the eggs, molasses, and vanilla and beat well.

5. In a separate bowl, whisk together the flour, baking soda, salt, cinnamon, and ginger until well blended.

6. Add the dry mixture to the sugar mixture in several additions, alternating with the buttermilk until well combined.

7. Drop the cookie dough by teaspoonfuls (or, if you want monster-sized cookies, use tablespoons) spaced 2 inches apart onto the prepared half-sheet pans.

8. Bake for about ten minutes, until golden around the edges.

9. Remove from the oven and allow the cookies to cool on the cookie sheet for 5 minutes and then transfer them with a spatula to wire racks to cool completely.

Peanut Butter Cookies

Makes 36 large cookies • Prep time: 25 minutes • Cook time: 45 minutes

This peanut butter cookie recipe was submitted in a contest we held looking for the ultimate peanut butter cookie. Our contests are open to our employees, so it wasn't surprising when the winner was one of the bakers who worked in our Bakehouse. We had lots of entries to this contest among our staff, but this college student from Idaho was definitely the winner. Nothing tastes better than the chopped peanut butter cups on top. This recipe has been retired, but we know you will enjoy making it at home.

---

2 cups butter, softened

2 cups granulated sugar

1½ cups light brown sugar

4 eggs

1 teaspoon vanilla

2 cups chunky peanut butter

5½ cups flour

1 teaspoon salt

3 teaspoons baking soda

4 peanut butter cups, chopped

1. Preheat the oven to 375 degrees F. Line a half-sheet baking pan with parchment paper.

2. Using a stand mixer with paddle attachment, cream butter, sugar, and brown sugar for 3 to 5 minutes until light and fluffy. Scrape down the sides of the bowl.

3. Add eggs one at a time, mixing each in. Add vanilla. Mix until blended. Scrape down the bowl. Add peanut butter. Mix until blended.

4. In a separate bowl, whisk together the flour, salt, and baking soda. Incorporate dry ingredients into creamed mixture. Scrape the sides of the bowl. Do not overmix.

5. Using an ice cream scoop, place leveled scoops of dough two inches apart on half-sheet pans. Using the bottom of a glass dipped in sugar, slightly flatten each cookie. Press chopped peanut butter cup pieces into the top of each cookie.

6. Bake for 15 minutes. Allow to cool on the pan.

Tasty Tips

- Try using almond butter or cashew butter in place of peanut butter for a different flavor. Top with chopped toasted almonds or cashews, respectively.

Pumpkin Chocolate Chip Cookies

Makes 6 dozen cookies • Prep Time: 15 minutes • Total Time: 30 minutes

This recipe comes from Dave's mother, Diana Vincent. Dave remembers her putting raisins in these cookies instead of chocolate chips (although his siblings are pretty sure they were chocolate chips). Included here is the chocolate chip version. Diana loved Kneaders and she came in often. When she grew older, her daughters would bring her to Kneaders drive-thru to pick up one of her pumpkin cookies. We think of her every time we eat these cookies. They are so good, they just may become your tradition as well.

---

3 sticks butter, softened

1½ cups brown sugar

2 eggs, slightly whisked

1 (16-ounce) can pumpkin puree

2¾ cups all-purpose flour

1 tablespoon baking powder

1 teaspoon cinnamon

½ teaspoon nutmeg

½ teaspoon salt

¼ teaspoon ginger

1 cup nuts (optional)

1 cup raisins (optional)

1 cup chocolate chips (optional)

1. Preheat oven to 400 degrees F. Using a stand mixer with paddle attachment on medium speed, cream together butter and brown sugar until butter starts to lighten and the mixture becomes fluffy.

2. Add eggs and pumpkin puree. Mix for one minute on low speed. Scrape down the sides of the bowl. Mix again for one minute.

3. In a separate bowl, whisk together flour, baking powder, cinnamon, nutmeg, and salt.

4. Add the dry ingredients to the wet and mix on low speed for one more minute until incorporated. Fold in the optional items, if desired, by hand.

5. Using a 2-ounce cookie scoop or a spoon, scoop into 2-inch balls. Place on a half-sheet baking pan lined with parchment paper.

6. Bake for 15–17 minutes, until the outside edges are brown.

7. Remove from the oven and let sit on the pan for 10 minutes to finish baking, then allow to cool on cooling racks.

Tasty Tips

- Once you've got the chocolate chip version down, give the raisins or nuts a try.

Spider Cookies

Makes 2 dozen cookies • Prep Time: 20 minutes • Total time: 20 minutes

Thanks to Dave Vincent (our CFO here at Kneaders) for sharing this family recipe.

We've thought about making spider cookies at the bakery, but they're even more fun for you to make at home as a family with all of your little (and big!) helping hands. This easy recipe requires no oven time and there are just four ingredients. They are the perfect Halloween cookie because they look like hairy spiders. These spooky treats are both creamy and crunchy. You can't beat the combination of chocolate and butterscotch with the saltiness of peanuts and noodles.

---

1 (12-ounce) package chocolate chips

1 (12-ounce) package butterscotch chips

1½ cups peanuts

6 ounces chow mein noodles, such as La Choy

1. Melt chocolate chips and butterscotch chips in a double boiler, stirring constantly.

2. Remove from heat and stir in nuts and noodles.

3. Spoon onto wax paper one spoonful at a time.

4. Cool in the refrigerator until the chocolate is set.

Tasty Tips
- This is one cookie you can eat as you make.

White Chocolate Chip and Cranberry Cookies

Makes 36 (1.5-ounce) cookies or 18 Kneaders size (3-ounce) cookies • Prep Time: 25 minutes • Total Time: 1 hour

Everyone knows that we make many, many gift baskets at Christmastime. We often include this cookie in our baskets because they look so much like the holidays, with their red cranberries and white chocolate chips. Tuck them into a gift for a neighbor or leave them out for Santa with his glass of milk.

---

1 cup butter, softened

1 cup light brown sugar, packed

1 cup granulated sugar

2 eggs

1 tablespoon vanilla

3 cups all-purpose flour

1 teaspoon baking soda

1½ cups white chocolate chips

1½ cups dried cranberries

Pistachio or macadamia nuts, as desired

1. Preheat the oven to 375 degrees F. Line 3 half-sheet baking pans with parchment paper.

2. In a large bowl, cream together butter, light brown sugar, and granulated sugar until fluffy. Beat in eggs and vanilla.

3. In another bowl, whisk together the flour and baking soda. Stir this into the sugar mixture. Do not over mix, as this will cause the cookies to be tough.

4. Fold in white chocolate chips, cranberries, and preferred nuts.

5. Drop by heaping spoonfuls onto the prepared half-sheet pans, leaving about 2 inches of space between cookies. Bake for 10–12 minutes, until slightly brown on the edges. Allow to cool for 10 minutes on the half-sheet pan before placing on a cooling rack.

Tasty Tips

• These are perfect cookies for a holiday cookie exchange.

Almond Citrus Bars

Makes 12 bars • Prep Time: 20 minutes • Total Time: 2 hours

January is the perfect time for citrus. We began making these bars in January several years ago. We all love the taste of the almond crust, the citrus topping that incorporates both lemons and limes, and the careful dusting of confectioners' sugar on top. These treats will brighten your day and take you straight to summer, even if there is snow outside.

CRUMB CRUST

Nonstick cooking spray

1½ cups all-purpose flour

½ cup confectioners' sugar

6 tablespoons (3/4 stick) butter, chopped in cubes

⅛ cup sliced almonds

1. Preheat the oven to 340 degrees F.

2. Spray a 9x13 baking dish with nonstick cooking spray.

3. In a medium bowl, combine flour and sugar. Using a pastry blender, cut the butter into the flour until mixture resembles coarse breadcrumbs. Stir in almonds.

4. Press crumb crust into the 9x13 baking dish. Bake for 20 minutes or until light golden brown.

CITRUS FILLING

6 eggs

2¼ cups granulated sugar

½ cup all-purpose flour

¾ teaspoon baking powder

¼ cup lemon juice

⅛ cup lime juice

Pinch of ground nutmeg

1 teaspoon lime zest

1 teaspoon lemon zest

Confectioners' sugar, for garnish

1. While crust is baking, combine eggs, sugar, flour, baking powder, lemon juice, lime juice, and nutmeg in a medium bowl. Beat on medium speed for 2 minutes.

2. Stir in lemon zest and lime zest by hand. Pour filling over the hot crust.

3. Bake for 20 minutes or until the edges are browned and the center appears set. Cool in refrigerator for 1 hour.

4. To serve, sprinkle with confectioners' sugar.

Tasty Tips

- For over-the-top Citrus Bars, decorate with candied citrus slices.

CANDIED CITRUS SLICES

¼ cup water

¾ cup granulated sugar

2 small lemons, thinly sliced, or
   10 key limes, thinly sliced

1. In a large skillet, combine water and sugar and bring to a boil.

2. Add the sliced lemons or limes. Simmer gently, uncovered, for 2 minutes or until just softened.

3. Transfer to rack to cool. When the slices reach room temperature and are completely dry, place them on top of the citrus bars.

Raspberry Crumble Bars

Makes 12 bars • Prep Time: 15 minutes • Total Time: 35–40 minutes

Raspberry seems to resonate with our guests. Whether we make raspberry croissants, raspberry lemon tarts, fresh fruit eclairs with raspberries, or raspberry lemon cupcakes, we always have a winner. We worked on this recipe during the COVID-19 quarantine of 2020. The research and development committee made them several ways before deciding on this recipe. Our neighbors, families, and friends were our tasters. I think you'll enjoy the results.

Nonstick baking spray

1 cup unsalted butter, room temperature and cut in cubes.

2⅛ cups all-purpose flour

½ cup granulated sugar

½ cup brown sugar

1 cup rolled oats

¼ teaspoon fine sea salt

1¼ cups Kneaders Raspberry Jam

1. Preheat the oven to 350 degrees F. Spray a 9x13 baking pan generously with baking spray.

2. Add flour, granulated sugar, brown sugar, salt, and oats to a food processor. On the pulse setting, press the button a few times in 1-second intervals to mix. Add the cubed butter. Pulse until you have formed crumbles the size of a small pea. Set aside 1¾ cups crumbles.

3. Press the remaining crumble mixture onto the bottom of the prepared pan. Consistency is the key to making a good crumb bar. Each layer needs to go to the edges of the pan.

4. Spread the raspberry jam over the top of the crumble crust.

5. Sprinkle the remaining crumbles on top of the jam.

6. Bake for 25–30 minutes, or until the crust is golden brown.

Tasty Tips

- Make a tasty variation by using Kneaders Strawberry Jam or Kneaders Apricot Jam. The crumble is also very good made with biscoff cookies instead of oats.

Rich Chocolate Brownie Base

Makes 12 brownies • Prep Time: 5 minutes • Total Time: 40–55 minutes

These brownies are seriously fudgy. You might even think they *are* fudge on your first bite. As our CFO Dave Vincent likes to say, the more chocolate the better. That's why we make four different kinds of brownies or bars every day. I once had the pleasure of meeting Olympic gymnast and gold medal winner Peter Vidmar. He shared with me that his favorite bar at Kneaders is the Ultimate Cookie Bar (a brownie with an Oreo cookie layer topped with a chocolate chip cookie layer). No matter which of our brownies is your favorite, this brownie base will give you a great start.

⅔ cup Dutch process cocoa

1½ cups granulated sugar

½ cup powdered sugar

¾ teaspoons salt

1 cup unbleached all-purpose flour, such as Lehi Mills

½ cup vegetable oil

2 tablespoons water

3 large eggs

1 cup semisweet chocolate chips, such as Ghirardelli

1. Preheat the oven to 350 degrees F.

2. In a mixing bowl, whisk together the cocoa, granulated sugar, powdered sugar, salt, and flour.

3. In another bowl combine oil, water, and eggs and mix until incorporated.

4. Pour the egg mixture into the dry ingredients and mix until combined. Add chocolate chips and stir lightly to incorporate.

5. Pour into a 9x13 quarter-sheet baking pan that has been sprayed with oil.

6. Bake in the oven for 33–35 minutes. It's tricky to determine when these brownies are done. The top should be shiny with a slight crust, but the inside should still be chewy. The best way to determine doneness is with a probe-type thermometer. The internal temperature should be 180 degrees—test in 3 different places.

7. Remove from the oven and place on a cooling rack for about 1 hour before cutting. Covered and unrefrigerated, they will keep for 3 days.

Marshmallow Brownies

1½ cups miniature marshmallows

1. Allow brownies to cool for 10 minutes. Top with miniature marshmallows.

2. Return to the oven and bake until the marshmallow tops are a light gold.

Rocky Road Brownies

1½ cups miniature marshmallows

1½ cups semisweet mini chocolate chips

1½ cups mini butterscotch
chips (optional)

1. Allow brownies to cool for 10 minutes. Top with miniature marshmallows, mini chocolate chips, and mini butterscotch chips, if desired.

2. Return to the oven and bake until the marshmallow tops are a light gold and the chips are soft.

Caramel Marshmallow Brownies

10 caramels, unwrapped,
Kneaders caramels preferred

1½ tablespoons heavy cream

1. Add caramels and cream to a small microwave-safe bowl. Microwave in 20 second-intervals, stirring to incorporate, until smooth.

2. Drizzle warm caramel sauce over either of the marshmallow variations when they are removed from the oven. Allow to cool completely.

Tasty Tips

- Topping ideas are endless. Make this recipe your own—how about crumbled pretzels as a topping?

Salted Caramel Nut Bars

Makes 12 bars • Prep Time: 20 minutes • Total Time 30 minutes

You will love the salty, sweet taste of these nut bars. They're such a great holiday treat that we served at Kneaders at Christmastime. Dr. Don Runyan, the original owner of the Yuma AZ Kneaders stores, shared this recipe with us. It was given to him by one of the ER nurses who worked with him. Something about this recipe always makes you want more.

1½ cups all-purpose flour

¾ cup packed brown sugar

¼ teaspoon salt

½ cup + 2 tablespoons unsalted butter, softened, divided

2 cups salted mixed nuts without peanuts

1 cup butterscotch chips

½ cup light corn syrup

1. Preheat oven to 350 degrees F.

2. In a medium bowl, mix flour, brown sugar, and salt. Using a pastry blender, cut in ½ cup butter. Mix evenly.

3. Press crust evenly into the bottom of an ungreased 9x13 baking pan. Bake for 15 minutes and cool slightly.

4. Sprinkle nuts evenly over the crust.

5. In a 1-quart saucepan over low heat, mix the butterscotch chips, corn syrup, and remaining butter, stirring occasionally, until the chips are melted.

6. Drizzle butterscotch mixture evenly over the nuts, being careful to cover the edges of the crust.

7. Bake for 5 minutes.

8. Cut into 12 pieces while still warm.

Tasty Tips
- This is also very good using only cashews instead of mixed nuts.

PIES and PUDDINGS

Blueberry Sour Cream Pie

Serves 6–8 • Prep Time: 40 minutes • Total Time: 1 hour

Full of contrasting textures, this pie is impossible to resist. Having sour cream in the name takes everyone by surprise. But once you take a bite, you realize it's the perfect ingredient. The sour cream filling is mixed with lemon juice and improved by adding freshly ground nutmeg. The result is a pie that tastes both tart and sweet.

My favorite time of year to serve this pie is July. For a great summer holiday dessert table, try this trio: Blueberry Sour Cream Pie, Fresh Strawberry Pie (see recipe on page 291), and banana cream pie—red, white, and blue. I promise these pies taste like summer on a spoon.

BLUEBERRY FILLING

½ cup warm water, divided

5 teaspoons cornstarch

½ cup sugar

½ teaspoon lemon powder or
   1½ teaspoons lemon juice

¼ teaspoon salt

2 cups frozen wild blueberries, thawed

SOUR CREAM FILLING

⅓ cup sugar

1 tablespoon cornstarch

1½ teaspoons flour

⅛ teaspoon salt

1 cup + 2 tablespoons whole milk

1 egg yolk, beaten

1 tablespoon butter

½ teaspoon vanilla

½ cup sour cream

½ teaspoon lemon juice

1. To make the blueberry filling, combine ¼ cup warm water and cornstarch in a small bowl until smooth. Set aside.

2. In a saucepan, combine remaining ¼ cup water, sugar, lemon powder or juice, and salt. Add blueberries. Be careful not to break the berries. Cover and bring to a boil over medium-high heat.

3. When the blueberry mixture has come to a full rolling boil, gently stir in the cornstarch mixture. Stir with a spatula until the mixture bubbles and thickens. Turn off heat. Cover and allow to sit for at least 10 minutes.

4. Gently stir again, then refrigerate until cool to the touch.

5. For the sour cream filling, combine sugar, cornstarch, flour, and salt in a saucepan over medium heat. Gradually stir in milk. Bring to a boil, stirring constantly. Boil for 2 minutes. Remove from heat.

6. Temper the beaten egg yolk by gradually pouring ½ cup hot milk into the egg yolk while stirring. Add yolk mixture back into remaining filling and return to a boil, stirring constantly. Boil for an additional 2 minutes.

7. Remove from heat. Stir in butter and vanilla. Cover with plastic wrap so that it touches the top of the pudding. This prevents a skin from forming. Cool to room temperature.

8. When the filling has cooled, stir in sour cream, lemon juice, and nutmeg. Pour into the baked pie shell and chill.

9. Once sour cream filling has chilled within the pie shell, carefully spoon cooled blueberry filling on top, starting at the outer edge and working toward the center. Refrigerate until ready to serve.

10. When ready to serve, top with Whipped Cream Topping (see recipe on page 227) and garnish with fresh blueberries.

Tasty Tips

- Using powdered lemon (available online) will give a delightful tanginess that you won't forget.
- Wild blueberries are smaller than regular blueberries and have more flavor, making them great for this pie recipe.

Chocolate Cherry Cream Pie

Serves 6–8 • Prep Time: 10 minutes • Chill Time: 1 hour • Total Time: 1 hour 10 minutes

This recipe was shared with us by my sister Linda Kimball Runyan. The bottom of this pie is not the usual plain cream cheese filling. It will surprise you with its creamy lemon flavor.

For years at Kneaders we made this pie every Valentine's season. With its chocolate cookie crust and cherry filling, it looks just like a valentine. We recommend you make it and give it to someone you love.

---

1 (6-ounce) premade chocolate cookie crumb pie crust, such as Oreo

CREAM FILLING

1 cup heavy cream

1 (14-ounce) can sweetened condensed milk

⅓ cup lemon juice

1 teaspoon vanilla extract

½ teaspoon almond extract

CHERRY GLAZE

1 (14.5- or 15-ounce) can cherries

¼ cup sugar

1 tablespoon cornstarch

1. In a medium bowl, whip heavy cream (do not add sugar) until medium peaks form. Set aside.

2. In a large bowl, stir together sweetened condensed milk, lemon juice, vanilla, and almond extract. Gently blend until incorporated, about 2 minutes.

3. Gently fold whipped cream into milk mixture until incorporated. Spoon the mixture into the cookie crumb crust and chill for 1 hour before serving.

4. While the pie chills, make the cherry glaze. Drain cherries, reserving juice. Heat cherry juice, sugar, and cornstarch in a medium saucepan until thick and clear, about 10 minutes. Allow to cool. Add cherries and chill until ready to serve.

5. Before serving, add the cherry glaze or cherry pie filling to the top of the cream pie and enjoy!

Tasty Tips

- If you want to skip making the cherry glaze, you can use 1 (21-ounce) can cherry pie filling instead. We like Duncan Hines Wilderness brand best!
- For a great party dessert, leave off the cherry filling. Serve each slice plain. Provide a topping bar with bowls of cherry filling, raspberry filling, blueberry filling, lemon filling, or your favorite pie filling. Let your guests top their own slice of pie.

Cream Cheese Lemon Truffle Pie

Serves 6–8 • Prep Time: 20 minutes • Total Time: 2 hours 20 minutes

We owe so much to those who came before us. Lemon pies always make me think of my mother, who always brought a lemon pie to the family Thanksgiving. With such a large crowd (some years as many as a hundred people), it was not uncommon to wash out a pie tin and fill it up with leftover slices for later. What fun it was to eat such good food with such wonderful people. How thankful I am for Ruth, Althea, Lucretia, Mary, Bona, and Eda—the amazing Ashby women, who were strong and caring and surrounded me with love.

This lemon truffle pie is our answer to a lemon meringue pie, but better. We have tried lemon meringue, lemon blueberry, and lemon cream, but this recipe is still our guests' favorite. White chocolate mixed with lemon curd is only one of the three layers in this perfect pie. I hope you enjoy it—and, perhaps, share it at Thanksgiving with those you love.

---

1 (9-inch) pie shell, baked (see recipes on pages 300 and 302)

Candied nuts, for topping

FILLING

1 egg

1 tablespoon cornstarch

½ cup water

3 tablespoons sugar

Zest of ½ lemon

1½ tablespoons fresh lemon juice

2 teaspoons butter

1 cup vanilla chocolate chips or melting wafers

1 (8-ounce) package cream cheese, softened

WHIPPED CREAM

1 cup heavy cream

¼ cup confectioners' sugar

1. In a large mixing bowl, combine the egg and cornstarch. Set aside.

2. Put the water, sugar, and lemon zest in a saucepan and bring to a boil. Slowly add the egg mixture. Stir continually and heat until thickened.

3. Remove from heat. Add lemon juice and butter. Stir until mixture has cooled to 100 degrees F. Pour half of the hot filling in a bowl and set aside. This will be used as the second layer of the pie.

4. Add the vanilla chips to the filling remaining in the pan. Stir until the chips are melted. Pour in a bowl and add the softened cream cheese. Beat together with an electric mixer. Spread this mixture in the bottom of the pie shell.

5. Spread the set-aside lemon filling on top. Chill for 2 hours.

6. In a mixing bowl, beat heavy cream and confectioners' sugar with an electric mixer to form whipped cream. Top pie with whipped cream and garnish with nuts. Keep refrigerated until it's time to serve.

Tasty Tips

- We like to top our pies with almonds. See toasted almond instructions on page 8.
- To get the most juice out of lemons, heat whole lemons in the microwave for 10–20 seconds. When juicing, cut the lemon in half lengthwise. More surface area equals more juice. Stick a fork in and break up the membranes. Squeeze.

Fresh Strawberry Pie

Serves 6–8 • Prep Time: 10 minutes • Total Time: 30 minutes

This retro pie recipe, a favorite from my childhood, makes me think of two great women. The first is my mother, Althea Kimball. Some of these pie recipes are ones she shared with me. But much more important, she was a monumental example of motherhood. I couldn't have had a better or sweeter example. She was always happy to make this pie for us if I would go to the garden and pick the ripest berries. She passed away when I was in my early twenties.

This recipe also makes me think of a dear woman named Colleen Mott. Colleen helped me with some of the pie recipes for Kneaders, and she was also a wonderful mentor to me as I parented my children after the loss of my own mother. Colleen passed away this last year, but she, like my mother, will forever be in my heart. I am so grateful that I have been able to carry on their heritage of loving and serving my family and others through sharing food made with love.

To create this decadent pie, choose the best strawberries you can find. Make sure they are deep red, ripe, and flavorful. Pile the strawberries high in the middle of the crust and serve with sweetened whipped cream. This sweet recipe tastes like summer. Be sure to share it with someone you love.

---

1 cup granulated sugar

2 tablespoons cornstarch

1 cup boiling water

1 (3-ounce) package strawberry gelatin, such as Jell-O

2 pounds strawberries

1 (9-inch) pie shell, baked (see recipes on pages 300 and 302)

Whipped Cream Topping (see recipe on page 227)

1. In a small pan, mix together the sugar and the cornstarch. Add boiling water and cook over medium heat until the mixture thickens, about 5 minutes. Remove from heat.

2. Add the strawberry gelatin and whisk until smooth. Let the mixture cool to room temperature.

3. Remove the green leaves from the strawberries and cut in half lengthwise.

4. Layer the strawberries, cut side down, in the baked pie shell. Continue until you have filled the pie shell with three layers. Each layer is smaller than the first. Cover with the cooled strawberry glaze mixture.

5. Refrigerate until set. Serve with Whipped Cream Topping.

Tasty Tips

• Make this pie when berries are in season, ripe and full of color.

Grated Apple Pie

Serves 6–8 • Prep Time: 20 minutes • Total Time: 1 hour 5 minutes

This is the very first apple pie made at Kneaders. Shirl Thomlinson, a lifelong friend of Kneaders and a professional apple grower, shared his family recipe with us. Akane apples are a Japanese apple sometimes called Tokyo Rose because of the beautiful streak of red in their skins. They have a thin skin and are both tart and sweet, which makes them the perfect apple for pies.

These unique apples are only available in August, September, and October, and Shirl is one of the only growers in the USA. I have included Shirl's suggestion of the two apples that you could use together to get a similar taste. You will need to peel the tart Granny Smith apples because of their thick skin, but you don't need to peel the sweet Fuji apples. They have a thin skin that will give a beautiful color to your pie.

---

2 (9-inch) pie crusts, unbaked (see recipes on pages 300 and 302))

3 cups grated (unpeeled) Akane apples or 2 cups peeled and grated Granny Smith apples with 1 cup grated (unpeeled) Fuji apples

½ cup sugar

½ cup brown sugar

2 tablespoons cornstarch

¼ teaspoon salt

¼ teaspoon cinnamon

1 teaspoon maple syrup

¼ teaspoon lemon juice

1 tablespoon butter

1 egg

2 tablespoons water

Turbinado sugar, for topping

1. Line a pie plate with one pie crust and set aside. Place grated apple in a bowl. Set aside.

2. In a medium bowl, mix sugar, brown sugar, cornstarch, salt, and cinnamon. Add apples. Combine until evenly distributed. Add maple syrup and lemon juice. Pour into the lined pie plate.

3. Cut the butter into 8 pieces and dot the apple mixture with butter. Add the top crust. Flute the edge as desired.

4. To make an egg wash, whisk egg with water. Brush the surface of the dough with egg wash and then sprinkle with turbinado sugar.

5. Pierce the top of the dough in several places to allow steam to escape while baking. Bake the pie for 40–45 minutes or until the crust is golden brown.

6. If possible, let the pie cool on a rack for 5 hours before serving.

Tasty Tips

- Come up with your own combination of apples. The variations are limitless.

Lime Pie with Pretzel Crust

Serves 6–8 • Prep Time: 15 minutes • Total Time: 55 minutes

Every year we make thousands of caramel-coated, chocolate-dipped pretzel rods. We take the pretzel ends and broken pieces and use them to make this fantastic crust. When you take a bite of the pie, make sure to savor the salty, sweet, juicy lime flavor. This pie is a Kneaders family favorite.

CRUST

Nonstick baking spray

1 cup + 2 tablespoons very finely ground salted pretzel crumbs, + more rough crumbs for garnish

3 tablespoons sugar

7 tablespoons butter, melted

FILLING

3–4 limes (or 6–8 key limes)

4 egg yolks

1 (14-ounce) can sweetened condensed milk

Whipped Cream Topping (see recipe on page 227)

1. For the crust, preheat the oven to 350 degrees F. Lightly spray a 9-inch pie plate with nonstick baking spray. Set aside.

2. In a bowl, combine finely ground pretzels, sugar, and melted butter. Press the mixture into the bottom and up the sides of the prepared pan. Bake for 8–10 minutes. The crust won't change color much, but it will firm up. Remove from the oven and set aside.

3. For the filling, zest the whole limes until you have 4 teaspoons. Place zest in a bowl and set aside. Cut the limes in half and squeeze out the juice, being careful to not include any seeds, until you have ½ cup lime juice. Set aside.

4. Whisk the lime zest and egg yolks together until eggs are tinted light green. Beat in the sweetened condensed milk, then the lime juice, and set aside at room temperature until it thickens, about 30 minutes. Do not stir.

5. Pour the finished filling into the baked pie crust and smooth with a spatula.

6. Bake the pie at 350 degrees F. for 28–32 minutes, until the filling is set, with a small spot (size of a quarter) in the middle that still looks soft. Cool for several hours before serving. Add Whipped Cream Topping and garnish the outside edge with crumbled pretzels.

Tasty Tips

• Processing pretzels in a food processor for 30 seconds works well for grinding them. Use waxed paper to press the crust into the pie pan.

Nana's Pumpkin Pie

Serves 6–8 • Prep Time: 30 minutes • Total Time: 1 hour

Unless you're making a deep dish pie, you will surely have two large pies and one little pie from this recipe. I think by now you know what to do with the little pie.

Read Colleen and Gary's story on pages 1–3.

1½ cups granulated sugar

6 teaspoons ground cinnamon

4 large eggs

1 (29-ounce) can Libby's 100% Pure Pumpkin

2 cans evaporated milk

2 (9-inch) unbaked pie shells

1 (3-inch) unbaked pie shell

Whipped Cream Topping (see recipe on page 227)

1. Preheat oven to 425 degrees F.

2. In a small bowl, mix sugar and cinnamon.

3. In a large bowl, beat eggs until frothy.

4. Stir in pumpkin and cinnamon-sugar mixture. Gradually stir in evaporated milk. Mix until evenly distributed.

5. Pour into unbaked pie shells.

6. Bake for 15 minutes. Reduce temperature to 350 degrees F. for 40 minutes, or until a knife inserted in the middle comes out clean.

7. Cool on a wire rack for 2 hours.

8. Add a dollop of Whipped Cream Topping, dust with cinnamon, and decorate with leaves cut from crust scraps.

Tasty Tips (according to Nana)

- Never, never use any canned pumpkin except for Libby's.
- After you add the pumpkin from the can, rinse it with the evaporated milk to make sure you get every bit of pumpkin in your pie.
- When the pie is baking, it isn't done until it starts to puff slightly in the middle. When it does, take it out immediately.

Pecan Pie

Serves 6–8 • Prep Time: 20 minutes • Total Time: 1 hour

This pecan pie is exceptional. Once you take a bite, you'll see why. On a visit to my daughter in Texas, we were lucky enough to be there at pecan harvest time. It was so engaging to see her and her family vigorously shake the pecan trees until all the nuts fell off. The pecan farmers sold all kinds of pecan treats in the orchard stores: turtles, tassies, salted pecans, sugared pecans, pecan ice cream, and—of course—three different kinds of pecan pies. During the last twenty-five years at Kneaders, we have made our share of different pecan pie recipes. This one is my favorite because every bite is packed with pecans.

---

1 (9-inch) pie shell, unbaked (see recipes on pages 300 and 302)

⅓ cup butter, melted

⅔ cup brown sugar, lightly packed

¼ teaspoon salt

1 teaspoon vanilla

1 cup light corn syrup

3 eggs, beaten

1½ cups roughly chopped pecan pieces + about 1 cup pecan halves (only use the perfect ones)

1. Preheat the oven to 350 degrees F. Press pie shell into a pie plate. Set aside.

2. In a medium mixing bowl, cream butter and brown sugar. Add salt, vanilla, and corn syrup. Mix with a hand mixer on the lowest speed until completely incorporated.

3. Add beaten eggs and chopped pecan pieces by hand. Be careful not to incorporate a lot of air into the filling.

4. Pour into unbaked pie shell. Do not overfill. You will need room to arrange the pecan halves on top of the pie, and the filling will expand a bit during baking.

5. Starting at the outside edge of the pie and working in a spiral, place the pecan halves on the filling until you have completely covered the pie.

6. Bake for 30 minutes. Cover loosely with foil or an inverted pie tin and continue baking for an additional 10–20 minutes. Pie is done when it reaches an internal temperature of 200 degrees F. or when it jiggles slightly just in the middle. Filling will continue to set as it cools.

Tasty Tips

• Buy extra pecan halves because several will be broken. Use the broken pieces to chop up for the filling.

Pie Crusts

Kneaders Basic Pie Crust

Makes enough crust for 1 (9-inch) double-crust pie, 2 (9-inch) single-crust pies, or 6 hand pies
Prep Time: 10 minutes • Total Time: 20 minutes

Something I love about pie dough is how it serves as a blank canvas for many different fillings. At Kneaders we use this recipe for cream pies, double-crusted pies, and even hand pies. One year it served as the crust for a deconstructed chicken pot pie. We hope this multipurpose recipe will be as useful for you in your homes. Don't be afraid to get creative with your fillings!

---

2 cups bread flour

½ teaspoon salt

1 teaspoon sugar

¾ cup high ratio shortening, such as Sweetex

5–6 tablespoons ice water

1. In a mixing bowl, combine flour, salt, and sugar. With a pastry blender, cut shortening into flour until it resembles coarse bread crumbs. Using a fork, stir in ice water a little at a time until you can form a ball. Dough should be soft and pliable but not sticky. For a flaky crust, you should be able to see small chunks of shortening throughout the dough, giving it a marbled look.

2. Roll and bake according to individual recipe directions, or use half the dough and follow the directions here to blind-bake a single crust.

3. To blind-bake a single-crust pie shell, roll and fit dough into a metal 9-inch pie plate, leaving enough to hang over the edge. Trim ½-inch beyond the rim of the pan and fold under to make a high edge. Press the edge between the thumb and forefinger at intervals around the top edge of the pie.

4. Poke bottom and sides with a fork; this will keep the crust from bubbling up. Bake at 450 degrees F. for 10–12 minutes.

Tasty Tips

- To make a cream cheese pie crust, take out 4 tablespoons shortening and add 4 tablespoons cold cream cheese that has been cut into cubes. Proceed as indicated in the recipe.
- Use pie scraps to make savory hand pies, in the style of the Pineapple Hand Pies on page 305. Fill with scrambled eggs, chopped ham, and cheese, then sprinkle with garlic salt.

Grandma Worthington's Beginners Pie Crust

Makes enough crust for 1 (9-inch) double-crust pie, 2 (9-inch) single-crust pies, or 6 hand pies
Prep Time: 10 minutes • Total Time: 20 minutes

As a young bride in the 1940s, Gary's mother, Mary Hale Worthington, cut this recipe out of the *New York Times*. It's a no-fail pie crust, one even beginners can succeed with. You will enjoy the flaky texture as well as how easy it is to position on a tin without tearing. It is worthy of any pie you want to put in it. Mary made the very best pies I have ever tasted.

¾ cup + 1 tablespoon shortening

1 tablespoon milk

¼ cup boiling water

1 teaspoon salt

About 2 cups flour

1. In a mixing bowl, mix shortening, milk, and boiling water with a fork. Add salt and just enough flour to clear the sides of the bowl (about 2 cups).

2. Mix until all ingredients are incorporated, but don't go crazy. If it looks marbled, you have done it just right.

3. Shape into two rounds. Put each round between two 12-inch square sheets of waxed paper to roll out. Do not add flour. Start in the middle and work toward the outside edge, turning as you go.

4. To blind-bake a single-crust pie to fit into a pie plate, remove one side of waxed paper from a round. Set an empty pie plate on top face-down. Holding onto the waxed paper, flip over the tin and crust together. Carefully peel the waxed paper off the crust, and carefully fit the crust to the tin, leaving an inch on the outside. Fold the crust under and press a fork along the edge. Poke holes in the crust with a fork.

5. Bake at 475 degrees F. for about 8 minutes, until golden brown.

6. To make a double-crust pie: Follow step 4 above to fit one round into a pie plate. Fill the pie as desired. Peel the waxed paper off one side of the second round. Using the still-attached waxed paper, drape the round over the filled pie and gently peel the waxed paper off. Cut the excess crust off ½ inch from the tin. Fold both crusts under and decorate the edge with a fork or fingers. Cut slits in the top crust. Bake according to recipe directions.

Tasty Tips

• Be sure family recipes are passed from generation to generation. Food sparks some of the best memories and connects us together. Food is a language of love.

Pastry Cream and Vanilla Sauce

Makes 2 cups • Prep Time: 20 minutes • Total Time: 30 minutes

PASTRY CREAM

1¾ cups whole milk

¼ cup butter

1 cup sugar

¼ cup water

¼ cup cornstarch

2 egg yolks

1 teaspoon vanilla extract

Pinch of salt

½ teaspoon vanilla bean paste

1. In a 2-quart saucepan, add milk, butter, and sugar. Do not stir and do not place on heat yet. Set aside.

2. In a separate bowl, whisk together water and cornstarch, making sure there are no lumps. Add egg yolks, vanilla extract, and salt. Whisk together until completely smooth.

3. Place the saucepan on the burner over medium-high heat. Bring to a boil without stirring. When it has come to a full boil, add the cornstarch mixture, stirring thoroughly and constantly. When it starts to bubble and thicken, remove from heat and continue stirring for 1–2 minutes to keep bubbles from forming. Add vanilla bean paste and stir.

4. Cool for 10 minutes, stirring occasionally. Pour into a bowl. Place plastic wrap directly on top of the filling to keep a skin from forming. Chill until completely cool.

VANILLA SAUCE

1 cup Pastry Cream

1½ cups heavy cream

⅛ teaspoon vanilla bean paste

Place pastry cream, heavy cream, and vanilla bean paste in a mixing bowl. Mix well to combine.

Tasty Tips

- You can use extra pastry cream as a fruit dip. For a lighter, fluffier dip or filling, fold in whipped cream or a nondairy whipped topping.

Pineapple Hand Pies

Makes 18 hand pies • Prep Time: 30 minutes • Total Time: 50 minutes

In 2013, Cilla came to a store operator training in Orem. Cilla's energy and desire to help others is unparalleled, and we enjoyed her Polynesian charm. As a thank-you at the end of training, she brought us huge pineapple half-moon pies. We loved them! With Cilla's permission, we sold a smaller version of these hand pies in 2014 as part of our Aloha Summer. They were a big hit. Pineapple Hand Pies remain one of our most requested recipes. Thank you for sharing, Cilla.

---

3 recipes (a triple batch) pie crust (see recipes on pages 300 and 302)

ice water, for moistening

PINEAPPLE FILLING

1 (20-ounce) can crushed pineapple, drained, juice reserved

½ cup pineapple juice, divided

1 cup sugar

⅔ cup heavy cream

2 tablespoons cornstarch

TOPPING

2 egg yolks

1 tablespoon water

3 tablespoons sugar

1 teaspoon cinnamon

1. Preheat the oven to 365 degrees F.

2. Start by making the pineapple filling. In a medium saucepan, combine ¼ cup pineapple juice, crushed pineapple, sugar, and heavy cream. Bring to a boil over medium heat, stirring frequently.

3. In a separate bowl, combine cornstarch and remaining ¼ cup pineapple juice to make a slurry. Add to the boiling mixture. Heat until it starts to thicken and bubble. Do not overcook; the filling will continue to thicken as it cools.

4. Roll out dough on a lightly floured surface to about ¹⁄₁₆ inch thick. Cut 5-inch circles. Continue rolling and cutting until you have 18 circles.

5. Moisten the edges of one circle with ice water. Place about 2 tablespoons pineapple filling in the center of the dough. Fold in half so edges meet, making a half-moon. Seal around the edges. Use a fork to form a decorative edge. Repeat until all 18 pies are filled. Prick each pie 3 times with a fork to vent.

6. Make an egg wash by whisking together egg yolks and water in a shallow bowl. Using a pastry brush, brush each pie lightly with egg wash.

7. Combine sugar with cinnamon. Sprinkle cinnamon sugar over pies.

8. Bake for 20 minutes or until golden brown.

Tasty Tips

- For a quick hand pie, buy canned pie filling and substitute it for the pineapple filling.

Raspberry Bread Pudding

Serves 6–8 • Prep Time: 20 minutes • Total Time: 1 hour 50 minutes

While bread pudding was at first a way for frugal cooks to use up dry bread, it's now made a name for itself as the ultimate comfort dessert. Once when I was sick, a neighbor brought me this bread pudding to cheer me up. After tasting it, I knew it was something we should be making at the bakery. It was the first of many extraordinary bread puddings sold at Kneaders, and it remains a favorite of our guests. The secret to its amazing taste is our world-class bread. And I have to smile at how many guests eat it for breakfast. Bread, eggs, milk, fruit—sure, it's breakfast!

---

2 loaves Kneaders Country White bread, set out to dry for 3 hours

1 quart heavy cream

3 cups sugar

1 egg

1 teaspoon vanilla extract

5 cups frozen raspberries, broken into smaller pieces

1 cup sugar

½ cup apple juice

1 recipe Vanilla Sauce (see recipe on page 303)

1. Preheat the oven to 375 degrees F.

2. In a large bowl, whisk together cream, sugar, egg, and vanilla extract by hand.

3. Tear bread into 2-inch pieces. Mix cut bread with custard mixture, making sure all bread gets separated. Allow the bread to soak for 30 minutes, stirring every 5 minutes.

4. In a medium bowl, combine raspberries, sugar, and apple juice. Stir until sugar is dissolved.

5. Dish ¾ of bread mixture into a 9x13 baking dish. Pour raspberry filling over the bread and spread evenly.

6. Top with remaining bread mixture. Bake for 40 minutes, until golden brown.

7. Remove bread pudding from the oven and let cool for 10–15 minutes.

8. Serve bread pudding warm with cold vanilla sauce.

Tasty Tips

• The secret to this recipe is to use Kneaders Country White Bread. Any other bread won't taste quite as good!

Sticky Toffee Pudding

Serves 8–10 • Prep Time: 20 minutes • Total Time: 1 hour

Late one night I was watching a story on the Food Network about the Häagen-Dazs contest for the ice-cream flavor of the year. The winning flavor for the year 2006 was Sticky Toffee Pudding. It sounded delicious. The next day I was obsessed with finding recipes for this amazing dessert. I wanted to make it in our stores. Here is what I came up with. Don't leave out the dates—they are the secret ingredient. Enjoy!

STICKY TOFFEE PUDDING

2 cups flour

1¼ teaspoons baking powder

1¾ cups dates, pitted and finely chopped

1¼ teaspoons baking soda

1 cup boiling water

⅔ cup butter

1 cup granulated sugar

4 eggs

2 teaspoons vanilla

TOPPINGS

1 (8-ounce) jar Kneaders Famous Caramel Syrup

1 recipe Vanilla Sauce (see page 303)

Whipped Cream Topping (see page 227)

Toffee bits

1. Preheat the oven to 340 degrees F. Grease and flour a 9x13 baking dish. Set aside.

2. In a small bowl, combine flour and baking powder. Set aside.

3. In another bowl, add dates and baking soda. Pour boiling water over dates. Set aside.

4. In a large bowl, combine butter and sugar. Cream until light and fluffy, about 3 minutes. Add eggs and vanilla. Blend well.

5. Add flour mixture to butter mixture. Mix until combined. Fold in date mixture by hand until combined.

6. Pour batter into prepared dish. Bake for 35–40 minutes, or until pudding springs back when touched in the center.

7. To serve, drizzle each piece with caramel syrup, add a dollop of Vanilla Sauce and Whipped Cream Topping, and sprinkle with toffee bits.

Tasty Tips

- Lightly sugared pitted chopped dates can be found in the grocery store.

SWEETS *and* TREATS

Butterfinger Caramel Apples

Makes 10 caramel apples • Prep Time: 30 minutes • Total Time: 35 minutes

Fall is a favorite time of year for everyone at Kneaders. Once we start making our caramel apples, that makes the season even better! We make four kinds of caramel apples at Kneaders: a cinnamon white chocolate, a drizzle of white and dark chocolate with walnuts, an Oreo with white chocolate, and a milk chocolate Butterfinger. We are delighted to share this Butterfinger caramel apple recipe with you.

---

10 Granny Smith apples,
  room temperature

10 wooden craft sticks

2 pounds top-grade caramels

2 pounds tempered milk chocolate
  coins, or 2 pounds semisweet
  chocolate chips, divided

8 large Butterfinger candy bars, crushed

1. Prepare a half-sheet baking pan with a silicone mat, parchment paper, or nonstick spray. Set aside.

2. Wash the apples and dry them. Make sure they are at room temperature so that the caramel and chocolate will adhere properly to the apple. Insert the wooden craft sticks halfway into the apple core. Set aside.

3. In a glass bowl, microwave the caramels at 30-second intervals, stirring in between, until melted and caramel reaches 185 degrees F.

4. Dip apples completely into caramel, making sure the caramel touches the stick. Shake off excess caramel. Stand apples on prepared half-sheet baking pan to cool.

5. Once the apples have cooled and set, pinch off any caramel that has pooled around the base of the dipped apples.

6. In a glass bowl, microwave 1½ pounds chocolate coins at 1-minute intervals, stirring in between, until chocolate reaches 120–125 degrees F. Seed the chocolate by adding additional coins and stirring until it cools to 100 degrees F.

7. Dip apples in chocolate, leaving 1 inch caramel showing at the top. Shake off excess chocolate. Immediately roll apples in crushed Butterfingers. Stand apples on prepared half-sheet baking pan. Put immediately in the refrigerator and let cool until the chocolate sets, about 10 minutes. The quicker you can get them cooled, the more shine your apples will have. Cut and enjoy!

Tasty Tips
- For a more sturdy option, replace the craft sticks with heavy-duty (6-inch by 5.5-mm) bamboo skewers.

Chocolate Fudge

Makes 5 (½-pound) blocks marshmallow fudge • Prep Time: 20 minutes • Total Time: 50 minutes

About five years into starting the Abbie & Ellie candy company, we were talking about how much we love fudge. We decided we would like to sell fudge in the store. Where could we find the perfect recipe? We asked everyone we knew. At last one of our food reps gave us his grandma's go-to recipe. It was creamy, it was soft, and it had a rich decadent taste—just what we were looking for. We hope you enjoy it.

Nonstick cooking spray

2¼ cups granulated sugar

¾ cup evaporated milk

¼ cup butter

2 (7-ounce) tubs marshmallow creme

1 pound dark chocolate wafers, such as Ghirardelli Intense Dark (86% Cacao Dark Chocolate)

1. Spray a 9x13 baking dish with nonstick cooking spray. Set aside.

2. In a large nonstick pot, bring sugar, evaporated milk, and butter to a rolling boil. Boil for 4 full minutes. Turn off heat and immediately add the marshmallow creme and chocolate. Stir until well incorporated.

3. Pour into the prepared pan and place in the refrigerator to set, about 30 minutes. Remove from the refrigerator and cut into blocks.

The DESIGNER

Mark Orton

One of the most enjoyable parts of building a business is the chance it gives us to create. Another is the opportunity we have to meet other people who love to be inventive. Mark Orton, the creative director of KorCreative, is an expert at making things look and feel wonderful. He graduated from ArtCenter College of Design in Pasadena, and he has designed the world—airports, businesses, products, offices, and much more. When Mark comes to visit, we all want to be in the room. His energy and excitement are contagious.

The first time we engaged Mark was to help us with our logo redesign in 2013. We were on the cusp of growth and expansion and wanted to evolve our brand into something that felt more "grown-up" and that could compete nationally. What I loved most about his process was that he really tried to understand our needs and listened to what we thought and felt about the brand. Then he presented us with multiple options to choose from that could help us achieve our goals. The one we loved from the start is the one we ended up moving forward with, and it's been a pleasure to see it on our stores and elsewhere over the years. It just fits. Since then, Mark has designed all things Kneaders—ads, boxes, catalogs, menus, posters, signs, vehicle wraps, websites, tags, bags, swag, and packaging for the holidays.

Mark is a combination of down-to-earth and reach-for-the-sky. He knows how to work hard and how to dream big. Mark grew up in Idaho and was raised by wonderful parents, Mark and Annette Orton. His family didn't have much, but they enjoyed the simple pleasures of being with family and making things that were fun to eat. Mark has fond memories of making taffy at Christmastime with his mother as she told him stories about making that very same taffy with her own grandmother, Harriet. He loved spending time together pulling the taffy until it was just right. (And he says not to be scared of the fact that vinegar is one of the ingredients—the recipe is delicious!) Mark also loved eating the Christmas English toffee that his mother (now known as Gramma Annette to his kids) made each year. When you come to those recipes in our Sweets and Treats section, you'll see that those recipes are written by the women who made them. We haven't changed a thing. I love the personality and the way you can hear their voices even in a few short sentences and descriptions. These are the kinds of things that make recipes come alive—and that keep the people who made them alive in our hearts all through the years.

Mark's father worked in church education and had also studied art for a semester in Los Angeles. There was no art class available for Mark in high school, so his dad helped him create an art portfolio and take it to Ricks College (now BYU–Idaho). The faculty were kind and gave him a small scholarship and accepted him into the program. While he studied at Ricks College, Mark took a lettering class and knocked it out of the park. A professor asked Mark if he'd ever thought about going to school in graphic design—and Mark didn't even know what that was! But he loved the idea. Several of Mark's professors had attended ArtCenter College of Design and that became his goal as well. Mark's professors helped him prepare his portfolio to apply there after he finished up at Ricks. Not only was he accepted, ArtCenter also gave him advance standing and a half-tuition scholarship.

After graduation, Mark went on to work for Hamagami/Carroll in Santa Monica, California, and then Pederson/Gesk in their Seattle and Minneapolis offices before starting his own firm, KorCreative. He did all of this while raising a family of six with his wife, Robin, and serving in his church. His work ethic is unparalleled, and yet he always brings a sense of enjoyment and play to the projects he does for us. It's so exciting when someone can take what you have in mind and make it better and easier to see. Mark's superpower is that he knows how to listen to people and to take what they feel and know in order to design a product that accomplishes what they need.

When I asked Mark what his favorite thing was that he'd designed for us, he said he loves seeing our logo "out in the wild"—on cups or bags people are carrying, or when he goes to an event and sees that the catered food is in Kneaders boxes. He thinks *There are my children!* when he comes across his work out in the world. We feel that way, too—we love seeing what we've made out and about, and we're honored when you invite our creations into your homes.

See HERITAGE CANDY recipes on page 319.

Heritage Candy

Read Mark Orton's story on pages 316–17.

Gramma Annette's Christmas English Toffee

Serves 16 • Prep Time: 15 minutes • Total Time: 1 hour

1 cup real butter

1 cup brown sugar

Chopped nuts

Large Hershey's bar, coarsely chopped (can use chocolate chips instead if desired)

Butter a half-sheet baking pan and set aside. Melt sugar and butter together in a heavy pan, stirring constantly. Bring to a boil, stirring constantly. When the mixture reaches a boil, turn down the heat so it is just simmering. Continue simmering, stirring as little as possible, until it reaches the "crack" stage (300 degrees F.). As soon as the "crack" stage is reached, pour out onto prepared pan. Do not spread. Place pieces of chocolate bar on top and let them melt. When melted, spread the chocolate evenly over the top of the candy, and sprinkle with chopped nuts. Let set until chocolate is hardened. Break into pieces.

Words of Advice from Gramma Annette

- Only make this when the sun is shining, or it will go sugary, so they say. Don't ask why, I don't know. Have your chocolate close by, along with your chopped almonds or walnuts.

Grandma Harriet Walker's Old-Fashioned Vinegar Taffy

Makes 30 pieces • Prep Time: 30 minutes • Total Time: 1 hour, not including pulling time

2 cups sugar

2 tablespoons butter

½ cup white vinegar

Combine sugar and vinegar in a heavy saucepan. Bring to a boil to hard-ball stage (250 degrees F.). Add butter. Pour onto buttered plate to cool. When cool enough to handle, butter your fingers, take a blob of it and stretch and pull it so that the air mixes in and turns it from gold color to white or until it is too hard to pull. Twist it and place on plate. Break off chunks for eating.

Peppermint Bark

Serves 10 • Prep Time: 10 minutes • Total Time: 30 minutes

Peppermint bark is a twenty-year tradition at Kneaders. You'll be surprised at how delicious three ingredients can taste. We hope you love it—we sure do.

Read Tami and David Vincent's story on pages 74–75.

---

1 pound milk chocolate (wafers, chips, or broken candy bars)

1¼ pound white chocolate (wafers, chips, or broken candy bars)

¼ pound peppermint candies, such as Starlight Mints

1. Add the unwrapped peppermint candies to a gallon ziptop bag, then insert that bag into another gallon ziptop bag. Using a rolling pin, crush the candies into small (¼-inch) pieces. Set aside.

2. Making sure the baking pan is clean and dry, line with parchment paper.

3. In a large microwave-safe bowl, melt milk chocolate in the microwave in 15-second increments, stirring each time, until the chocolate reaches 125 degrees F.

4. Pour melted milk chocolate into the pan, using a spatula to make sure the chocolate reaches the edges. Refrigerate while melting the white chocolate, at least 5 minutes.

5. In a medium microwave-safe bowl, melt white chocolate in 15-second increments, stirring each time, until the chocolate reaches 130 degrees F.

6. Pour melted white chocolate into the pan, using a spatula to make sure the chocolate reaches the edges. While the white chocolate is wet, immediately sprinkle peppermint across the white chocolate. Refrigerate until all is hardened, then break or cut into 2- to 3-inch chunks.

Tasty Tip

- Use an instant-read thermometer to make sure the chocolate is the correct temperature before spreading: about 125 degrees F. for the milk chocolate; 127–130 degrees F. for the white chocolate. Getting the white chocolate hot enough bonds the two chocolates together.

Chocolate Almond Cream Puffs

Makes 12–14 cream puffs • Prep Time: 45 minutes • Total Time: 2 hours 30 minutes

One summer, Monica Kate, our executive pastry chef, toured the stores teaching an éclair and cream puff class. Our guests had so much fun learning from this expert pastry chef. The grand finale was helping make a croquembouche tree out of cream puffs. What a magnificent centerpiece for a Christmas dinner.

Kneaders offers different classes on a monthly basis. Please call for times and locations.

---

1 batch Pâte à Choux (see recipe on page 324)

CREAM FILLING

2 cups Pastry Cream (see recipe on page 303)

12 ounces white baking chocolate, chopped

½ cup + 1 tablespoon heavy cream

1. Make a batch of Pâte à Choux, but pipe 2½- to 3-inch circles rather than 4-inch rectangles. Bake according to instructions and allow to cool after drying in an open oven.

2. Make pastry cream and cool to a little below room temperature.

3. Place white chocolate in a small bowl and set aside.

4. In a small saucepan over medium heat, or in the microwave in 30-second intervals (about 1½ minutes total), heat heavy cream just until it comes to a simmer.

5. Pour hot cream over white chocolate. Whisk until smooth. Cool to room temperature, stirring occasionally. This will take about 20 or 30 minutes.

6. Once cooled, beat with an electric mixer for 2–3 minutes until doubled in size.

7. With a spatula, mix in pastry cream until incorporated. Chill.

CHOCOLATE MOUSSE FILLING

4 egg yolks

4 tablespoons granulated sugar, divided

2 cups heavy cream, divided

8 ounces semisweet chocolate, melted

½ teaspoon vanilla extract

⅛ teaspoon almond extract

1. In a 1½-quart saucepan, whisk together egg yolks, 2 tablespoons sugar, and ¾ cup heavy cream. Cook over medium heat, stirring constantly, until mixture coats the back of a spoon. Do not boil. Remove from heat.

2. Whisk in melted chocolate and extracts. Continue stirring until smooth. Chill until cool.

3. In a separate bowl, beat remaining 1¼ cups heavy cream and remaining 2 tablespoons sugar with an electric mixer until stiff peaks form.

4. Stir ⅓ of the whipped cream into the cooled egg yolk mixture. Gently fold in the rest with a rubber spatula. Chill.

ASSEMBLY

Cut cream puff shells in half horizontally. Put one level ice-cream scoop of cream filling on the bottom half of a cream puff shell. Put one level ice-cream scoop of chocolate filling on top of cream filling. Replace top of cream puff. Repeat with remaining shells.

Tasty Tips

- Use instant chocolate mousse mix in place of chocolate filling. It will take 2 (4-ounce) boxes to equal approximately the same amount. Add ⅛ teaspoon almond extract to milk before beating.

Éclairs

Makes 18 éclairs • Prep Time: 55 minutes • Total Time: 2 hours

About three years after we opened our first store, we decided that we wanted to expand our pastry line. One thing that appealed to us was making éclairs. Our good friend John Olejko from ProBAKE helped us develop the pâte à choux recipe. We then filled this light and tasty pastry dough with creamy filling and dipped it in our chocolate ganache. We're sharing all three recipes with you so that you can have this elegant dessert whenever you'd like.

In 2018 we came out with a brand-new éclair—our open-faced éclair. We had a contest, this time with our pastry chefs, to invent variations on this open-faced éclair. They came up with the Chocolate Strawberry Éclair, the State Fair Éclair, the Unicorn Éclair, and the Banana Split Éclair. Each month we gave our guests a new whimsical eclair to try. Pastry chefs and guests alike enjoyed this fun-filled promotion.

PÂTE À CHOUX

1 cup water

½ cup butter

1 teaspoon granulated sugar

½ teaspoon salt

1 cup all-purpose flour

5 eggs or 1 cup liquid egg

1. To make the pâte à choux, preheat the oven to 425 degrees F. Line a half-sheet baking pan with parchment paper. Set aside.

2. In a medium saucepan over medium-high heat, combine the water, butter, sugar, and salt. Bring to a boil, then immediately remove from heat.

3. Stir in the flour. Incorporate well and return to heat. Stir constantly for 4 minutes or until the mixture pulls away from the sides and forms a film on the bottom of the pan.

4. Transfer to a mixing bowl fitted with a paddle attachment. Mix on low speed for 3 minutes. The mixture should cool slightly while mixing. Add the eggs one by one, incorporating after each egg. The batter will be smooth and shiny.

5. Immediately put the mixture in a pastry bag with no tip and pipe onto the prepared half-sheet baking pan. Each piping should be 4 inches long.

6. Bake for 15 minutes, then decrease the oven temperature to 350 degrees F. Bake for 25–30 minutes, until the pâte à choux is golden brown.

7. Turn off the oven, prop the door open, and allow the pâte à choux to dry in the oven for 15–20 minutes.

CREAM FILLING

1 (4.6-ounce) box vanilla pudding, such as Cook and Serve Jell-O

2 cups milk

1 cup whipped topping, such as Cool Whip, thawed

4 teaspoons vanilla extract

CHOCOLATE GANACHE

2 cups semisweet chocolate chips

2 cups heavy cream

2 teaspoons vanilla

Prepare the vanilla pudding according to package directions and cool. Fold the pudding, whipped topping, and vanilla together in a medium-sized mixing bowl. Refrigerate until ready to use.

Tasty Tips

• This is a difficult recipe. Worth it, but hard! Make it when you have enough time to not be distracted.

1. Place chocolate chips in a large bowl and set aside.

2. Pour cream into saucepan and bring to a boil. As soon as the cream boils up to the top of the pan, quickly remove from heat and pour it over the chocolate chips. Let stand for a minute. Stir with a whisk until smooth. Stir in vanilla.

ASSEMBLY

1. Once pâte à choux, cream filling, and chocolate ganache are all ready, assemble the éclairs. With a wooden skewer, make a small hole in the top of each pâte à choux and break any webs inside. Fill a pastry bag fitted with a large round tip with cream filling. Using the pastry bag, fill each pâte à choux with the cream filling from the hole you made with the skewer. Dip the top half of each éclair into the chocolate ganache. Set on wire rack to dry.

2. Serve immediately. Éclairs can be refrigerated for up to 24 hours.

Tart Shells

Makes 12 (3-inch) tart shells • Prep Time: 25 minutes • Chill Time: 2 hours or overnight • Total Time: 2 hours 45 minutes

Yermonia, our first pastry chef (see her story on pages 216–18), introduced fresh fruit tarts—one of our signature desserts—to Kneaders. She asked me to buy her tart molds, and I was happy to oblige. Yermonia hand-pressed each tart shell. The tarts became so popular that we were making too many for her to continue hand-pressing each shell. We have now moved to using premade tarts from our Swiss supplier. They are still delicious, but this recipe will let you make the shells the Yermonia way.

DOUGH

10 tablespoons butter, softened

¾ cup confectioners' sugar

½ teaspoon vanilla

2 eggs

2 cups all-purpose flour

EGG WASH

¼ cup milk

1 egg

1. Using an electric mixer, beat butter until smooth. Add confectioners' sugar and vanilla. Slowly alternate adding the eggs and flour until just incorporated. Press dough flat, but do not knead. Wrap in plastic and chill overnight, or for at least 2 hours.

2. Preheat the oven to 325 degrees F.

3. Grease tart shell pans. Divide cold dough into 12 parts. Roll to make 2-inch balls. Roll out individual dough balls to desired thickness and gently press into 3-inch pans. Cut off extra dough on the edges.

4. Bake for 20 minutes, until light brown.

5. Whisk together ingredients for egg wash. Brush each tart with egg wash and bake for a few additional minutes, until tarts are golden brown. Cool before filling.

> *Tasty Tips*
> • Prepare tart shells the day before you need them.

Peach Tarts

Makes 12 tarts • Prep Time: 20 minutes • Total Time: 40 minutes

One of our longtime pastry chefs at Kneaders was Amber Wurth. Amber loved the pastries, and it showed. At Kneaders we change pastries with the seasons. As we hunted for a new pastry for the late summer, Amber came up with this incredible peach tart. At the time we had nothing peachy on our menu. Who knew peaches would be such a big hit?

SPICED APRICOT GLAZE

½ cup apricot jam

1–2 teaspoons water

¼ teaspoon cinnamon

1 generous dash nutmeg

SPICED MOUSSE FILLING

2 (2.7-ounce) packets Dr. Oetker French Vanilla Mousse

Milk, for preparing mousse

1½ teaspoons cinnamon

¼ teaspoon nutmeg

PEACH FILLING

2 peaches

12 (3-inch) tart shells, baked (see recipe on page 326)

Whipped Cream Topping (see recipe on page 227), for garnish

Ground cinnamon, for garnish

⅛ teaspoon almond extract

1. For the spiced apricot glaze, puree jam with an electric mixer. Add a little water if needed to make it a smooth, spreadable consistency. Stir in cinnamon and nutmeg. Store in the refrigerator until ready to assemble the tarts.

2. For the spiced mousse filling, measure out the milk according to package directions but do not add to mousse packet yet. Add cinnamon, nutmeg, and almond extract to milk. Then finish preparing mousse according to package directions. Store in the refrigerator until ready to assemble the tarts.

3. Peel peaches. Remove stones and slice. You will need 36 slices, so make sure you get at least 18 slices per peach.

4. To assemble the tarts, spread a thin layer of spiced apricot glaze on the bottom and sides of each tart shell. (You won't use all the glaze here. Save some for brushing on the tops.)

5. Using a pastry bag fitted with a large shell tip, pipe a rosette of spiced mousse filling into each tart shell large enough to cover the bottom of the shell and tall enough in the center to come slightly above the shell.

6. Place 3 peach slices on top of each tart in a fan shape.

7. Thin the apricot glaze with an equal amount of hot water. Brush lightly over the top of the peaches.

8. Top each tart with Whipped Cream Topping and garnish with a sprinkle of cinnamon.

Tasty Tips

• Be sure to look for clingstone peaches.

Haupia Tarts

Makes 12 tarts • Prep Time: 20 minutes • Total Time: 30 minutes

All of our family loves Hawaii. If we could go every year, we would. We do manage to make it there every three or four years. On the south side of Oahu there is a little bakery that makes haupia pies, where we always stop. When we decided to do the Hawaiian summer promotion at Kneaders, we thought it the perfect time to make our own version, but as a tart. We are thrilled to be sharing it with you. Aloha!

---

12 (3-inch) tart shells, baked
  (see recipe on page 326)

HAUPIA FILLING

⅓ cup cornstarch

1¾ cups water, divided

1 cup cream of coconut

1 cup whole milk

⅔ cup granulated sugar

TOPPINGS

½ cup cream of coconut

6½ cups whipped topping, such
  as Cool Whip, thawed

2 (3.1-ounce) packets Dr. Oetker
  Dark Chocolate Truffle Mousse

Chocolate curls, for decorating
  (see instructions on page 212)

Toasted coconut flakes, for decorating

1. In a medium bowl, whisk together cornstarch and 1¼ cups water to make a slurry. Whisk until there are no lumps. Set aside.

2. In a blender, blend cream of coconut and remaining ½ cup water until smooth. Transfer to a saucepan over medium heat. Add whole milk and sugar. Heat, whisking continually, until it begins to boil. Add slurry and continue whisking until the mixture boils again. Be very careful not to burn the bottom of the mixture.

3. Remove from heat and put in a bowl. Cover with plastic wrap touching the top of the mixture so it does not form a skin. Cool before using.

4. While filling cools, prepare the toppings. Whisk cream of coconut and whipped topping in a bowl until combined. Refrigerate until needed.

5. Prepare mousse according to package directions. Refrigerate until needed.

6. Once filling is cool and toppings prepared, assemble the tarts. Fill a piping bag fitted with a large round tip with chocolate mousse. Fill each tart shell halfway full.

7. Place haupia filling in a measuring cup with a pour spout. Fill each tart to the top of the shell with haupia filling.

8. Fill a piping bag fitted with a large closed star tip with whipped coconut topping. Pipe whipped coconut topping to cover the top of the tart. Decorate with chocolate curls and toasted coconut.

Tasty Tips

• Cream of coconut and coconut cream are not the same thing. Make sure you get the right one—cream of coconut.

Lemon Meringue Tarts

Makes 9 tarts • Prep Time: 25 minutes • Total Time: 35 minutes

At Kneaders, we love any kind of citrus flavor. This lemon tart is a variation of our key lime tarts. The difference (besides the flavor of the citrus) is that instead of having a whipped topping like the key lime tarts, our lemon tarts have meringue on top. We don't always carry these in our stores, so we wanted to share this recipe in case you love citrus as much as we do. This way, you can have them any time you'd like.

---

9 (3-inch) tart shells, baked
(see recipe on page 326)

LEMON FILLING

4 egg yolks

1 (14-ounce) can sweetened
condensed milk

Zest of 1 lemon

½ cup lemon juice

MERINGUE

5 large egg whites, room temperature

½ teaspoon cream of tartar

½ cup granulated sugar

⅛ teaspoon salt

1. Preheat the oven to 350 degrees F. Line a half-sheet baking pan with parchment paper. Set aside.

2. Whisk egg yolks by hand until they begin to turn a lighter yellow color. It will take a couple of minutes. Drizzle sweetened condensed milk into beaten egg yolks as you continue to whisk. Mix until thoroughly combined. Add lemon zest and juice. Mix until blended.

3. Spoon mixture into prepared tart shells, filling to within 1/16 inch of the top. Place tarts on the prepared half-sheet baking pan. Bake for 10 minutes. While tarts are baking, whip up the meringue.

4. For the meringue, in a mixing bowl, beat the egg whites and cream of tartar together with an electric mixer on medium speed for 1 minute. Increase to high speed until soft peaks form, for about 4 more minutes. Add sugar and salt. Continue beating until stiff peaks form.

5. Remove tarts from the oven. Change the oven to broil on high.

6. Top each tart with a generous dollop of meringue, ensuring the meringue touches the crust to prevent weeping (beads of liquid forming between the filling and the meringue). Return to the oven and broil for about 3 minutes or until the meringue is golden brown. Watch them closely, as they can burn quickly. As an alternate method, you can use a culinary torch to brown the meringue.

Tasty Tips

- You will get quite a bit more juice from a lemon if you microwave it for 15 seconds and then roll it on the counter before you slice and juice it.
- For a nice stiff meringue, make sure your bowl and utensils are free of any grease.

INDEX

RECIPE INDEX

DIPS AND SPREADS

STUFFINGS AND CROUTONS

CAKES AND TRIFLES

COOKIES AND BARS

PIES AND PUDDINGS

SWEETS AND TREATS

RECIPE INDEX

ACKNOWLEDGMENTS

We feel so lucky to work with Nick and Erin Bayless. Nick and Erin have been working with Kneaders for over ten years, and they truly went the extra mile helping us get all of the photographs for this cookbook finished in time. Nick is a Utah-based photographer and videographer who has been working with food and lifestyle for over twenty years. Erin is a designer and stylist who started out working for Martha Stewart in New York City and now primarily focuses on food styling. They love cooking, eating, and working together on food and lifestyle shoots. Through lighting and patient attention to detail, they make every image mouth wateringly delicious.

Erin and Nick Bayless.

Nick and Erin collaborate with Kneaders to produce photography for their website, billboards, store signage, and marketing to help build a strong brand. In addition, they produce video for various advertising needs. One fun project was promoting the Kneaders elephant cookie campaign to raise money for cancer research. Their kids, some of the Worthington grandkids, and other kids dressed up as flour-dusted bakers in a kid-sized kitchen to narrate this incredible story.

We also want to thank Ally Condie for her helping in compiling the essays and other written items for this cookbook. Ally is a #1 *New York Times* best-selling author, the mom of four great kids, and a longtime Kneaders fan. Her favorite thing to order at our stores is the Chunky Cinnamon French Toast after a long morning run.

Ally Condie.

ABOUT *the* AUTHOR

More than twenty-five years ago, Colleen Worthington rolled up her sleeves and built a baking empire out of her own kitchen, which provided a place for her children and now grandchildren to learn hard work, dedication, and creativity.

Together with her husband, Gary, the Worthingtons pursued their interest in scratch-made artisan breads by training at both the American Institute of Baking and San Francisco Baking Institute. They worked closely with Lehi Mills to develop an exclusive flour mixture and located an ideal, traditional Italian hearth-stone oven. Their first bakery opened in Orem, Utah, in 1997, where they served European hearth breads. Within a few months, they expanded to offer a variety of sandwiches, soups, salads, and pastries. In their first quarter-century, they have expanded to forty-nine stores in six southwestern states.

Gary and Colleen Worthington.

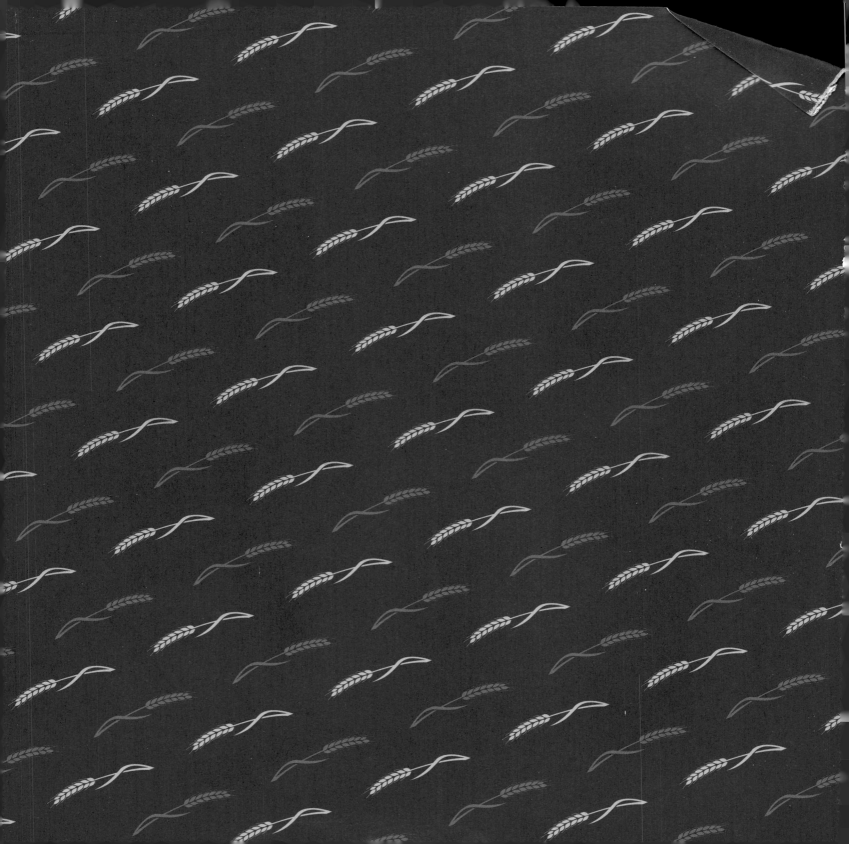